Mont Blanc

and the Aiguilles Rouges

a guide for skiers

*To Danielle, who put up with all the absences
that were necessary for the creation of this book,
and to my beloved son Edouard, who left to join
all our dear friends still up there…*

*Front cover: Opposite Mont Blanc (skier: Edouard Baud)
Back cover: At the top of the south couloir on the Aiguille de l'Éboulement*

Mont Blanc
and the Aiguilles Rouges
a guide for skiers

Anselme Baud

Published under licence in Great Britain by Cordee Limited, Leicester, October 2004
www.cordee.co.uk

Printed in Belgium

ISBN 1 904207 27 8

British Library Cataloguing Publication Data
A catalogue record for this book is available from the British Library.

English translation by Josephine Cleere
jo@basecamp.co.uk

Original title: *Mont Blanc et Aiguilles Rouges à ski*
First published in 2002 by Nevicata Editions, Brussels, Belgium
www.nevicata.com
© Paul-Erik Mondron, publisher.

Skiing and mountaineering are inherently dangerous activities. The author and publisher accept
no liability whatsoever for any loss, injury or inconvenience resulting from the use of this guide.

Anselme Baud

Mont Blanc
and the Aiguilles Rouges
a guide for skiers

Mont Blanc and the Aiguilles Rouges

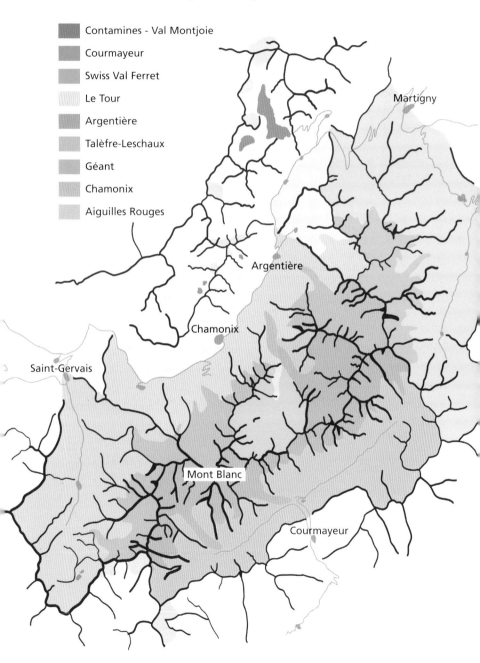

- Contamines - Val Montjoie
- Courmayeur
- Swiss Val Ferret
- Le Tour
- Argentière
- Talèfre-Leschaux
- Géant
- Chamonix
- Aiguilles Rouges

Martigny

Argentière

Chamonix

Saint-Gervais

Mont Blanc

Courmayeur

Contents

INTRODUCTION

MONT BLANC

Unique and majestic, basking in glorious light or vexed by troublesome storms, Mont Blanc is the king of Europe. It presides in stately fashion over its glaciers, deep valleys, and delicately crenellated granite ridges. Its summit has always been prized; its deadly rages terrifying some and fascinating others.

The first to tread on its snowy dome were the Chamoniards Gabriel Paccard and Jacques Balmat on 8th August 1786. Since that time the mountain has enjoyed no respite: first came the caravans of hopeful conquerors, then there were the intrepid unguided parties, those in eager pursuit of discovery, and adventurers of all kinds. Latterly, with the aid of advances in technology, we have witnessed, or indeed participated in, some more irreverent assaults on the mountain's dignity: Jansen's laboratory (financed by Eiffel), a banquet sponsored by a leading brand of champagne, a car on the summit that subsequently remained stranded in a snowdrift on the Petits Mulets Ridge (4690m) for several months, to name but a few...

Happily, however, man is not only motivated by fame or greed. He needs to climb Mont Blanc for himself - for his ego, to know his own limits. The desire to share enthusiasm for, and the pleasure in accomplishing the climbing of this mountain justifies the suffering and pain that such a venture involves. Back in the valley he is filled with a feeling of vitality and serenity, and memories that will last infinitely longer than his tracks, soon to be reclaimed by the drifting snow.

Mont Blanc is elusive: it is there to be admired, never dominated, never conquered. It will forever be the source of dreams and ambition, of peace and respect for nature. These are memories to be cherished, this is a mountain to preserve and protect against man's mischievous and perverse power of destruction. We need to demonstrate our respect for Mont Blanc. It must be spared from man's disgraceful abuse of his home; the reopening of the Mont Blanc Tunnel to heavy lorries being a case in point.

Mont Blanc and the Vallée Blanche

The pure line of a telemark turn

In the Mont Blanc Massif the skier has a fantastic choice of descents and routes, ranging from great introductory tours to extreme descents requiring a high level of technical ability. The enormous geographical and technical diversity of routes, the equally diverse weather conditions, and the ease with which one can pass from one side of a mountain, or indeed a frontier, to another, have made for a very sophisticated system of ski tours in this area. Moreover, the numerous ski lifts, especially on the French side of the Massif, have made Chamonix a veritable "Mecca" for both mountaineers and skiers.

Geographically the Mont Blanc Massif is defined by the deep valleys that surround it. These are the Chamonix Valley, Val Montjoie, the Chapieux Valley, Italian Val Veni, Swiss Val Ferret and the Trient Valley. These valleys belong to France, Switzerland and Italy who share a language as well as a culture. (On the Italian side of the Massif, in the Valle d'Aoste, the inhabitants speak a dialect of French).

Geologically, however, this crystalline massif is much closer to its neighbour to the north, the Aiguilles Rouges. Owing to their proximity, and the ease of access to them from the Chamonix Valley, I have included the Aiguilles Rouges in this guide rather than grouping them with the surrounding Chablais area. I have also decided to include a selection of 'belvedere' routes in the neighbouring areas that offer stunning views of the Mont Blanc Massif. There is a spectacular view of the north face of the Massif, for instance, from the Aiguilles Rouges; and the Miage area is clearly visible from Mont Joly, Col de la Fenêtre and Col de la Cicle (Les Contamines). The south face of Mont Blanc (Val Veni) can be seen from Col Chécrouit; as can Val Ferret from Testa Bernard. From the Vichères-Bavon ski lift system at the Grand Saint Bernard, Switzerland, you can access the top of Val Ferret and the start of the descents into Switzerland from La Fouly to Martigny. Finally, the Arpille, the Bel Oiseau and Fontanabran (Finhaut) areas offer great views of the Trient side of the Mont Blanc Massif.

CHOICE OF ROUTES

Some of the routes that appear in this book I have simply had to include, whereas others represent a personal preference. The rapid advances in skiing over the past few years have made it simply impossible to list every single new line, skied and boarded by countless dozens, that starts near the top of a ski lift. It is also a little difficult to give safety advice when the rules of the game seem to change so quickly. The advice to wait two days after a big fall of snow has become, or so it would seem, obsolete. Now, the day after a huge dump of snow, the more foolhardy will eagerly embark down extreme lines on the Rond Glacier, or the Mallory Couloir on the Aiguille du Midi... And I do have to question the wisdom of such a decision. Since 1995, the numbers of skiers and boarders attempting ever steeper slopes have increased markedly. Fortunately, the steeper sides of the Massif in Switzer-

On the north face of the Trident

land and Italy remain less well equipped and in some senses more wild. These are the slopes that offer extreme tests of willpower and technique, and which really stick in the memory...

This guide features 156 main routes and for most of them I have included several variants and secondary descents. All the principle routes have been selected because of their popularity and a need to inform the majority of their potential visitors. Other factors in my choice have included: the mountain, access conditions, historical importance, an anecdote begging to be told, and of course the aesthetic value of the route itself. The majority of them are described in detail.

These routes are divided into two types:
- there are the 'grand public' type that are well known and well used and are, for the most part, easy to moderately difficult (Crochues – Bérard, Passon...).
- then there are the 'steeps', the more or less well known couloirs that offer more difficult descents (Couloir de l'Éboulement, Rond Glacier, Milieu Glacier...).

Most of the main variants are described in detail. There are other routes, however, that I have not described in detail because they are of less interest, are exposed to more objective dangers or are rarely in condition (and require rappels etc) and consequentially I have only given them a technical grading.
These include:
- routes that can only be accessed by a (serious) climb or by helicopter and

should only be attempted by the most experienced ski-mountaineers (The Shroud, north face of the Triolet, Pilier d'Angle, Innominata…) and it seems rather unnecessary to add that they are rarely descended.

and routes that I myself have not skied and cannot describe in sufficient detail (North face of Triolet).

Moreover, there are a few lesser known routes, similar to other descents, that I have chosen to keep back in reserve…

It is true that skiing as we now know it will continue to evolve, and who would have thought 20 years ago that all the descents in this book can now be done with just one board attached your feet?

In the end, the choice of routes and tours in this book is very personal, and there is, therefore, always the possibility that one of these days someone will produce a guide with a completely different selection of routes.

This book could have been written at some stage or another by any one of a number of pioneers and extreme ski addicts. The list of sadly missed companions, however, is already too long and includes: the fiery Patrick Vallençant; Heini Holzer, the purist; the king of balance and opportunism, Jean-Marc Boivin; not forgetting the superbly talented snowboarders such as the visionary Bruno Gouvy, Alain Moroni, killed on the north face of the Aiguille du Plan, Marco Siffredi who was lost on Everest in September 2002, and Dédé Rhem, killed under Helbronner in 2004.

Happily, many of the Massif's extreme skiing and boarding pioneers survive: Yves Détry, Daniel Chauchefoin, Serge Cachat-Rosset, Jacky Bessat, Laurent Giacomini, Jean-Pierre Mansard, Dominique Pottard, Eric Bellin, Jérôme Ruby, Stéphane Dan, Véronique Périllat the monoskier, the guides Jean-Franck Charlet, Roland Cretton, Sam Beaugey, Rémy Lécluse, Francis Bibollet, the ever young Swiss veteran Sylvain Saudan, the Genevan Dominique Neuenschwander, the Italians Stefano de Benedetti and Toni Valeruz, and Pierre Tardivel who has devoted most of his life to extreme skiing. I should perhaps also mention here two of the younger extreme skiers, Emmanuel Ballot and Eric Monnier. These extreme skiers and boarders have plenty of tales of adventure, hair-raising descents and feats of self-composure and inner struggles to tell. Like skiers and mountaineers across the world they will dream from time to time of that unforgettable descent on that unforgettable day and the signature they carved into its snowy mantle.

CHOOSING YOUR DESCENT ACCORDING TO SNOW CONDITIONS AND THE WEATHER FORECAST

For ski-mountaineers the Mont Blanc region, which gets a decent covering of snow virtually every year, offers a large range of routes. The three different approaches (from France, Switzerland and Italy via the Mont Blanc tunnel) give access to three areas with distinctly different snow coverage and weather patterns. It is, therefore, rare to be stuck for something to do owing to poor conditions. The significant climate differences between the three countries is where the richness of this varied and yet relatively small Massif lies.

The western part of the Massif, around Les Contamines, gets snow early in the season. To the south, in Italy, the snow usually arrives later unless the foehn (a warm southerly wind) comes in. On the Swiss side, as in Italy, the climate is milder and at the beginning of the season there is often not enough snow. Moreover, in both Switzerland and Italy by the end of the season at middle and low altitudes the snow has already melted. However, the glaciated and rocky terrain of the Chamonix Valley needs a heavy covering of snow for there to be good ski conditions. While the northerly and westerly weather systems drift in and out of the valley, the snow stays and the skiing is good until quite late in the spring (May).

In terms of the quality of the snow, the weather conditions again dictate certain choices. In the Aiguilles Rouges, for example, the least effect of the foehn produces a noticeable difference in the quality of the snow from one side of the range to the other. Snow on the north side stays longer and is often better than the snow on the south side, and the snowfall is heavier from the west.

The wind from the north-east is the cause of certain unusual windslab formations that create a big avalanche risk on south-west and north-west faces, and these slabs sit on a layer of transformed snow (eg on the Pas de Chèvre, Rond Glacier etc…). Having said that, depending on the base layer it is the east faces that usually remain unstable after a big fall of snow. This was evidenced by the two huge slab avalanches that were set off on the Point de Vue pistes by the pisteurs/ski patrol at the Grands Montets in 2002. In short, it all depends on the wind and the frequent fluctuations in temperature as these create the 'mille feuilles' effect, the build-up of layer upon layer of hard and soft snow.

If you want to ski couloirs, then the Massif's east and south faces are in condition relatively early (March). The other faces, notably the north faces, are icy and rarely in condition before around mid-May, and the best time to ski them is between then and mid-June. During the coldest part of winter the snow cannot bind to the ice. When the spring comes, however, the warmer conditions mean the wetter snow can stick to the ice. This is why the north faces along the Argentière Glacier are often in condition only after the Grands Montets lifts have closed! In fact, some of the best and most difficult descents (such as the Bionnassay, Miage etc) can be done in the first snows of autumn. If it wasn't for the difficult approaches and lengthy walks out, this would be an almost ideal option because the new snow adheres very well to the soft ice.

Quite apart from these bewildering meteorological considerations, you can't beat experience, or intuition. An experienced skier's 'sixth sense' will help him to detect the subtle variations in the quality of snow simply by examining its texture and colour. By picking out tiny contours in the snow the skier can find his way down an

Precision telemarking...

otherwise unpromising and possibly dangerous slope. Although the point of skiing off-piste and ski-touring is get away from it all and discover untracked slopes, there are also times when it is prudent to follow tracks left by guides or more experienced skiers. Copying the right choice can be useful and a good learning experience. Even though the guide may feel he is being followed by too many people, he is from time to time pleased to have helped or even protected his little band of followers. Do remember, however, to keep your distance and try not to set off an avalanche above the people you are supposed to be following.

50° on hard snow!

STEEP SKIING
TECHNIQUES AND EQUIPMENT

The development of wider carving skis caused a revolution in terms of technique. They can be used in any kind of snow, they are faster, the initiation of turns is much quicker, they carve really well, perform well in competition and in freeride conditions, and are great for linked turns. However, when it comes to serious off-piste skiing these great advances have a flip side. For instance, the faster you ski on a glacier the faster the crevasses appear and the more alert you have to be. It is difficult to control side-slipping on hard snow on a steep slope with skis with a large side cut. Moreover, in the 70s and 80s relatively hard and narrow slalom skis were best for skiing steeps. This is no longer the case and the current designs are too short and provide less control over your balance lengthways and hardly side-slip at all. One of the main criteria for ski-tourers and freeriders when choosing from the less parabolic skis remains the weight. Most of the new carving skis are heavier than their predecessors which can be a real inconvenience if you have to carry them for long periods.

The basic principle behind steep skiing technique is keeping your speed down. The risk of falling is much greater on steep slopes, so it is extremely important to keep your speed to an absolute minimum when initiating a turn. This lack of speed (speed usually helps to make the turn) should be replaced with a more-controlled unweighting of your skis. I have been teaching my clients and aspirant guides at the École Nationale de Ski et d'Alpinisme a technique that remains well suited to steep skiing (solid, easy to initiate and simple turns): a turn from standing (the 'frappé-tiré' turn).

Turn from standing

Preparation
Start a side-slipping position: bend your body (with your chest facing downhill), have your weight on your downhill ski, and your uphill ski well forward. Stop any side-slip by flexing the lower knee inwards (uphill) ie. increase edging.
Plant the poles (upper pole near the ski tips, lower one towards the middle of the ski).

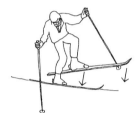

Initiating the turn
Weight both poles.
Lift then stamp down your uphill ski, which can be in a slight stem to help initiate the turn.

The resulting unweighting of the lower will automatically rotate it in the direction of the turn.

Bring the skis together by quickly flexing your knees: 'pull' up your knees as the tails of the skis cross the slope (push down on both poles while unweighting the upper ski).
You will find that you will be sitting back-slightly for a short time at this point, but your skis will not be touching the snow.

Finishing the turn
Land softly, increasing the pressure on the skis progressively.
Control your side-slipping, keep your speed down, putting your weight over your downhill ski and flexing your knees.

Note: In this turn it is essential that you lean on both your poles. The uphill pole will not get in the way of the skis as they rotate. Push the grip of your downhill pole down the fall-line as you finish the turn.

Turning while moving

When the slope is less steep or the conditions are better you can try turning while moving at a moderate speed. Start with smooth side-slipping:
– be in a flexed position with your weight on your downhill ski;
– place your uphill ski quite far in front of you and diverging from the lower one (the tip angled slightly uphill; the opposite of a stem-christie).
– your speed, even though moderate, will help you initiate the turn.
Initiate the turn with a stamp of the uphill ski, which will cause the lower ski to unweight. Now flex your knees by bringing your knees up.
Note: The stamping movement is not designed to transfer your weight to the uphill ski, rather it is a brief motion that quickly unweights your downhill ski so it can rotate downhill.

Summary

From a standstill, firmly plant your poles and weight your downhill ski.
Lift your uphill ski and give a hard stamp that will unweight the lower ski. It is then easier to unweight this ski and bend your knees to make the turn.
It is the downhill ski that drives the turn.
Another, I think less elegant, technique uses the rapid pivoting movement of the initial unweighting of the downhill ski as the motor for the turn. This 'pédalé-sauté' or standard 2-footed hop turn (pioneered by Patrick Vallençant in the 70s) is more physically demanding. You only plant one pole, the downhill one, and the bigger jump required could make the landing less easy to control.

NUMBERS SKIING AND BOARDING STEEP SLOPES

In the past few years there has been a huge increase in the numbers of people skiing and boarding the Massif's steepest and most exposed slopes. As soon as there is enough snow on the steep faces and couloirs, the more audacious skiers and boarders set about descending them. The rapid evolution of snowboarding in the past few years has opened up routes that had previously been considered unthinkable. The enthusiasm and determination of the top boarders, such as Gouvy, Siffredi, Rhem, Ruby etc, has demonstrated that many of these descents can be attempted earlier and earlier in the season. More often than not they are skied and boarded in soft snow where we wouldn't have dared to set foot a few years ago for fear of setting off snow slides.
After carefully studying the descent, and armed with a lot of experience and even more bare-faced cheek, the new experts seem to hesitate less and less and there are, in fact, fewer accidents than before.
Nowadays it is not unusual to see several people on the north face of the Aiguille du Midi in May, and in the afternoon! Speed seems to have become the order of the day. Set off a few snow slips at the top, move out of the way if they come past you, but otherwise ski the slope as quickly as possible. You not only need good technique and agility, but you also need to be level-headed and cool under pressure for some of the most serious descents. It is true that several descents of the

Rond Glacier and the Mallory will give you a certain amount of experience. It is, however, also true that Marco Siffredi and the Slovenian Karnicar's descents of Everest on snowboard and skis makes the Aiguille du Midi's 1000 metres or so seem a little small… but even so, it's still quite a ski! Let us not forget the laws of balance…

PRACTICAL INFORMATION

At the start of each of the main routes you will find a practical information section. These tables give a brief resumé of the essential information for the route, and include information on access, starting points and technical data about the descents themselves. Most of the route descriptions also include more precise advice and tips, and provide the reader with a detailed introduction to the route in question. The descents described in this book are generally the most popular or the most practical route for a particular slope, and those that I have skied and have enjoyed.

Below is a description and explanation of the data given in the practical information sections, together with their symbols.

STARTING POINT: This indicates where you start the route proper on skis or snowboard. Access to these points is, in general, included in brackets after the altitude (ski lift, road etc). Where the descent finishes in a different place from the starting point, this is described later on.

HEIGHT GAIN AND LOSS: A single set of arrows shows the height gain and loss for a day tour and a double set indicates a two-day tour (D1, D2).

ORIENTATION: This corresponds to the overall orientation of the route or, for certain routes, the orientation of a key point in the descent (main couloir etc). However, depending on how far into the season it is and the temperature, this does not necessarily give a good indication of the quality of the snow. This is especially true of those slopes that are exposed to low-angle sunlight at the beginning of the winter and in May and June.

PERIOD: This indicates the optimal point in the season for a descent. Nevertheless, this period can change quite significantly from one year to the next and it is strongly recommended that you check the conditions with the ski patrol, local weather forecasts and snow report, guides bureaux etc…

TIME: The times given for the routes are based on a fit ski-mountaineer going at a steady pace. The timings given are from the Starting Point (see above) and include any climbing up and stops along the way as well as the descent itself. Obviously these times are going to be just a guide as the snow conditions, the level of fitness and size of rucksack of each group member will have a bearing on how long the route takes. Where necessary the timings are broken down per day and are based on a rate of ascent of 350 to 400 metres per hour.

PHOTO: This refers to the page containing a photograph of the numbered routes and/or any variants. These photos are merely a useful tool to help you identify the routes and are not intended to replace the relevant IGN map for the area.

Unbroken blue lines indicate the main route and any variants.

Dotted blue lines represent the part of a route that is hidden in the photograph.

Broken blue lines show short descents that link two or more routes or slight variants that are very near the normal route.

Orange arrows show routes that have not been included in this book because they are too rarely in condition and are too hazardous for most of the time.

Green arrows show descents that are not included in this book because they are exceptionally difficult (ABO), and require helicopter lifts, and rappels etc.

 TECHNICAL LEVEL: This grading system has a direct correlation with the skier and his or her technical ability. The grading system I use here is divided into four levels each of which have three sub-divisions. There is also a fifth level with an indefinite number of sub-divisions. This is only an indication of technical difficulty and is defined by the angle of the slope and the nature of the terrain. I have used the traditional mountaineering grading system for the overall feel of the route that takes into account the approach, the level of commitment, the time it takes and the route's difficulty. In this system F means 'facile' or easy, PD is 'peu difficile' or not moderately difficult, AD is 'assez difficile' or quite difficult, D is 'difficile' or difficult, TD is 'très difficile' or very difficult, ED is 'extrêmement difficile' which is extremely difficult and ABO stands for 'abominablement difficile' and refers to a very, very difficult route that is also extremely hazardous.

The level of technical ability required for a descent corresponds to the control that the skier has over his or her skis on firm snow (hard snow or snow slightly softened by the sun, or snow that you cannot really get your edges into). Conversely, when the snow is very heavy or when there is lots of powder and where falls are much easier to stop, the technical rating is very different. If this is the case, why not just ski in soft snow conditions? There are various factors to take into account when responding to this question:

– the top layer of snow must be stable enough to support a skier;
– the objective dangers such as rock fall, cornice collapse, slides caused by melting snow and ice etc should be minimal or one should be able to monitor and check them;
– on the way up to the start of the descent you should be able to get a good idea of the terrain and of the potential hazards (ice patches, rocks etc).

However, given the increasing numbers of extreme skiers and snow-boarders attempting these kinds of slopes in soft snow, it would appear that these conditions are less rigorously adhered to than before… In any case, the technical grading can only be defined by using hard snow as the reference point.

- **Level 1** : beginner off-piste skier or boarder who can ski/board up to 30° slopes, sparsely wooded areas, wide couloirs and combs of less than 800 metres descent with minimal risk of avalanche.
  EG: Pré du Rocher (Plan de l'Aiguille), Arpille de la Ravoire, Bec-Rond à Bavon, Col des Dards, Lacs Jovet.
- **Level 2**: comfortable on more uneven terrain, in more densely wooded conditions, on firmer and more difficult snow, and on 35° slopes that are longer than 800 metres.
  EG: Aiguillette des Houches, Col Infranchissable
- **Level 3**: beginning to tour with good control over skis or board in couloirs, 40° and other longer and more committing slopes.
  EG: Mont Blanc du Tacul, traverse of the Dômes de Miages, Armancette Glacier.
- **Level 4**: can descend steep slopes with short sections reaching 50°, narrow couloirs and very difficult terrain including very uneven glacier areas.
  EG: Rond Glacier, Milieu Glacier, Spencer Couloir, Grandes Jorasses.
- **Level 5**: extreme skier or boarder who can descend long and sustained steep couloirs and slopes that are over 50°. The skier or boarder's technical ability is very advanced as is his or her mental preparedness. This level is open-ended and includes slopes above 55° that are very rarely in condition and are even more rarely skied or boarded.
  EG: Couturier Couloir, north/north-east face of the Courtes.

SLOPE : Gradients for the slopes have been calculated using the 1/25000 IGN maps for the relevant area and in certain cases from measurements taken on the slopes themselves. These figures are always open to adjustment. It goes without saying that the quality of the snow on the day will ultimately determine the difficulty of the descent. An icy 35° slope is clearly going to be more difficult to safely ski than a 45 or 50° slope of thick powder snow. The quality of the light (how much you can make out of the terrain and even the gradient of a slope) is an additional factor. North facing slopes, for example, become more difficult when they are in the shade.

Moreover, although the gradient of a slope is an essential piece of information you also have to take in account its length. For this reason I have tried to avoid putting average gradients and have instead noted the length of the steepest sections of the descent (eg. 45°/250m). The gradient of some short sections at the top of certain slopes (which can be icy or have lots of snow) can vary considerably from the average gradient of the slope as a whole. The average gradient, for example, in the middle of the Gervasutti Couloir on the Tour Ronde or the south couloir of the Col Armand Charlet is 45°, but the slopes to the side that you have to ski or board get as steep as 50°!

DANGERS: I use the term 'dangers' instead of 'seriousness' as I prefer to set out the objective dangers (avalanches, rock fall, serac fall, collapsing cornices, possible blows from a slip etc), rather than focusing on the subjective risks that the ski-mountaineer must overcome him or herself. The known and recorded dangers of hidden crevasses on a broken glacier, and rocks loosened by the fœhn or the sun, or of a slide that can start in a hidden corner of a face, for instance, must be included in any guide to the area. That is not to say that we encounter these obstacles on every trip into the mountains, but they form an integral part of the off-piste skier and boarder's alpine adventures and they do perhaps bring their own special piquancy...

• **Danger 1**: small risk of sliding after a fall and few objective dangers. This is off-piste skiing not far from protected areas such as ski lifts, roads, villages etc.

• **Danger 2**: there is a risk of serious injury or worse from hitting a rock or tree while sliding after a fall. The objective dangers (rock and serac fall, cornice collapse, avalanche etc) are quite high especially in unfavourable weather conditions (wind, hot spell etc). The route is remote or technically committing.

• **Danger 3**: you simply cannot fall and only chance or luck will save you if you do. The remoteness and/or the technical difficulty of the route increase the risk. It is imperative that the skier or boarder attempting these routes is technically capable and experienced enough both mentally and physically to make the right decisions.

 EQUIPMENT: The list below is by no means exhaustive. I do think, however, it is important to mention a few items now so that the gear list can be efficiently adapted and personalised by each skier and boarder. Some people find gear lists very useful while for others they are the start of great debate and argument. They are nevertheless necessary.

• **Off-piste day pack (DP)**: This should contain a shovel, probe, and ARVA (transceiver for locating people, and being located, after an avalanche). You should also carry a hat, spare pair of light gloves, sunglasses or goggles and a T-shirt in a small plastic bag. In a different colour plastic bag put a basic repair kit (spare ski pole basket, sturdy sticky tape), a piece of bicycle inner tube for securing skis to packs, spare batteries for ARVA, knife, matches or lighter, basic first aid kit, small head torch, skins (if necessary).

• **One to two-day ski-touring pack (SP)**: in addition to the above items you should carry a kit for repairing your bindings and ski boot buckles (wire, string, pliers, penknife/leatherman). Think about taking a change of clothes and maybe a good light duvet jacket... More often than not for these kinds routes you will need a harness, ice-axe, crampons and a rope (for use as a handrail or for rappelling past cornices)... Try to carry a few spare plastic bags as they can come in handy in all sorts of situations, and can even be used as snow anchors. It is also not a bad idea to carry a small stove in case of emergency. For glacier travel you will need the necessary safety equipment (ice screws, slings or Prussik loops, carabiners, crevasse rescue kit).

- **High mountain and steep skiing pack** (HP): as well as the day pack and ski-touring equipment, you should take the necessary ski-mountaineering equipment for your chosen route (snow stake, Abalakov kit, helmet etc).

I haven't mentioned here the usual pieces of mountaineering equipment (map, compass, altimeter, mobile phone, GPS, sun cream, whistle, distress flares etc) that are no less indispensable.

You might think about adding aspirin, throat lozenges, cough sweets, something to soothe upset stomachs, plasters and antiseptic for cuts and burns, and arnica for bruises and cramps to your usual first aid kit and whatever else your doctor or chemist has suggested you carry.

Where you will be in very remote places you might consider taking a splint (inflatable devices and new light-weight materials that set to protect the injury now available). If there is a group of you, you might even think about taking a kit to convert skis and poles into a compact rescue sledge.

DEVELOPMENT AND EVOLUTION OF EQUIPMENT

Equipment is constantly changing and evolving which in turn creates advances in technique, comfort and safety on the mountain. In short, thanks to the advances in equipment design, ski-mountaineers and boarders can now relatively quickly and easily reach a good level of competence. We are presented with a bewildering array of new products and innovations and it is sometimes difficult to make the distinction between what are essentially gadgets and what is actually useful. Moreover, the appropriate use of equipment comes from being well informed. These days it is not uncommon to see skiers and boarders at the top of the Aiguille du Midi, the start of the Vallée Blanche, with all sorts of slings and automatic blocking devices hanging from their harnesses. If they only had these things properly stowed there would be less risk of them catching their crampon points in them and sending themselves down the north face! It

Danielle in the first snow on the Grands Montets

is also not unusual to come across ski-tourers on a flat area or slightly inclined slope getting out their ski crampons (couteaux) and heel risers.

I sometimes suspect that this improper use of gear has little to do with actual need.

The most important considerations for ski-mountaineers and boarders are weight, efficiency and versatility.

- CLOTHES: I recommend you take thin and light clothes such as thin jumpers (fleeces or other) and windstopper layers, but you should think about doubling them because they are not necessarily warm enough on their own. The same goes for trousers and gloves. The advantage of this is that you can take off or put on layers according to the time the route takes, its difficulty and the weather. It is equally important to be able change your damp base layers. Apart from the super fit among us who 'never stop' and even with the new breathable fabrics, it is still useful to be able to change out of wet clothes to avoid getting cold which can be a real handicap in the evening or the next day. With a wet base layer you will not be able to get warm again when you stop (and sometimes not even on the way down) even if you put more layers on over the top. For your head: you may not be warm or dry enough in a bandanna, and a hat (or warm cap) is always better.
  On your legs: you will find that you can wear two layers of thin wool long johns or fleece trousers under a pair of light over-trousers. Otherwise, long johns and Gore-tex trousers are great and the elastic or zip systems at the bottom of the Gore-tex trousers means you don't have to wear gaiters.
  One-piece suits are not practical or very well suited to winter off-piste skiing. Moreover, on steep slopes it is not a good idea to wear something that will let you slide too far in case of a fall.
- BOOTS: There is a huge choice of ski boots on the market now and you are sure to find a boot that is comfortable and suits your style of skiing. Touring boots these days can be almost as stiff as downhill boots and they have soles with moulded grips. For a long time I used very light, rear-entry, downhill boots which had two buckles and a vibram sole. The advantages of these were that they were light, good for skiing technical slopes and comfortable (with very light customised Thermoflex inner boots). Having said that, it is better not to use very stiff, high cut and heavy boots for touring, especially on the descents. The lack of forward and back flexibility at the ankle can be a problem especially in wooded areas and narrow couloirs.
  You can adapt your ski touring boots by replacing the laced inner boots with unlaced downhill inners which are more comfortable and technical. If you find that the front of your foot is loose in the boots, an in sole between the shell and the inner boot will lift your foot up and hold it better.
- SKIS: The new wide carving skis are so good that it would be a shame to carry on skiing on the long and narrow old-fashioned variety. However, for touring you should avoid the really heavy, wide skis with big side cuts, which are great nevertheless for off-piste skiing and heli-skiing. The current touring skis are excellent in all snow conditions and will do the job in hard snow and couloirs. I think that the hole in the end of touring skis is essential. Do take good care of your skis and make sure they are regularly waxed and the edges are kept sharp. You will really notice the difference in 'soapy' fresh, wet snow.
- BINDINGS: From the simple, ultra-light performance bindings to the heavier and more practical touring bindings, the choice is enormous. There are also plates that you can add to alpine bindings to convert them into touring bindings when you need them. There are two models available at the moment, the original and difficult to adjust 'Sécurafix' and the more practical 'Alpine-Trekker'. These devices allow you the benefits of your downhill boots and skis in a touring situation. They are, however, best kept for short tours or for accessing a serious couloir.

My father Jacques Baud (2nd on the left) with friends in Morzine around 1930

- SKINS : With the light, carving skis you don't have to cover the whole ski with the skin. If you are using narrow skins on wide skis the trick is to zig-zag the skin across the ski in an S-shape.
  The hook system on some skins is very convenient and also serves as a back-up in case the glue fails. The hook is attached to a piece of rubber and a metal loop for adjusting the length of the skin. This makes it easier to change the length of the skin or to remove the skins without taking off your skis. When folding the skins take care not to stick the tail end directly onto the middle of the skin as this will be difficult to unstick later. To avoid this problem, keep a bit of plastic handy to cover the tail. Alternatively, fold the end with the hook down first, then fold the tail end down on top of the hook. Waxing your skis will also help and will extend the lifetime of the skins.

A FEW TIPS

Before you set off

Find out about the amount and quality of the snow from the local weather reports, the guides bureaux, ski schools and ski patrols etc.
Watch out for the southerly and south-westerly winds that can have a huge effect on the conditions in the Massif. Even the local weather centre, despite its best efforts and extremely high standards, has difficulty now and then with the huge variations in conditions from one valley to the next that the fœhn brings.

The group leader should prepare the map of the route and have the altitudes, directions (orientation), distances, landmarks, estimated times and any necessary GPS readings noted down. Plan an alternative route or trip if the weather changes, there is a delay at the lift station or there are too many people on the mountain that day. A great morning's outing can in fact finish very late and in horrendous snow conditions and at the limits of good sense and caution. You should know when is the right time to attempt a descent and watch and listen to the mountain. Use all the available information (contacts on the ground, books, topos etc), but also be prepared to do save it for another day or do something else. Always check your equipment.

Once you are there

Once you have arrived find out if the wind direction has changed since the last fall of snow. Has the isotherm changed, or is there more sun on a particular face and is the wind stronger than normal?
Check if the ski lifts, trains and buses (if necessary) are running.
If you start the tour by skinning up a slope, try to avoid sweating too heavily by taking off layers sooner rather than later. Think about where you stop and make sure you are not in the line of a snow slide, in the wind or in the blazing sun. Try not to stop in the middle of a slope and look for a slightly less steep area where you can set off again more easily.
It is important to keep your distance from the skier in front of you. This will keep you out of each other's way, make for a more pleasant skiing experience, and reduce the risk of overloading the slope. If the slope does go, there is a smaller risk of all of you being caught in an avalanche if you are spread out. It is also easier to turn around or to make a detour at your own pace when you are not bunched together.
When climbing a slope using skins you should set off at a slow and steady pace using long strides and trying not to use heel risers! Keep your feet quite far apart and try to take a route that will avoid the use of kick turns. Try to maintain a pace with a steady height gain and, where it is safe to do so, use the whole width of the slope. Unless you are looking to set a record, avoid steep climbs. Generally, a regular pace without stops will be as quick as a steep climb using heel risers during which you have to keep stopping for breath.
If there are more than two of you on a glacier, I would recommend that you rope up using a 'téléphérique' system (see below) and one or two prussik loops or shunts.

On the descent

Where large amounts of snow have built up, carry out soundings to ascertain the depth of the snow (anything from a simple sounding with your pole to digging a snow pit).
Where the snow is hard, have a look at the slope and the terrain. Check for any cracks or breaks in the snow, and rocks that you should be aware of in the event of a fall or a slide.
When you are skiing through a powder field keep your distance from other skiers and get in the habit of skiing 'en traces de peigne' (as if the slope was being

combed). There are many advantages to this technique: it uses a minimum of the slope, you can descend one by one while watching each other, it does not overload the slope and you follow (to one side) the tracks of the person in front of you while leaving room for skiers coming after you. If you stick more or less together there is less likelihood of the fragile top layer of snow being cut and destabilised elsewhere and you will leave the slope as more than just a bowl of spaghetti.

Plan ahead where you are going to stop and try to find a sheltered spot (a ridge, bowl, rocks or a tree) even if this means more than just traversing off the slope. If you have to traverse a slope that is steeper than 30° and you are not sure how stable the snow is, check for other safer routes across. Before starting across it imagine you are alone, without an ARVA and there are no available rescue services as this may help to avoid taking unnecessary risks! Wrap up warm at this point (scarf, face mask, balaclava, goggles…), make sure your rucksack is good and tight (unless it is too heavy and it is likely to impede any sudden movements) and take your hands out of the ski poles straps.

If a slab does break away push hard with your poles towards a stable surface. In certain circumstances you can use sliding blocks to extricate yourself from and get uphill of a snow slide. This specialised technique demands a great deal of agility and very highly developed reactions!

In the vast majority of cases it is inadvisable to head straight down the slope as avalanches accelerate very rapidly and a powder snow avalanche can reach up to 300 kph!

If you are likely to be buried the only advice is to try to stay on top of the avalanche, without swallowing too much snow, and try to keep an air cavity in front of your mouth and nose. This, of course, is all totally hypothetical but is worth bearing in mind as it might speed up your reactions should you find yourself in such a situation. It is useful to note here that the Avalung and ABS systems have already proved, in some cases, to be effective.

In soft snow or in a couloir always keep out of the line of the skier uphill of you in case they set of a slide or fall.

Think about tightening your bindings.

I could write more here about safety do and don'ts, but most accidents are caused by simple and basic mistakes or happen as a result of a combination of several minor errors…

Roping up on a glacier

It is not always easy to ski on a glacier while roped up, and I recommend the following methods.

- **For two people:**
  1. Tie, or attach with a locking carabiner, one end of the rope to your harness.
  2. Pass the rope two or three times over your shoulder and around your chest (on top of your rucksack straps), or, if the rope is long enough, each skier ties on roughly three metres from the end of the rope and carries the spare rope in their rucksack.
  3. Now tie a clove hitch or a figure of eight and attach the rope to your harness using one (or two) locking carabiners.
  4. Attach an automatic locking system (Klemheist, prussik loop or Petzl 'shunt') to the rope and to the tie-in loop of your harness.

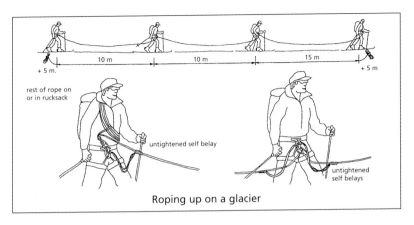

Roping up on a glacier

The advantages for this system, where the skiers are roughly 15 to 25 metres from each other, are:

– If your partner falls in a crevasse you can hold his or her fall immediately and can set up a crevasse rescue system using the extra rope in your bag.

– If you fall into a crevasse you can set up another automatic locking system (alpine clutch etc for your foot) so that you can release the knot on the carabiner on your harness as you already have one automatic locking system already attached to the rope. You can then start prussiking out of the crevasse yourself.

• **For three or more people:**
The first and last skiers rope up as above. The remaining members of the group are attached to the rope with a long cow's tail (maximum length 30 cm). This is for glaciers with relatively few crevasses and obstacles.

When travelling over more heavily crevassed and difficult glaciers I recommend using the 'téléphérique' system for roping up those not at the front or the back of the group:

1. Pass the rope through a locking carabiner that is securely attached to your harness.

2. Set up two automatic blocking devices on the rope (one either side of the locking carabiner). These can be attached to the harness's tie-in loop using or a short sling and a locking carabiner. This is a much more versatile system to use when crossing heavily crevassed terrain requiring lots of turning, crossing cracks in the slope and snow bridges. The other members of the group can belay the skier at the front who uses the extra rope lengths to cross an obstacle. All the other skiers have to do is release the automatic blocking device at the front (the one behind will release automatically as it is stopped by the carabiner that has therope running through it) to pay out extra rope to the first skier. The skiers behind the belayer merely have to move towards the belayer to give him or her more rope.

This technique helps to avoid frustrating and dangerous situations caused by the rope lengths between skiers not being appropriate for the distances between the hazardous areas.

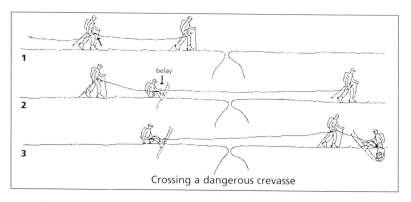

Crossing a dangerous crevasse

This also allows you to adjust your pace of ascent or descent, and more importantly allows proper belaying.

On very rare occasions it is possible for two people to rope up this way using knots in the middle of the rope to help check someone's fall if they go into a crevasse. However, in this situation it is imperative that each skier has enough rope to rescue their partner from a crevasse. The knots in the main rope bite into the lip of the crevasse checking the skier's fall. As the knots have checked the fall they are also going to prevent the belayer pulling the first skier out, or the trapped skier from prussiking up the main rope. Therefore, extra rope is required to set up a crevasse rescue pulley system. Other group members, if substituted for the knots, would make very useful and live snow anchors. The equipment manufacturers, such as Petzl, provide detailed and helpful drawings to explain how their gear works.

FUNDAMENTAL RULES FOR SKIING IN THE MOUNTAINS

Jean Coudray, a guide and teacher at ENSA, has been taking his students, future guides and clients across the Alps and to the world's highest mountains, from K2 to Kangchenjunga, for over 30 years. An old climbing partner of mine, Jean suggested a series of important points and basic rules to bear in mind before and during any outing on skis. Thorough and methodical preparation before a trip together with careful observation on the day, will help prevent numerous errors of judgement. The continuing work of the Swiss guide Werner Münter, author of the method of 'reduction' (a great checklist for reducing avalanche risk), should also be mentioned here. The following is a list of fundamental rules that should be adhered to before and during any trip to ski in the mountains.

Assess the risks and spot the dangers

It is essential to gather data (local avalanche forecasts etc) about a particular route or face, but this in itself is not enough as these are only probabilities. You must nevertheless therefore assess this information and make your own evaluation of the risks you are taking. In order to do this you should take the follow-

ing three factors into consideration:
1. the snow conditions and weather forecast
2. the topography of the terrain (gradient of the slope, its orientation, profile and avalanche gullies)
3. the other members of your group and other skiers on the mountain (the all-important human factor)

Be aware of, and look out for, the possible negative signs associated with each of these factors. Beware!

- after big falls of snow the risk of avalanches being set off by other skiers and other factors arises much earlier than the risk of spontaneous avalanches
- fresh snow accompanied by wind is the main cause of avalanches
- the first good weather day after a snowfalls is undoubtedly the most dangerous. This, though the danger can also persist for several days, even weeks.

Manage the risks and make your decision

Consider the three main factors at the three main stages of your trip:
1. before (preparation)
2. during (at the beginning of each observable section of the route, to be done partly on ground)
3. during (at every stage that you anticipate will be difficult or delicate).

Procedure to follow for each of these factors:
- identify the dangers (negative signs, alarms signals)
- analyse the danger (faint slight doubts, doubts, strong doubts, very serious doubts) and make your decision (yes or no)

If you decide to continue try to minimise these dangers.

Procedure to follow to minimise the probable dangers:
1. appropriate distances between each member of the group
2. choice of precise route (with respect to the terrain)
3. speed and mode of progression adapted according to the conditions
4. stay where you can see and hear each other
5. take care when choosing places to meet up/regroup
6. avoid critical zones and tricky areas (convex slopes with fresh or deep snow)
7. never start down a steeper steepening slope without first having stopped to check the terrain downhill
8. be properly equipped (ARVA, shovel, probe…)
9. never ski uphill or downhill directly above or bellow another skier
10. follow the single track when necessary

Conclusion

- Humility (towards the natural environment which we cannot control)
- Modesty (towards others)
- Curiosity (learn about the snow)
- Prudence (don't forget to think!)
- Saying no is not a form of cowardice! It sometimes takes more courage and intelligence to turn back. To feel the danger or fear the worst is not the same thing as being afraid. On the contrary, listen to what your instinct and your gut feelings are telling you.

One more thing: remember, the avalanche does not know you're an expert.

ABOUT THE AUTHOR

Anselme Baud

Anselme Baud was born in Morzine, Haute-Savoie, in 1948 and has been a major force in the development of extreme skiing in the Alps for many years. He became a mountain guide in 1973 and has an impressive number of extreme first descents to his name including the north face of the Aiguille Blanche de Peuterey, the north face of the Aiguille du Midi, the Peuterey Ridge, and the Col Armand Charlet among others in the Alps. His first descents in the Andes include Vintinani and Huayna Potosi; and in Antarctica they include the north-west couloir of Vinson; and Dhaulagiri and Yalung Kang in the Himalayas. Anselme Baud teaches at ENSA (the French National Ski and Mountaineering school based in Chamonix), and has taken his students on expeditions to Bolivia and Nepal. In addition to his work at ENSA, Anselme also regularly runs ski and mountaineering expeditions across the globe and has successfully climbed the 'Seven Summits' (highest summit of each continent) with clients.

MAPS

France: IGN 3531 ET Saint-Gervais-les-Bains (Top 25)
              IGN 3530 OT Chamonix-Mont-Blanc (Top 25)
Switzerland: 1345 Orsières (1:25000)
              1344 Col de Balme (1:25000)
              1324 Barberine (1:25000)
              1325 Sembrancher (1:25000)
              1365 Grand Saint Bernard (1:25000)
              282 Martigny (1:50000)
              292 Courmayeur (1:50000)

ABBREVIATIONS

km	kilometre(s)	OP	off-piste route
m	metre(s)	ST	ski-tour
hr(s)	hour(s)	HM	high-mountain route
min(s)	minute(s)	CAF	Club Alpin Français
ref.	mountain hut (refuge)	CAI	Club Alpino Italiano
bel.	'belvedere' route with stunning views of the Mont Blanc Massif	CAS	Club Alpin Suisse

PHOTO CREDITS

All the photographs in this book are from the author's collection with the exception of the following: Emmanuel Moy (cover, p.274), René Robert (p.167), Jean-Pierre Mansard (bottom of p.37), Toru Nakano (top of p.139)

LES CONTAMINES-VAL MONTJOIE

PRACTICAL INFORMATION

Les Contamines Tourist Office: +33 (0)4 50 47 01 58 - Fax: +33 (0)4 50 47 09 54
Guides Office, Les Contamines: +33 (0)4 50 47 10 08
Guides Office, Saint-Gervais: +33 (0)4 50 47 76 55
Weather forecast: 08 92 68 02 74 / www.meteo.fr
Snow report: 08 92 68 10 20
Mountain rescue (Gendarmerie de montagne): +33 (0)4 50 78 10 81

SKI LIFTS

Les Contamines: +33 (0)4 50 47 02 05
Mont Joly: +33 (0)4 50 93 20 14
Bellevue (Les Houches): +33 (0)4 50 54 40 32
Tramway du Mont Blanc (Le Fayet, Saint-Gervais): +33 (0)4 50 47 51 83

ROAD ACCESS

From Geneva or Annecy, take the A40, in the direction of Sallanches. From Grenoble head towards Albertville, then follow the Gorges de l'Arly to Megève.

Crozat car park (Bionnassay, 1400m)
From Sallanches or Chamonix go to Le Fayet and up to Saint-Gervais. From Megève go to Saint-Gervais. Take the D902 in the direction of Les Contamines and just after leaving Saint-Gervais take the small road on the left that goes to Bionnay and Bionnassay. The car park is at the end of this road.

La Gruvaz (Saint-Gervais, 1100m)
From Saint-Gervais follow the road to Les Contamines and about 3km (2 miles) after the turning for Bionnay there is a small road on the left that goes to La Gruvaz. The car park is after the small village, beside the Torrent du Miage.

Le Cugnon (Les Contamines, 1200m)
From Saint-Gervais go through Les Contamines and take the small road on the left to Le Cugnon. The car park is after the village.

Les Chapieux (Bourg-Saint-Maurice, 1550m)
From Albertville (Grenoble – Albertville; Annecy – Faverge – Albertville; Sallanches – Megève – Albertville; Chamonix – Saint-Gervais – Megève – Albertville) take the D925 to Beaufort, continue past the lake and the Cormet de Roselend and follow the small road to Les Chapieux. The road is closed in winter from the Thermes de Bonneval (1050m) up.

There are several reasons why I chose to start the book on this side of Mont Blanc. This part of the Massif generally gets snow early in the season and you get a real sense of its majesty and grandeur from this, its west side. I hope that the skiers and boarders who read this book will understand and agree with this choice. If not, well, it will give them something to talk about during the long winter evenings in the numerous mountain huts around the Mont Blanc Massif!

At the beginning of the winter season there is often an early fall of snow, sometimes before the opening of the Les Contamines ski lifts, here at the Massif's

Previous page: Skiing 'en traces de peigne' in the Miage Massif.

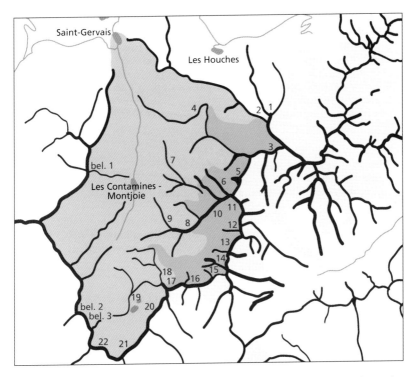

grassy edge. A wander along the belvedere that goes from Mont Joly to the Aiguille Croche provides a great view of the Bionassay—Miage—Col du Bonhomme area, the north-west side of the Massif. After the first snow falls you can do the Col de Tricot, Mont Truc, Monts Jovets tours as well as the Cols de la Fenêtre, de la Cicle and des Chasseurs that form the border of Haute-Savoie with Savoie. Within the Massif itself the two mountain huts that are manned in spring (from the end of March) are on the same route as the popular Tré la Tête glacier route.

In this first group there is a whole range of descents from easy one-day routes to moderately committing weekend tours to atmospheric traverses into Italy and extreme north face descents.

MOUNTAIN HUTS

Ref.1 ▪ Tête Rousse Hut (3167m, AD)
Run by the Saint-Gervais CAF, this hut currently has 57 places (40 in the winter room) and there is a new hut under construction. It is guardianed from mid-June to the end of September. The winter room has gas stoves and blankets.
Tel: +33 (0)4 50 58 24 97 or +33 (0)4 50 93 95 91

From Saint-Gervais follow route number 2 (this section) to the Chalet de l'Are. Cross the plateau and the moraine to get on to the Bionnassay Glacier. Go up its left bank to the foot of the Pointes de Tricot. Depending on the time of year and the conditions, this section can be quite difficult with crevasses, seracs and a small ice wall. When you get to the large plateau (2150m) cross over to your left and climb along the west face (up to 2500m) and then follow the right bank of the glacier that takes you to just below the hut. To get to the hut you have to go round or cross several steep rock spurs and then follow a small couloir.

⌐ 1400m   ⊘ 5-6hrs

↗ 1770m

Ref.2 ▪ Plan Glacier Hut (2713m, PD)
Private hut with 20 places. Not guardianed during the ski season.
Tel: (Saint-Gervais Guides Bureau) +33 (0)4 50 47 76 55

From the village of La Gruvaz (on the Les Contamines road) follow the forest path up to the Chalets de Miage (1 1/2 hrs). Climb up the wide valley that leads to the glacier. At around 2100m get onto the steep moraine on your left and follow it up to the hut which is on the right under a rock.

⌐ 1100m   ⊘ 4hrs

↗ 1610m

Ref.3 ▪ Tré la Tête Hut (1970m, F)
Private hut with 80 places. Closed in winter and open from mid-March.
Tel: +33 (0)4 50 47 01 68 or +33 (0)4 50 47 05 26

From Le Cugnon (after Les Contamines) follow the summer track that leads to the Tré la Tête Hut (sign). From Les Plans traverse south (Nant des Tours Couloir and the Grande Combe). Continue above the trees (steeper slopes with risk of snow slides) to the last step and the hut is 15 minutes after this.

⌐ 1200m   ⊘ 2hrs

↗ 770m

Ref.3.a ▪ Tré la Tête Hut by the Combe Noire (F)

Although slightly longer, this route is more varied and involves much less risk of avalanche after a big snowfall. From Notre-Dame de la Gorge take the Roman road that leads south. After the

Up to the Col de Tricot

Pont de la Téna (bridge) turn left towards the Combe Noire waterfall. Go round the Tête Noire on its south-east side to get to the hut.

P   1200m   ⊘   2hrs

↗   770m

Ref.4 ▪ Conscrits Hut (2580m, PD)
A CAF hut with 80 places (16 in the winter). Guardianed in the spring.
Tel: +33 (0)4 79 89 09 03

Follow ref. 3 to the Tré la Tête Hut, now head uphill and east. There is a cairn 400m further on. After the cairn climb down through the two rock bands (this is the Mauvais Pas which is exposed but not very difficult) and traverse to the foot of the glacier. Move up the centre of the glacier at first and follow its right bank to avoid the crevasses and seracs. At around 2400m climb up the sustained slopes on the south face that take you to the new hut at 2580m.

P   1200m   ⊘   4-5hrs

↗   1450m

Ref.5 ▪ Robert Blanc Hut (2750m, AD) via the Tré la Tête Glacier
Private hut with 45 places in summer (open from mid-June). Not guardianed in the ski season but has one room open where you can sleep and there is wood for cooking. Tel: +33 (0)4 79 07 85 64 or +33 (0)4 79 07 23 33 (Bourg-Saint-Maurice Mairie/Town Hall).

From the Tré la Tête Hut follow route number 17 (this section) to the Col du Mont Tondu (2895m) which is above and to the left of the slope that narrows after the Aiguille des Lanchettes cliff. After a 50m traverse to the east, drop down in a diagonal line on foot in places or descend directly beneath the col where there is steep rock band (cables). Put your skis back on at the top of the small Glacier des Lanchettes (possible bergschrund) and keep left to go round the rocky spur at about 2760m. There is now a long, virtually flat traverse (over 1km) to the hut which stands on a headland at 2750m.

P   1200m   ⊘   6hrs

↗   1700m   ↘   280m

Ref.5.a ▪ Robert Blanc Hut via les Chapieux (PD)

From Bourg-Saint-Maurice take the road to Les Chapieux (open in winter at least as far as Thermes de Bonneval, 1050m). Take the road on skis up to Les Chapieux then follow, on the right bank, the track passing under the cliffs. Carry on up the entire length of this valley (des Glaciers). The Refuge de Chapieux is closed in winter although the Refuge des Mottets (further up the valley, 1864m) can hold 10 people. You will pass the Chalet des Lanchettes as you continue up the valley on

its south-eastern side. Depending on how much snow there is you can either follow the summer track and cross the rock band here or move left to go round it
higher up. You should be able to see the hut beneath the Pointe des Lanchettes.

P   1060m   🕰 5-6hrs

↗ 1700m

'BELVEDERE' ROUTES

Bel. 1 ▪ Mont Joly (2525m, PD)

P 2130m (ski lift)	🗺 December-April	↳ sect. of 35-40°
↗ 395m	🕰 2-3hrs	⚠ 1
↘ 725m	🎿 2.3	🏠 DP
⊕ South-east		

From Saint-Gervais (or Saint-Nicolas de Véroce) take the cable cars up to Mont
Joux and the chair lift to just above the Pavillon du Mont Joly. From here, the first
part of the walk up the ridge to the summit of Mont Joly is hard going, but it soon
turns into a pleasant walk as you approach the cairn at the top (2525m, 30-45
mins). From the summit of Mont Joly follow the line of the ridges as they gently
descend to the Tête de la Combaz (2445m). You can now either ski across the
south-east face of the ridge to the foot of the Véleray drag lift or, if there is good
snow cover, follow one of the combes on the right that leads to Les Contamines.
Beware: do not try to ski the south-east face between Mont Joly and Tête de la
Combaz as the shale (schist) and steep grassy slopes are very avalanche prone.

Bel. 2 ▪ Col de la Fenêtre (2245m) et col de la Cicle (2377m) (PD)

P 2100m (ski lift))	🗺 December-April	↳ sect. of 35°
↗ 145m	📷 56	⚠ 1
↘ 1035m	🕰 2hrs	🏠 DP
⊕ East	🎿 2.1	

Take the cable car in La Gorge (télécabine de la Gorge) which starts just beyond
Les Contamines and opposite the car park. Then take the lifts up to the ridge that
leads to the Aiguille de Roselette, to the west of the Col du Mont Joly. Drop down
the back of this ridge under and to the west of the Aiguille de Roselette and climb
up (150m) to the east to get to the Col de la Fenêtre (2245m). Ski down from the
Col to meet up with route number 22 at around 1800m. Instead of climbing back
up to the Col de la Fenêtre, continue south and go round the Tête de la Cicle
(35°/100m) to arrive at the Col de la Cicle by the south side of this last combe. The
ski back down in a north-easterly direction is a bit steep (35°/100m), but there is
often good snow on the. Now you meet up again with route number 22 and you
can ski (without using the lifts) back to where you started (1167m).

Bel. 3 ▪ Col des Chasseurs (AD, 2688m)

⌐ 1210m (road)	🗻 December-April	⊾ 35°-40°/650 m
↗ 1478m	📷 56	⚠ 1
↘ 1478m	◷ 5hrs	⊕ DP
✧ North/North-east	✗ 3.1	

This tour, that starts in Notre-Dame de la Gorge, can be done before the season starts. The climb up the final combe gets narrow and steep (35-49°/150m) and requires a lot of kick-turns, but you often get powder on the descent.

1 MONT BLANC - DÔME DU GOÛTER   4807m
Grand couloir west   TD

⌐ 1400m (road)	🗻 April-June	⊾ 45°-50°/250m
↗ D1 + D2: 1800m + 1100m	📷 34, 239, 244	⚠ 3
↘ D1 + D2: 0m + 2900m	◷ 6-8hrs	⊕ HP
✧ West	✗ 5.3	

This route is for experienced ski mountaineers only. The best time to do it ranges from March (after a long spell of cold but fine weather) to the end of May, while in summer the couloir is too dangerous. At the Goûter Hut there is a winter room to the right that is always open. If you are going to ski this route you should make sure you have carefully marked landmarks on your map because poor visibility can lead to disaster. If, once on the summit of Mont Blanc, the weather and snow conditions change or you do not feel physically or mentally up to the task you can always ski down via the Grands Mulets by route number 133 (Chamonix section).

The west couloir was skied for the first time on 4th June 1973 by Jacky Bessat from Saint-Gervais. The same man holds the record for the longest skied descent in the Alps. There was enough snow (a rare occurrence) for him to ski from the summit of Mont Blanc to the station in Le Fayet (560m). That is a 4250m descent of both difficult (Goûter Couloir) and unusual terrain (train tracks). The commune of Saint-Gervais can therefore boast the longest ski route in the world. This is matched only by Mount McKinley, at 6100m, with a descent of over 4000m and the phenomenal descent on Alaska's Mount Logan where you go from 6000m to sea level! Nothing more than a dream for most skiers, this is undoubtedly a hugely ambitious route with which to open this guide to the Mont Blanc Massif. Nevertheless, I think the highest mountain in the Alps is not a bad place to start a book that brings together some of the most amazing descents in the world. In any case, the conditions have to be very special in order for this route to be skied and any plans to ski or board it require patience and perseverance.

D1 ▪ Saint-Gervais to the Tête Rousse Hut (ref. 1).

D2   From the Tête Rousse Hut climb in the direction of the Grand Couloir. Climb over the rock step (equipped with a cable) and cross the couloir. A mixed climb (PD) of 100m or so will get you onto a ridge. The frequent and unpredictable rock falls in the Grand Couloir make the climb up by the normal summer route the best option. The route now continues up on one or the other side of the ridge until about 150m before the Goûter Hut where you traverse a little to your right (cable). From the hut (3800m) you climb a small snow bank to get to the first summit of the Aiguille du Goûter (3817m). Ski along the horizontal ridge to reach the north-west face of the Dôme du Goûter. After a long, even slope (two small crevassed areas) turn left and either pass under the Dôme du Goûter or climb to its summit. From the Col du Dôme go to the Refuge Vallot (4362m) and from there climb to the summit of Mont Blanc via the Arête des Bosses route number 134 (Chamonix section). The descent follows the same route down to the Goûter Hut. Just beneath the hut (where the cables end) enter the couloir on foot as there are almost always exposed rocks here. Now follow route number 1a (below). If the snow conditions are good you can ski to the Bionnassay Glacier, but make sure there is enough snow at the bottom of the couloir.

1.a   Aiguille du Goûter, north face (TD). Walk to the top of the couloir (see route 1 above). It can also (on rare occasions) be accessed by the north-east ridge (exposed, steppening progressively to the entrance of the couloir). When it was first skied (12th January 1973) by Serge Cachat-Rosset there was snow on the entire length of the couloir (50-55°/500m).

1.b   North-west couloir (the length of the Arête Payot, D+). Start on the west of the snow dome. This is a long 40° couloir that steepens up at the end above the Glacier de la Griaz. The access from the summit is exposed and the rocks are not in good condition. You can also access it from the Grand Couloir near the small col or narrow gully at 3650m followed by an exposed 50m traverse. The first descent was by Dominique Chapuis and Roland Gignoux on 6th September 1971. NB. There are two west-north-west couloirs which are often skiable (D+).

Dôme du Goûter and the Aiguille de Bionnassay

2   TÊTE ROUSSE GLACIER   3200m
North-west face   PD

⌐	1400m (road)	⟨⟩	February-May	⌐	40°/250m
↗	1800m	⟨⟩	34, 37	⚠	2
↘	1800m	⟨⟩	6-8hrs	⊕	SP
⊕	North-west	✗	3.1		

This route requires good snow cover on the Bionnassay Glacier as there is a very uneven section at 2100m and on the lower parts of the route and the bushes on parts of the route can prove problematic if there is not enough snow. For this reason the route is hardly ever in condition before March (although it is not unknown for it to be well covered by February). The route along the glacier and the Torrent de Bionnassay is not obvious at times especially if there are bushes showing. In good conditions, however, this route is much more interesting than the classic route up via the Chalet de l'Are and Le Planet.

From Saint-Gervais go up to Bionnassay (Crozat car park, 1400m). Follow the high tension cable to the chalet at Le Planet. Traverse under the south facing avalanche couloirs to the Chalet de l'Are. Climb up to the Tramway du Mont Blanc (TMB), which passes under Mont Lachat, to the Col du Mont Lachat. If there is lots of snow or it is not stabilised avoid this route as the slopes that you have to cross are steep and grassy. If this is the case, take the TMB (from Saint-Gervais or Le Fayet) to the Col de Voza and skin up the line of the tracks. From the Col du Mont Lachat continue up to the Nid d'Aigle (Eagle's Nest) at 2372m. This is a sustained climb and you will need mountaineering equipment as there is an exposed section where you have pass round on the outside of the last tunnel. Now head up and north-east in the direction of the Cabane des Rognes (open shelter marked as Baraque Forestière on IGN map) and the Tête Rousse Hut. Take the summer path when the snow cover is not good (AD climb), or, in the spring, the north couloir (35-40°/350m).

The descent from the hut includes a steep couloir that requires good technique and equipment that has been checked (tightened bindings, sharp edges) in the top section. A series of beautiful and sustained combes lead to the Bionnassay Glacier. Cross over to the left bank of the glacier to the last step at 2150m (crevassed section). Leave the glacier at the left of its snout and carry on through the trees towards the Torrent de Bionnassay if the snow is good, otherwise turn right and head towards the Chalet de l'Are and the way you came up.

2.a   Access from Bellevue (PD). Take the Bellevue cable car that starts in Les Houches and follow the tramway tracks to the Col du Mont Lachat.

2.b   Access from Le Dérochoir (AD). From the Col du Mont Lachat follow the tramway tracks to around 2100m and climb left (east) onto a steep grassy shoulder (Le Dérochoir, summer path). This takes you to a second (north-facing) bowl, and from here you take the left-right sloping couloir (AD, 35-40°) to cross the rock band and get onto the Rochers des Rognes. Take care if the snow is banking up.

Follow the summer path (continuation of the Arête Payot) across the plateau to the Tête Rousse Hut. Alternatively, you can access the bottom of the large, central couloir at the foot of the Tête Rousse Glacier.

3   AIGUILLE DE BIONNASSAY   D
North face   4052m

1400m (road)		October or May-July		50°/800 m	
D1 + D2: 1800m + 850m		34, 37, 41		3	
D1 + D2: 0m + 2650m		D1+D2: $7^{1/2}$ + $3^{1/2}$ hrs		HP	
North/north-west		5.1			

This north face is one of the best descents in the Massif. However, the route's northerly aspect and complex system of broken glaciers means that any attempt on it requires careful observation to determine the best line. You can do this from the hut the day before. You should also find out exactly what the snow conditions are like as the slopes are quite heavily crevassed. A firm underlying base of snow is preferable, and in ideal conditions there would be a thin layer of powder or softened snow on the surface. The first descent was done by Sylvain Saudan on 6th October 1969.

D1 Saint-Gervais to the Tête Rousse Hut (ref. 1).

D2 From the hut descend a short, steep slope and then traverse south/south-west to the foot of the glaciated face on the Bionnassay. Climb up this face (I recommend you rope up for this) to the Tricot Ridge at around 3750m and then follow the ridge to the summit. On the descent, ski on the headland that comes down from the summit and faces north-east (often hard snow owing to the wind or refreezing). This first section is exposed, and despite the size of the face your sense of security increases the further you go down the suspended glacier.

After this ridge (at around 3650m) move right towards the centre of the face. Now follow the route you took up, between the seracs and ice walls. At around 3000m cross the Bionnassay Glacier to get to its right bank and follow route number 2 down. The direct descent of the north face of the Bionnassay and the long diagonal descent through the seracs and rock bands

On the north face of the Aiguille de Bionnassay

North face of the Bionnassay

beneath it was first done by Pierre Tardivel, Bertrand Delapierre (on a snowboard) and Paul McLoed on 23 June 2001.

3.a   Aiguille de Tricot, north face (TD). Climb up the face in crampons to make sure there is enough snow to cover the ice and to acquaint yourself with the route down. After the sustained descent under the summit, stay right and head towards the rock spur that divides the glaciated face of the Bionnassay at around 3100m. This route avoids the band of seracs lower down. The first descent of this route was by Jean-Pierre Mansard (skis) and his son Yannick (snowboard) on 19th June 1999. Pierre Tardivel had previously skied this face from a helicopter drop on the Aiguille de Bionnassay (55°/400m).

3.b.   Alternative ascent route via the Plan Glacier Hut (2700m) and the Tricot Glacier (AD). After following a steep depression to the east, you come to a slight ridge which requires some mixed climbing. Rejoin the Tricot Ridge on the left. From here climb up to the summit of the Aiguille de Bionnassay (4hrs).

Jean-Pierre Mansard on the north face of the Tricot

4   COL DE TRICOT-MONT VORASSAY   2299m
North-east face   PD

🏁	1400m (road)	🗻	January-April	⤒	35°/150 m
↗	900m	📷	34, 38	⚠	1
↘	900m	⏱	4¹ᐟ² hrs	⊕	SP
✦	North-east	🎿	2.3		

You can ski quite early in the season in this lower altitude ('moyenne montagne') area, under the towering north faces of the Bionnassay and the Miage. Good training for some and a great route in itself for others, this is a route to do at the beginning of the season when the winter cold first penetrates the low and shaded Bionnassay valley. This is best done as a traverse. What makes a climb up in skins for the ski-tourer is the great descent that follows it, and I prefer to make smooth turns in the beautiful cold snow on the Bionnassay face than to fight my way through the sometimes crusty lumps on the Miage side. What's more, if you decide to start and finish the day at the Bellevue cable-car, it is only a 35-minute skin up from the tiny village of Le Crozat to the Col de Voza.

From Saint-Gervais go up to Bionnassay and follow route number 2 to the Chalet de l'Are. Head south and, at around 1850m, go over the moraine and cross the glacier. Cross the second moraine, on the other side of the glacier, to get to the Combe de Tricot. Climb up the combe to the col (2120m). From here climb 180m up the sustained slopes that take you to the summit ridge of Mont Vorassay (2299m). Watch out for the enormous cornices on the face opposite. The snow is often in excellent condition on the descent down the Combe de Tricot. Now follow route number 2 out. Do have a look at the descent while on the way up as the shrubs and bushes start at between 1500m and 1800m.

4.a   Traverse of the col towards the Chalets de Miage (PD). This variation of the route is not always in condition owing to its south-westerly aspect and the numerous avalanches that come down from the Pointe Inférieure de Tricot. In the spring on firm snow you can ski from the top of Mont Vorassay, but take care as the snow sits on loose dry grass... Cross the village of Miage and climb up the track on the face opposite. If there has been heavy snowfall this area is avalanche prone and it may be wise to climb 200m up to Mont Truc (1811m) to avoid the dangerous area. Follow the

Col de Tricot seen from the Miage chalets

path through the wood to the village of La Gruvaz depending where you have left your car(s) (7h, 35°/400m).

4.b   Access from Bellevue (PD). Take the Bellevue cable-car up from Les Houches. Cross the tramway and head south down through the wood to join route number 4 as it climbs up towards the Chalet de l'Are. If the snow conditions are good you can also traverse along the south face of Mont Lachat and loosing a little bit of height as you go. Just under the summit there is a hedaland that takes you down to the Chalet de l'Are.

4.c   Pointe Inférieure de Tricot, west face (2830m, D+). The first descent was by Daniel Chauchefoin on 11th March 1984 (40°/800m with some sections of 45°).

4.d   Pointe Inférieure de Tricot, east couloir (2830m, D). Very narrow at the summit, this couloir is accessed by a narrow gulley before the point marked 2204m on the map (40-45°/600m). The (south-facing) couloir on the left can be skied towards the end of the season.

5	COL DE MIAGE	3367m
	Durier Hut	AD

⌐ 1150m (road)	🏔 March-May	📐 40°-45°/350m
↗ 2200m	📷 41	⚠ 2
↘ 2200m	🕐 10hrs	⊕ HP
✪ North-west	🎿 4.3	

The Durier Hut is perched high on the Col de Miage, but the Plan Glacier Hut, at an altitude of 2713m, also has the air of an eagle's nest. It is well equipped and it can sleep 15 people. However, is not used much in the winter. This despite the fact that the Col de Miage is conveniently on the border with Italy and the descent from it into Italy is not too steep. In spring you can drive a 4x4 up to the Chalets de Miage and this route can be done there and back in a day (starting very early in the morning, obviously).
Other possibilities: traverse of the Dômes de Miage (10.b) or cross into Italy via the Miage Glacier.

Durier Hut and the Miage peaks

Climb to below the Plan Glacier Hut (see ref. 2) to around 2500m. Stick to the right of the glacier as you go round the base of the Aiguille de Tricot to avoid the crevasses and head for the pronounced couloir that leads to the Col de Miage. At the top of the Col, traverse 100m to the right to get to the Durier Hut. The descent from the Col de Miage is steep at first. The slope is slightly less steep on the right, steepens up again in

Return via the Miage chalets

the middle section and narrows at the bottom. Leave the glacier pretty soon by the old lines of moraine on its right bank and a small gorge. Move back left and follow the valley down. In spring, there are fewer avalanches down the right side of the glacier (from 2092m down) but it is steeper.

5.a   Durier couloir south (point marked 3358m on map, D+). This is similar to route number 5 but a little less steep. First descent by Daniel Chauchefoin (January 1976).

5.b   Col de Miage, north/north-west face (3342m, D+). Skied for the first time by Jacky Bessat on 8 September 1972, this slope is wider with an average gradient of 45°/600m.

6	**DÔMES DE MIAGE**		**3673m**
	Métrier Ridge		**D+**

⚑	1150m (road)	🏔	March-June	⬏	50°/400m
➚	D1+D2: 1450m + 1070m	📷	41, 42	⚠	3 (avalanches, seracs)
➘	D1+D2: 0m + 2510m	☺	D1+D2: 5 + 7hrs	⊕	HP
✥	North	🎿	5.1		

At the end of spring there is enough snow in the Miage valley to think about skiing the Métrier and you can even get to the Chalets de Miage with a 4x4. Bear in mind the fact that the suns hits the north-east facing bottom part of the slope very early. Snow slides can be set off from 3300m, and this is particularly true of the small east facing slope next to the rocks on the left. Thanks to the heavy snowfall in 1999, a group of 6 'volunteers' from the guide's scheme and I were able to put together a pretty exhausting itinerary (early June). Day 1: Start at Notre-Dame de la Gorge, climb up via the Col des Glaciers and descend the north face of the Dôme de Neige on the Aiguille des Glaciers. Day 2: Start from the Conscrits Hut, Bérangère-Miage traverse and descend the Métrier. Day 3: From the Plan-Glacier Hut climb to the summit of the Aiguille de Bionnassay via the Aiguille de Tricot and ski the powder on the north-west face. This proves that you can also access the Métrier from the Tré la Tête Glacier via the Conscrits Hut. The first descent of the Métrier Ridge was by P. Clément and A. Giraud on 22 June 1968. Pierre Tardivel successfully skied the north face direct in November 1988.

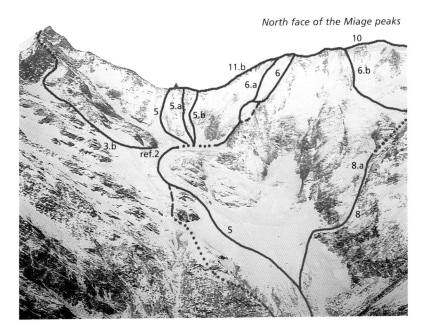

North face of the Miage peaks

D1 Climb up to the Plan Glacier Hut (see ref. 2, 2896m).

D2 From the hut descend to the glacier. Cross the glacier heading south towards the rocks opposite. Take the north-west facing couloir beneath the point marked 2944m on the map and join the Métrier Ridge. There is a bit of mixed climbing up the arête to 3300m where it steepens up and you have to cross a rock step. Watch out for possible sheets of ice on the left beneath the cornices on the summit. Now head right to join the ridge leading to the summit that comes up from the Col de Dômes (3564m). There is also a more committing route that continues under the summit on the left. The direct descent from the summit, at 3672m, rarely has enough snow and snow slides often uncover the sheets of ice beneath. I recommend you go up to the summit and back and then start your descent between the rocks on the right. Now drop onto the north face. After 200m continue on the left of the spur and then head east onto the glacier (these slopes get the sun early). Join the system of ice steps and gullies (50°/100m) on the left. After having crossed the bergschrund, join the glacier and the route that you took to climb up. The 'intégrale' descent of the Métrier Ridge is less easy to ski in the lower section.

Mont Truc

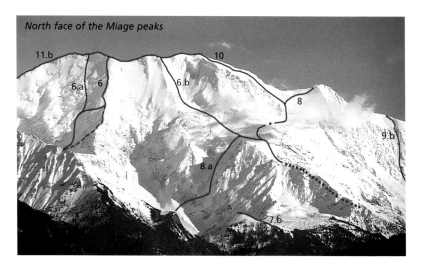

North face of the Miage peaks

6.a North face direct (TD). First skied by Pierre Tardivel in 1988 (50°/500, crevassed).

6.b Covagnet Couloir (TD). This route, which starts between the 3633m and
3666m summits, was first skied by Jacky Bessat on 10th August 1973 (50°/400m).

7	**MONT TRUC**	**1811m**
	Traverse	F

1150m (road)		Decembre-April		track	
660m		41, 42, 45		1	
660m		3hrs		SP	
North-west		1.2			

You can treat this easy tour as a training exercise at the beginning of the season,
as an alternative on bad weather days or a snow-shoe outing. Even though it is
not far from the Les Contamines ski area, this area still has a wild and isolated
feel to it. In fact, it also makes a great 'belvedere' route to reconnoitre the routes
from the Col de Tricot to the Les Contamines lifts to the west.

Follow the directions for ref. 2 and take the route to the Chalets de Miage. Then,
at 1380m, head right (sign) and get to the Chalets du Truc and the summit . You
can take the track that forks at 1550m down to Les Contamines via La Frasse.

7.a Access by the Chalets de Miage (PD). You can also climb up by the
Chalets de Miage and the east face of Mont Truc (see 4.a and the avalanche risk
owing to heavy snowfall on the traverse).

7.b ▪ Le Monthieu (F). It is also possible to go along the headland towards Le Monthieu up to 2100m. There are lovely views from here and an easy ski down.

8   AIGUILLE DE LA BÉRANGÈRE   3425m
Armancette Glacier   AD

⚑	1200m (road)	🏔	February-May		35°/200m
↗	D1+D2: 770m + 1455m	📷	41, 42, 43, 44, 45	⚠	2
↘	D1+D2: 0m + 2200m	⏱	D1+D2: 2 + 9hrs		SP
✦	North-west		3.3		

The Armancette Glacier is one of the most spectacular routes in the Massif. As you can see from the height gain, it is also quite an 'athletic' trip! The direct climb up the Armancette Glacier, however, is not recommended unless there are already lots of tracks in. Rather than stopping at the Tré la Tête Hut you can also spend the night at the new Conscrits Hut. If you do decide to take this

East ridge of the Bérangère

option, the climb up on the first day will be 2 to 3 hours longer. From this hut, you can also access the Aiguille de la Bérangère by climbing straight up to the Col de la Bérangère (3348m) by the shorter but steeper 'cheminée' (chimney). From there you can then get on to the Armancette Glacier and avoid the tricky descent from the summit along the east ridge and the cornices. The glacier was first skied by unknown skiers in 1925.

The Bérangère is quite a popular tour and although the top part of the slope is quite steep the south face is a very pleasant ski.

D1 ▪ See hut 3 and hut 3.a to get to the Tré la Tête Hut.

D2 ▪ From the Tré la Tête follow the directions given in ref. 4 to get to the new Conscrits Hut. There is a steady slope leading up to the Aiguille de la Bérangère until you reach a steep area that you can go round on the left side. Move back towards the south-east ridge to the right, climb over the high step and reach the summit on your left. Walk down the east ridge from the summit (cornices make roping up necessary). After an exposed 200m, traverse to the Col de la Bérangère. Ski down the middle of the Armancette Glacier and then stay on the right. Go round and under the rocky outcrop and leave the glacier on the right at around 3000m. Traverse northwards and after a wide headland traverse rightwards above a very steep slope, with a rocky section at the top, to get to the point marked 2772m on the map. If this looks dangerous go back to the right bank of the glacier, go round the outcrop and climb 15 minutes up the small combe to the south of the point

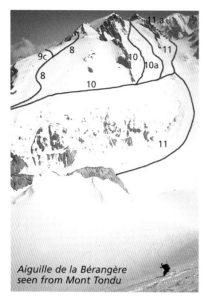

Aiguille de la Bérangère seen from Mont Tondu

marked 2772m. From this point head north into the large bowl under the Pointe de Covagnet. At around 2300m, and depending on the snow conditions, go round the rocky outcrop either on the right or the left and continue down the small valley that narrows.

When you start to see the first trees stay on the right bank of the stream and steer clear of the dangerous slopes on the left. Now join the summer track at the bottom of the rock band (a steep, tree-covered slope that is nevertheless protected from avalanches) that takes you to the Lac d'Armancette (lake). Follow the track through the wood (follow the sign on the left to Les Loyer-Le Cugnon at around 1450m) that takes you back to the car park after the small bridge. You can also follow the track on the right to La Frasse which is more comfortable but requires leaving one or more cars in two different places.

8.a   Covagnet Glacier (AD). For very strong skiers. Turn right at the Pointe de Covagnet (at 2650m) and descend the steep slopes on the left bank of the Covagnet Glacier. Come back right and traverse under the glacier along a steep ledge to the Miage Valley (exposed sections with a risk of serac fall). You should only try this route when there is very good snow cover and in cold weather conditions. For this reason, this route is not recommended. You finish in the village of La Gruvaz.

9   AIGUILLE DE LA BÉRANGÈRE   3425m
North couloirs   AD

⚑	1200m (road)	🗻	January-May	⤵	sect. of 40°
↗	2200m	📷	42, 44, 45	⚠	2
↘	2200m	◔	10hrs	⊕	SP
✦	all	🎿	3.3		

Accessing these couloirs from below is hard going, and the mixed climbing on the south-west ridge and the buttresses requires alpine mountaineering experience. I recommend you access variants b and c from the Conscrits Hut. While the long north-west ridge of the Aiguille de la Bérangère is not very popular in winter (classic access route via number 8), it is nevertheless the main way to access the couloirs for the variant routes described here. You can safely get to the Tré la Tête Hut from Notre-Dame de la Gorge, and in spring, when it is open, this is a good starting point for tours (in manageable stages) to the Aiguille de la Bérangère, Col des Glaciers and Mont Tondu. Moreover, you can start quite late on the forest trail from Notre-Dame de la Gorge as is not exposed to avalanches, unlike the path from Le Cugnon. There is often good snow on the north-west face of the Bérangère and the Armancette, so this area is definitely worth a visit. You can do the whole of this route in one day, although be prepared for a tough climb up.

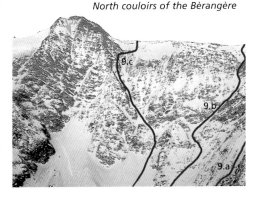

North couloirs of the Bèrangère

From Les Contamines go to Le Cugnon and follow the Tré la Tête path to 1810m. Go up the large combe to the southeast. The couloir that rapidly gets steeper takes you to a col between the Pointe de Chaborgne and the Pointe du Plan. You can continue along the crests to get to the Aiguille de la Bérangère. Pick out your descent route on your way up. When there is very good snow cover you can ski other routes on the north-west face.

9.a   Chaborgne Couloir (AD). Starts at 2458m, narrows at the bottom, 40°/400m section that is 50° in parts. Finishes in the Combe d'Armancette.

9.b   Têtes des Tré la Tête, north couloir (AD). Start at the point marked 2897m, to the east of the Pointe de Chaborgne. 40°/250m with a narrow start at 45°, the route forms an S shape and joins the Combe d'Armancette.

9.c   West couloir (D+). There is a third couloir that can be skied which starts at around 3250m. It faces west and its start is often both difficult to find and to

The Miage Massif seen from the west

access. It is sometimes accessed on foot. Start at the west headland and traverse rightwards over mixed ground and then head northwards under the Aiguille de la Bérangère. Stay on the left bank at the end of the route. First skied in March 1983 by Daniel Chauchefoin (40-45°/700m with sections of 50°).

10   DÔMES DE MIAGE   3673m
Traverse   AD

⌐	1200m (road)	🏔	February-May	⌐	35°
↗	D1+D2: 1380m + 1090m	📷	39, 41, 42, 44, 45	⚠	1
↘	D1+D2: 0m + 2470m	⏱	D1+D2: 5 + 6¹/² hrs.	⚐	SP
✦	South	🎿	3.1		

The Tré la Tête valley has all the ski tourer could ask for: a sense of isolation, superb views over a collection of north faces and suspended glaciers, a variety of easy and technical routes, and a new, well designed hut in a great location. You can't ask for a better guardian and cook – the welcome is warm and he is generous, polite, and laid back.

The classic traverse of the Dômes de Miage includes the descent of the Armancette Glacier from the Col de la Bérangère (route number 8). If necessary, you can take the 'cheminée' or chimney (40°/60m from the Col de la Bérangère), and join the Tré la Tête Glacier via the glacier sud or the Conscrits Hut.

D1   From Les Contamines climb to the Conscrits Hut following directions given in ref. 4.

D2   Traverse eastwards towards the old hut (moraine at around 2750m, rocks at around 2800m), and then move to the middle of the glacier. Climb up towards the spur that comes down from the summit marked at 3670m and avoid the crevas-

On the way up to the Dômes de Miage, opposite Mont Tondu

sed area by keeping near to the rocks. Traverse rightwards to the large south to south-east facing combe that takes leads to the col between the points marked 3633m and 3666m on the map. Follow the ridge to the summit. The descent follows the same route that you took to climb up. You can also traverse to the Col des Dômes and descend via the south-east combe (route 11).

On the traverse of the Dômes de Miage

10.a South-west face (PD). Start as for route number 10. Past the Aiguille de la Bérangère continue up the length of the glacier. Head under the crevasses towards the south spur of the Dôme (3169m). From there go right and climb up the combe to the Col des Dômes. Stick to the left bank of the combe (fewer crevasses at the top).

10.b Traverse of the Miage from east to west (AD). Take route 10 and descend the west slope towards the Col de la Bérangère. Move left and pass above the short steep 'cheminée' or chimney couloir to get to the top of the glacier. Climb up the atmospheric north ridge to get to the summit of the Bérangère. You can also descend via route 8 or ski the 'cheminée' couloir which is shorter.

11 DÔMES DE MIAGE   3673m
Col Infranchissable   PD

⚑	1200m (road)	🏔	February-May	⤵	not very steep
↗	D1+D2: 1380m + 1090m	📷	41, 42, 44	⚠	1
↘	D1+D2: 0m + 2500m	⏱	D1+D2: 5 + 6¹ᐟ² hrs	⊕	SP
✦	South-west	⛷	2.3		

Mountaineers and skiers rarely visit the highest 'dome' in the Miage chain as the climb to its summit is a little more exposed than on the more westerly peaks in the group. Nevertheless this is the first summit what has to be one of the best projects in any ski mountaineer's career: the traverse of the Mont Blanc Massif from the Col du Bonhomme to the Col Ferret. However, if you continue from the Col Infranchissable to the Col de Miage and cross into Italy (another atmospheric route), the tour does not go to this peak. You can carry on from here to the south side of the Massif and the descent starts on the left of a small hanging glacier (about 40°/150m, changes from year to year). From here, the Italian Miage

Descent from the Col Infranchissable skiing 'en traces de peigne'

Glacier, you can descend into Val Veni or continue your grand traverse by climbing up to the Gonella Hut (former mountain cabin) and spending the night there. Although rarely in condition, it is also possible to ski the east face of the Col Infranchissable (29.a). The traverse of the Massif from east to west includes skiing the Aiguilles Grises ridge, which can be quite exposed when it is icy. You can also get to the Gonella Hut via the Glacier du Dôme, starting at the couloir south of the Piton des Italiens, while the descent of the Bionnassay Glacier from the Col de Bionnassay is a quick way to get to the Durier Hut (450m of climbing). If you follow the traverse in this direction (east-west), it is easier to cross (on the climb up) the rocky sections of the Miage ridge. The differences in altitude, changes in orientation and exposure to the wind make this 'High Level Traverse of Mont Blanc' (Traversée Haute du Mont Blanc) a committing and delicate ski.

D1 Go to either Le Cugnon or Notre-Dame de la Gorge from Les Contamines and climb to the Conscrits Hut (see ref. 4).

D2 Traverse eastwards from the hut towards the old Conscrits Hut (under the rock, see 10). There is now an easy climb up the middle of the Tré la Tête Glacier. Continue to the Col Infranchissable (3349m). The climb does not have to end here, and you can continue into the large south-east facing combe on your left. This takes you to the east and above the Col des Dômes (sections of 35-40°) and from here you can walk up the snow ridge to the highest summit of the Dômes de Miage (3673m). Descend by the same route or by the small south-west facing slope (see 10.a) then back down the Tré la Tête Glacier.

11.a South-east face (PD). From the Col Infranchissable climb to the summit marked 3633m (on the left with a narrow ridge) and descend via the small crevassed south-facing valley and route 10.a.

11.b Traverse to the Col de Miage (Durier Hut) (D-). Go from the Col Infranchissable to the ridge that leads to the summit marked 3672m (slope sometimes icy, steep at the beginning and overlooks the Italian side of the Miage).

Traverse north to the point marked 3580m on the map. Follow the snowy headland and descend the rock ridge on foot (you will need to rope up for part of this).
This takes you to the Col de Miage (3367m) and the Durier Hut. Follow route 5
and the descent of the west face, or take the south slope to rejoin the Bionnassay
Glacier that takes you into Italy.

12   AIGUILLE NORD DE TRÉ LA TÊTE   3892m
North-west face   AD+

⚑ 1200m (road)	🗻 February-March	⌊ 50°/100m, 40°/250m
↗ D1+D2: 1380m + 1310m	📷 49	⚠ 2
↘ D1+D2: 0m + 2690m	☺ D1+D2: 5 + 6^1/2 hrs.	⊕ SP
✦ North-west	✗ 4.3	

Although not excessively steep, the north-west face of the Aiguille Nord de Tré la
Tête (also known as the Tête Blanche) is not often skied. At the end of winter the
highest section is often icy, and in May and June the lower slopes get a lot of sun
towards the end of the day which can create snow slips and crust. First skied on
23rd May 1926 by two guides, Armand Charlet and Camille Devouassoux, this
descent has an important place in the history of extreme skiing. It must have
taken a lot of bottle and a good dose of enthusiasm to set off on this kind of trip
with 2.15m long wooden skis that had no metal edges, and were attached to
their boots by only a single loop and leather straps... History does not record if
they skied the mountain from its
summit!

D1 From Les Contamines follow
ref. 4 to get to the Conscrits Hut.

D2 Join the Tré la Tête Glacier
(see 10) and follow it to 3250m.
Now climb right, to under the
Tête Carrée. Follow the rock line
south-east to join the ridge (at
3753m) that takes you to the summit (cornices). On the descent it is
a good idea to follow the north
ridge at the start and to use the
slopes you have had a good look
at on the way up. To descend
directly under the summit you
have to be absolutely sure that
there are no loose slabs or patches
of ice under the surface. You can
sometimes finish on the left
branch of the glacier (west of the
spur marked 3240m) after having
gone round to the right of the cre-

Aiguille nord de Tré la Tête

vasses in the middle of the glacier and you check out this descent route as you climb up the Tré la Tête Glacier.

12.a   Tête Carrée, north/north-west face (3732m, AD). An even slope that is often icy (40-45°/250m). Keep to the right bank.

13   AIGUILLE DE LA LEX BLANCHE   3697m
North-west face   D

1200m (road)		March-June			50°/300m
D1 + D2: 1380m + 1120m		50			3
D1 + D2: 0m + 2500m		D1 + D2: 5 + 6$^{1/2}$ hrs.			HP
North-west		5.1			

The best place to stand to check out your route on the Lex Blanche for the next day is a little higher than the old Conscrits Hut, at almost the same level as the glacier. It really is an impressive slope seen face on, and if, on the way up, the snow turns out to be too hard or even unstable you can always turn around. The first descent was by Jacky Bessat in 1974.

D1   Climb to the Conscrits Hut (see ref. 4) from Les Contamines.

D2   Follow route 11 to the Tré la Tête Glacier. Cross the glacier heading towards the point marked 2908m on the map and access the north-west face of the Lex Blanche, between the two rock spurs. The right-hand spur forms the base of the west ridge of the Lex Blanche. The route follows the small glacial valley to the

North face of the Lex Blanche

top of the left-hand spur (at around 3200m). Continue up the steep snowy headland (50°) to the summit. It is often easier to traverse to the Col de la Lex Blanche, and from there to follow the ridge to the summit (less steep and easier on your calf muscles!). If the snow conditions are good you can ski straight down the face or the route you climbed up. Otherwise, you can pick a line using the slopes in the centre of the face where it is not so steep (crevasses, bergschrund at the top).

14   DÔME DE NEIGE   3592m
North face   D

⌐	1200m (road)	🏔	March-June	⌐	50°/200m
↗	D1+D2: 1380m + 1010m	📷	50, 53	⚠	3
↘	D1+D2: 0m + 2390m	◷	D1+D2: 5 + 8½ hrs.	✛	HP
✣	North	🎿	5.1		

The Dôme de Neige is not considered a summit in its own right and you can combine the descent of its north-west face with that of the Aiguille des Glaciers. I managed to ski this route in perfect conditions in June after having set off from Notre-Dame de la Gorge at 8 in the morning (with the idea of skiing the Lex Blanche). The middle part of the face is often heavily crevassed with seracs that are difficult to cross. The year we skied it, the face was in good condition. Nevertheless, think about taking a snow stake or a wooden plank in case you need to abseil. The start, from the ridge marked 3706m, takes you down a 300m slope of 50° and the part of the route that goes through the seracs also has some very steep sections. It is easier to access the Dôme de Neige via the Col des Glaciers (15).

D1   Climb to the Conscrits Hut (see ref. 4) from Les Contamines.

D2   Follow route 11 to access the Tré la Tête Glacier at around 2700m. Try not to lose height and cross to the point marked 2807m on the map (rock below the small spur that is under the Col de la Scie). Climb up the small valley to the right of the point marked 2807m and traverse to the right of the face (3000m) to get past the narrow icy section (changes from year to year). Once you have got onto the higher and less steep section, climb up the large combe and follow the line of the bergschrund. Higher up, at around 3400m, the slope gets steeper again and turns to the left slightly up to the summit. 100m above the bergschrund, go to the right and avoid the summit step and climb to the wide col on the right of the Dôme de Neige. It is also possible to climb up the ridge on the right after having crossed the bergscrund at around 3200m (less monotonous route, but steeper at the beginning and often icy). The descent route depends, to a certain extent, on the conditions that you experienced on the way up. The slope to the left, near the west ridge, is more exposed and is often icy.

A great ski!

14.a ▪ **Alternative access route (AD).** You can climb up via route 15 if you are sure that the descent is 'ok' (the advantage being you spend less time underneath the seracs).

15   AIGUILLE DES GLACIERS   3816m
Via the Col des Glaciers   AD

⌐	1200m (road)	▨	February-May	ᒣ	sect. of 40°
⟋	D1 + D2: 1380m + 1300m	▣	46, 53	⚠	2
⟍	D1 + D2: 0m + 2610m	☉	D1 + D2: 5 + 8hrs	⊕	RM
⊕	All	⚔	3.1		

As its name suggests, this mountain rises up out of three glaciers and they form part of the border with Italy. The Aiguille des Glaciers and its rocky summit are definitely worth a visit, not least to ski the face that gets the afternoon sun. It was first skied in May 1926 by Armand Charlet and Camille Devouassoux. The Robert Blanc Hut, on the Les Chapieux face, has an interesting history. The first plans to put a hut near the 'rochers des Cabottes' or 'Les Cabottes Rocks' were put forward in the 1970s. These plans were abandoned in favour of a project to build on the site the hut currently occupies. In fact, the hut is ideally located and can be accessed from both Les Contamines and Chamonix to the north and by the normal route from the Tarantaise, to the south. Thanks to John, the hut's guardian, and his unusually fine wine cellar, the Robert Blanc Hut has become a gastronomic haven for the area's summertime visitors. The winter room is very comfortable in spring, and the magnificent sunrises in this part of the Massif are more reminiscent of the valleys to the south than its chilly alpine setting.

The guide Robert Blanc was a passionate skier and a true 'man of the mountains'. He was one of the key exponents of the development of the Les Arcs ski resort at its inception. He was also a committed amateur off-piste skier, ski-tourer and ski-mountaineer and he has a number of first descents of steep slopes to his name.

D1 ▪ Climb to the Conscrits Hut from Les Contamines via ref. 4.

D2 ▪ Descent directly under the hut and join the glacier. Cross the glacier roughly along the 2550m contour line and try not to lose height on the left. Climb up the left side of the glacier that comes down from the Col des Glaciers. At the top section under the col (steep, possible slabs), head for the Pointe des Lanchettes. Traverse along the west ridge on foot (rocks, cornices) until you get to the Col du Moyen Âge. The ridge gets wider now and leads to the Dôme de Neige (3592m). Continue above the south-west combe to the foot of the Aiguille des Glaciers (3700m). Leave your skis here and climb up the couloir that takes you to a notch near the summit (1hr of steep mixed climbing, AD). Collect your skis and descend along the route you took up. You can avoid some of the sections along the ridge, that you did on foot, by skiing along the top of the north face. (This can also be skied, has sections of 40° and can be exposed depending on snow cover.) The steep slope on the face in the shade, after the Col des Glaciers, can be dangerous so keep left and then move to the centre of the glacier (crevasses). This is not the standard descent route from this peak. You can also descend by the west face to

Mont Blanc and the Aiguille des Glaciers

Les Chapieux or the Robert Blanc Hut, or into Italy by the Col de la Seigne or the Col de la Scie (more exposed).

15.a Aiguille des Glaciers by the Robert Blanc Hut (AD). Descend from the hut and go round the spur that comes down from the Pointe des Lanchettes. Cross the steep moraine to get onto the Glacier des Glaciers. There is now an easy climb up the right bank of the glacier (a few crevasses between 3100m and 3300m if you cross to the centre), then continue up the big combe under the Aiguille des Glaciers. Pass the Dôme de Neige on the right to get to the last headland. The full descent of the south-west face by the Glacier des Glaciers finishes in Les Chapieux (route 18 in reverse). From here you can also cross into Italy via the Col de la Seigne.

16   POINTE DES LANCHETTES   3085m
North face   PD

⌐ 1200m (road)	🏔 January-May	⬦ 35°/100m
↗ D1+D2: 770m + 1115m	📷 46	⚠ 1
↘ D1+D2: 0m + 1880m	⏱ D1+D2: 3$^{1/2}$+4$^{1/2}$ hrs.	⌂ SP
⊕ North/North-west	⚒ 3.1	

Aspect of slope is essential when it comes to the quality of the snow, and a change in orientation of only a few degrees can make a huge difference. You must be able to alter your direction regularly to make the most of the snow conditions. If

Light and cold!

you get it right, you can move from breakable crust to perfect powder in just a few metres. This comes with experience, testing and observing the snow conditions and not necessarily always following other people's tracks.

Owing to its orientation, you can do this route in a day. You can also do it from the Conscrits Hut. If you start out from the Conscrits you will have to get onto the Tré la Tête Glacier (roughly 100m descent). You can also treat this tour as training for other tours or as a means of checking out the Glacier des Glaciers.

D1 Climb to the Tré la Tête Hut from Les Contamines (see directions in ref. 3 and ref. 3a).

D2 From the hut move onto the glacier. After the Mauvais Pas go past the Tré la Grande crevasses (between 2300m and 2400m) and continue on the right bank of the glacier. Head towards the north faces and to the left of the large white slope under the Col des Glaciers. Go the left of the rocks and continue up the slope so that you end up above these rocks. Now stay on the right of the glacier as you climb up to the col. You can walk to the summit of the Pointe des Lanchettes, and there is often enough snow on the north face for you to ski it. Descend straight down from the col and stay to the left to avoid the areas prone to slab avalanche.

16.a Aiguille des Lanchettes, north couloir (3073m, D+). descended by J. Labonne and P. Marin-Lamellet on 14th May 1982 (45°/350m).

17 MONT TONDU — 3169m
Pain de Sucre, north-east — AD

1200m (road)	March-May	40°/150m
↗ 1970m	46, 55, 57	1
↘ 1970m	9hrs	SP
North/North-west	3.1	

The north-east face of the Mont Tondu is an excellent introduction to steep skiing. However, do take care at the beginning of the season as the higher rock band does not have enough snow making the route more exposed. Moreover, the slope at the bottom of the combe can be prone to avalanches (convex and 30°). Ski this route in spring snow to give yourself the best choice of lines on the descent. If you are fit you can do this tour in a day, or if you prefer a more leisurely pace you can do it over two days with a night in the Tré la Tête Hut.

Follow ref. 3 or ref. 3.a to the Tré la Tête Hut from Les Contamines (Le Cugnon). Continue up the glacier and pass the Tré la Grande seracs (fewer crevasses towards right bank). Cross to the left bank of the glacier to the foot of the line of rocks that comes down from the Aiguille des Lanchettes. Climb diagonally up the first sustained slope to get on to the Mont Tondu Glacier. Cross a combe and climb up a second step on its right to join the summit ridge to the left of the Pyramide Chaplan. When the snow is firm enough you can also access the summit by the left (east) ridge. The descent from the Pain de Sucre starts at 20° and reaches 40° (more so on the left, in the centre of the small north face).

17.a   West and north-west faces (Nant Blanc) (AD). These routes can be accessed from the Tré la Tête side and from the Nant Blanc or the Lacs de Jovets (lakes). At the beginning of the season the route up via the Combe Blanche starts in Notre-Dame de la Gorge (2000m height gain), but you should not use this approach when there is lots of snow as there is a high risk of avalanche in this area.

17.b   Col des Chasseurs (AD). From the summit of the Pain de Sucre drop onto the west face and follow the line of the north-west ridge. Go past the Pyramide Chaplan and traverse up to the Col des Chasseurs (2720m). The north-east face is a bit tricky at the bottom (traverse across a steep slope), but is an interesting descent and takes you back onto the Tré la Grande area (possible sections of 40° at the bottom).

Mont Tondu

18   MONT TONDU   3169m
Tour   AD

⌐	1050m (road)	🏔	February-May	⌐	35°-40°/150m
↗	D1+D2: 1700m + 900m	📷	46, 55, 57, 59	⚠	2
↘	D1+D2: 0m + 2600m	🕐	D1+D2: 6 + 4hrs.	🏠	SP
✦	All	⛷	3.2		

This is a route for experienced ski-mountaineers only, as it is quite 'athletic' and has a steep north-west face to negotiate. If you think the slopes look dangerous (wind slab, icy conditions), you can go back via the Col du Tondu or do the tour via the Tré la Tête Glacier, Nant Borrant and the Col du Bonhomme (about 6hrs) before ending up back at Les Chapieux. You can also start this tour in Les Contamines, but this makes the first stage (the Col du Bonhomme and the climb to the Robert Blanc Hut) very long indeed. Even so, the other way round (from the Tré la Tête Hut south, return via the Col du Bonhomme) the stages are not well spaced.

D1   Follow ref. 5.a to the Robert Blanc Hut.

D2   From the hut traverse westwards and go round the south spur of the Aiguille des Lanchettes to get onto the top section of the glacier. Cross the rock band to join the Col du Tondu (cable, 2895m). Either follow the ridge or walk round the summit (crampons recommended) to get to the Pain de Sucre. As you can't see the descent route on the way up, take care as there can be icy patches and banks of snow built up by the easterly wind or the fœhn. At the bottom of the big slope (around 2500m) traverse left to cross the edge of the rock

View from Mont Tondu over the Lacs Jovet

band above the Lacs Jovet (lakes). You now join route 19. You can cut across to one of two cols that will take you to the Glaciers valley. The first one, Col d'Enclave (20), is to the north and is quite steep and the second is the Col des Tufs (20a).

19   MONTS JOVET   2468m
Normal route, Pointe Nord   F

⚐ 1200m (road)	🏔 December-April	⤵ 25-30°/80m
↗ 1260m	📷 56, 57	⚠ 1
↘ 1260m	☉ 6hrs	⊕ SP
✦ All	⚒ 1.2	

The Jovet lakes sector is quite a special area. Good snow cover means you can ski here from early on in the season, and although it is easy to access it still has a wild and untamed feel. The almost 1000m north face requires serious observation before you set off on one of its numerous

Mont Tondu from the Col du Bonhomme

routes as some of them are full of bushes and shrubs at the beginning of winter. The angle of the slopes varies from 25° to 35° and the snow stays cold here. However, the snow layers can be quite fragile as snow is deposited by the wind and at low altitudes grassy slopes do not form a good base for snow. Having said that, you should always be able to find a safe way down.

From Les Contamines go to Notre-Dame de la Gorge. Follow the summer path of the Tour du Mont Blanc to the Chalet de la Balme (1706m) and climb to above the small gorges (high tension cable) to Plan Jovet (1900m). Cross Plan Jovet eastwards (small EDF dams) to get to the Lacs Jovet (lakes at 2160m). From here turn north and head towards the point marked 2428m on the summit ridge of the Monts Jovet. Cross the north-west face to get to the north summit. There are two possible descent routes: the route you took up or the north-west face. The latter has a steeper slope (40°/200m) and can only be skied when there is good snow cover and the snow is stabilised. The lower slopes are sustained, and you head left above the wood to rejoin your route of ascent near the Plan de la Rollaz.

19.a ▪ North-west face (AD). Depending on the conditions you can sometimes ski just north of the point marked 2368m (small depression at 2350m on the north-west face) and the slope is less steep. The bushes and shrubs at the bottom of the other routes on the north-west face require a certain amount of snow cover.

20   COL D'ENCLAVE   2672m
North face   AD

P	1200m (road)		December-April		35 à 40°/400m
↗	1460m		56, 57, 59	⚠	1
↘	1460m		6¹ᐟ² hrs		SP
⊕	All		3.1		

This col is right on the edge of the Massif, and the long non-glacial descent down its north face can be skied throughout the winter. There is often good snow here and the traverse to the south via the Combe de Bellaval and Chalets de Bellaval can be a great ski.

From Les Contamines follow route 19 to Plan Jovet. If the snow conditions are good (stable top layer), you can traverse under the north-west face of the Têtes de Bellaval to the Col d'Enclave. Otherwise follow the headland on the right bank of the narrow valley up to the Lacs de Jovet (lakes). From the left bank of the lakes climb up the big north/north-west couloir (narrow and steep at the top) to the Col d'Enclave. The descent takes you down this same couloir. On the way up check out the conditions on the (skier's) left side of the couloir as they are often nicer to ski. At the bottom rejoin your approach route (19).

20.a   Col des Tufs (2651m, AD). From the the south end of Plan Jovet (1900m) head south-east towards the ridges. Go left to begin with and then move under the Têtes de Bellaval. You will recognise the steep couloir (35-40°/200m) that comes down from the col. The snow stays nice and cold in this area.

21   TÊTE NORD DES FOURS   2756m
North face   F

P	1200m (road)		December-April		35°
↗	1550m		59	⚠	1
↘	1550m		6hrs		SP
⊕	All		1.1		

This route gets snow relatively early on in the winter and can be done in a day. This is one of Zub's favourite routes. Endowed with boundless enthusiasm, Zub is a dedicated skier of all the couloirs in the area and is well known both for his solo outings and his study of local place names.

From Les Contamines and Notre-Dame de la Gorge follow route 22 to the Col du Bonhomme. Cross the first small valley that gets steeper towards the Rocher du Bonhomme. After having crossed this short section that can be exposed, carry on to the Col de la Croix du Bonhomme. Traverse north-eastwards and follow the headland up to the Col des Fours. The descent by the same route is easy and you may be skiing in transformed snow to the Col du Bonhomme.

21.a   Access via the south-west ridge (F). After the Col du Bonhomme and the first small valley, climb left. After having passed under the high tension cable (pylons), follow the south-west ridge to the summit.

21.b   Direct descent of the north face (PD). Climb by 22 and in the large combes on the north face, under the electricity pylon on the summit, heading west. There is often good snow on the descent. For the first 400m of the descent under the summit the slope is pretty steep (nearly 40°, cornices) and the slopes remain pretty sustained thereafter. Keep to the middle of the combe at the bottom.

21.c   S Couloir (AD). From the summit go back west, to the left of a headland, drop down a little way and traverse right to get into the S-shaped couloir, between the two rocks. Continue on the right to the north-west couloir that is narrow at the top. At the bottom and depending on the thickness of the snow you can traverse to the right (2200m) to avoid the lower rock bars.

21.d   Zub's Couloir (AD). You get to this couloir from the east of the summit. It is straight for 150m with a 40° slope at the top (very aesthetic).

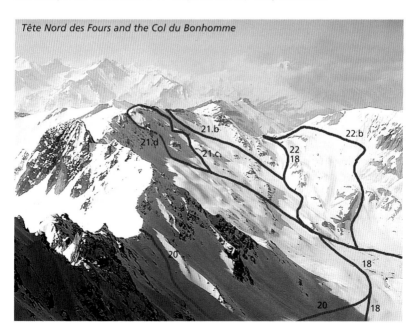

Tête Nord des Fours and the Col du Bonhomme

22 COL DU BONHOMME   2329m
North face   F

⌐	1200m (road)	🏔	December-April	⌐	sections of 30°
↗	1120m	📷	56, 59	⚠	1
↘	1120m	⏱	6¹ᐟ² hrs	⊕	SP
⊕	North-east	⚡	2		

The Col du Bonhomme is definitely worth a visit. As well as being the first col you cross on the Tour du Mont Blanc, this pretty valley gives you great views of the couloirs on Monts Jovet, Mont Tondu and the Col des Chasseurs. On the edge of Haute Savoie, this col also gives access to Savoie, and to the Tarentaise and Beaufortain areas. It is an ideal starting point for tours and trips into the surrounding lower altitude ('moyenne montagne') areas. However, do not underestimate the risk of avalanche in these lower, non-glacial areas. The grassy, moderate slopes of the mountains in this area are still prone to ava-lanche and the north-east face of the Aiguilles de la Penaz is not the only known danger spot. The Col du Bonhomme can be very windy in winter as it is a major crossing point for weather systems in Europe. As a result, as the snow is blown from one area the next it becomes hard and forms slabs. In the combes, on the other hand, there is good quality snow and lots of it.

Follow the path for the Tour du Mont Blanc (19) from Notre-Dame de la Gorge (up the valley from Les Contamines). After the Chalet de la Balme head south-west at first, then go round the Aiguilles de la Penaz on the left. A wide inclined plane above the gorge gives access to the Jovet plateau (around 2000m). Cross the plateau, going round left of the rock bands and narrow sections on the right, and continue south up the narrow valley that leads to the Col du Bonhomme. The des-cent is by the same route.

22.a Descent to Les Chapieux (PD). Traverse under the Rocher du Bonhomme up to the Col de la Croix du Bonhomme (2433m) (100m of quite steep ground, watch out for the slabs in the lower sections). From the Croix du Bonhomme Hut traverse down and to the left, staying above the steeper gullies, to the last head-land. Stay on the left bank of the main mountain stream to get to Les Chapieux. You can go to the left or the right of the small wood.

22.b Thavassets variant (PD). By crossing the Col du Bonhomme to the west, you can climb to the south edge of the Aiguilles de la Penaz (2605m) and can ski the whole east face down to 2200m, above the Plan des Dames. Traverse left again to get round the rock bars and meet up with route 19.

COURMAYEUR

PRACTICAL INFORMATION

International dialling code: 00 39
Courmayeur Tourist Office: 0165.84.20.60
Courmayeur Guides Office: 0165.84.20.64 or 0165.84.23.57
Weather forecast (Italy): 0165.441.13
Snow report: 0165.77.33.00 / www.ainev.it
Rescue: 0165.23.82.22

SKI LIFTS

Courmayeur
If the Val Veni road is blocked by snow, you can use the ski lifts (carpark for Val Veni cable-car 2 1/2 km from Mont Blanc Tunnel on the road to Courmayeur). At the top of the cable-car take the verde piste and then the Zerotta chairlift. From here you can use skins to skiup Val Veni. Alternatively, you can descend to Plan Chécrouit and take the Chécrouit and Youla (2624m) cable-cars. A magnificent off-piste run takes you to the Combal lake. Note: Only groups accompanied by a ski instructor or mountain guide are allowed to use the Tête d'Arp lift (2755m) that gives access to the long descent of the combe down to Courmayeur via Dolonne (1500m height loss).
Helbronner cable-car: 0165.89.925
Courmayeur ski lifts: 0165.84.66.58

ROAD ACCESS

From Chamonix take the Mont Blanc Tunnel (13km, tolls). If the tunnel is closed go to Martigny (Switzerland) via the Col des Montets, then take the Col du Grand Saint Bernard to Aoste and Courmayeur (2 1/2hrs).

Helbronner cable-car (La Palud) – From the Mont Blanc Tunnel go to La Palud (1 km after the Courmayeur exit). Park at the cable-car car-park (parking charges). The Helbronner service is divided into three sections: the first goes to Le Pavillon (2174m), the second takes you to the upper Torino station (huts at 3322m and 3371m) and the third to the Pointe Helbronner (3462m) from where there is a lift across to the Aiguille du Midi in France (closed in winter).

Val Ferret – From the Mont Blanc Tunnel go to La Palud and follow the road (usually cleared of snow) up to Planpincieux (shuttle service operates between La Palud and Planpincieux in winter). Where the road ends follow the cross-country ski courses.

Val Veni – From the tunnel head towards Courmayeur and just before the village of La Saxe take the small road on the right that heads uphill. Follow the signs to Val Veni and Notre-Dame de la Guérison. The road does not get cleared of snow in winter (for more information call the Courmayeur Tourist Office). In spring you can get to the roadhead at La Visaille (shuttles service from Courmayeur bus station).

Previous page: Patrick Vallençant on the first descent of the Peuterey Ridge, 1977.

The Italian part of the Mont Blanc Massif (Val Ferret and Val Veni) is home to some of the most imposing 4000m peaks in the Alps. While the Aiguille des Glaciers, Tre la Tête peaks and the Miage on the west face are great for skiing, few of the descents around Mont Blanc itself are regularly skied. Thanks to the relative ease of access to the Col du Géant there are numerous possible routes ranging from the Vallée Blanche to the magnificent, steep faces and couloirs nearby. To the east, on the Grandes Jorasses and on Mont Gruetta, there are a couple of major descents that are often skied. Finally, there is the Mont Dolent sector which forms the border with Switzerland and has a number of routes. Its altitude meant that the Col du Géant sector was a summer ski area until 1988. By that time, however, summer skiing had fallen out of fashion, the area was no longer profitable and the lifts were closed to protect the natural heritage of the site. The area is still very popular with ski-mountaineers. There are some marvellous 'belvedere' routes in this area, opposite the Massif, that are relative easy to get to. These routes give superb views of the Massif and provide ideal opportunities to reconnoitre complicated routes across glaciers and rocky areas. They are also great tours in their own right that can be done at the beginning of the season or even in the spring. Access to these two valleys opposite the Massif is from Courmayeur. For this reason I have grouped them together despite the considerable distance between the cols to the east and west. Moreover, there are only four main routes in the Val Ferret sector.

MOUNTAIN HUTS

Ref.6 ▥ Elisabetta Soldini Hut (2200m, F)
CAI Milan, (0165.84.40.80 in summertime), winter room can accommodate 24.

From Courmayeur take the Chécrouit cablecars to the Cresta de Yula. From the lift station climb up for a few metres then descend the north face (small valley, quite steep at the beginning) to 2350m. Now traverse left, staying high, under the crest that comes down from Mont Favre. Now climb up for about 5 minutes to pass the headland and continue traversing left to the Arp Supérieure and then the Arp Inférieure. From the bridge at the end of Combal lake (1958m) follow the road (right bank) to the hut. At the end of the season when the lifts are closed, follow the road to La Visaille (1700m) and climb with skins to the hut (2hrs).

⚑ 2624m   ⊘ 1¹/² hrs

↗ 230m

↘ 654m

Ref.7 ▥ Petit Mont Blanc or Montagna Hut (3047m, PD)
Not guardianed, 8 places, blankets, cooking utensils, no gas.

Follow ref.6 to the Elisabetta Soldini Hut. Continue to the right bank of the Lex Blanche Glacier (around 2400m). Cross the glacier at around 2600m and continue under a first spur and then round another spur, marked 2830m, that comes down from the Petit Mont Blanc. Climb diagonally eastwards until the first rock rib, which you pass, and access the headland (on which the hut stands) on the right. The slopes that lead to the hut are quite sustained, but if the snow is stable and you are climbing before midday this is a better route to follow as it is a more logical approach on skis. It is not recommended to follow the summer path as it is difficult in deep snow and is very dangerous in the afternoon.

⚑ 2624m   ⊘ 3-4hrs

↗ 1077m

↘ 654m

Ref.8 ▥ La Fourche Bivouac (3680m, AD)
Not guardianed, 12 places, poorly equipped.

From Entrèves go to the top Helbronner lift. Follow route 113 to the right bank of the Combe Maudite (foot of the north-west face of the Tour Ronde). Continue up the large north-east facing couloir that leads to the Col de la Fourche de la Brenva (45°/200m). The bivouac hut (3680m) is among the rocks a few metres south.

⚑ 3371m   ⊘ 2¹/²hrs

↗ 380m

↘ 100m

Ref.9 ▪ Boccalatte Hut (2804m, PD)
Guardianed in summer (0165.84.40.70), open in winter (25 places).

From Planpincieux (Val Ferret) follow the well marked path through the larches that heads up and right. Cross the mountain stream and climb on foot for about 150m up the steep left bank. Head straight and then left to traverse under the Planpincieux Glacier (risk of serac fall). Chains and cables lead to the hut 100m higher up.
Note: Large avalanches of melting snow in the afternoon.

⚑ 1560m   ⏱ 3hrs

↗ 1250m

Ref.10 ▪ Torino Hut (old hut at 3371m, new hut at 3322m, F)
Old hut open in ski season 0165.84.64.84, for summer hut call 0165.84.40.34.

Access from Entrèves via the Helbronner lifts. From the Aiguille du Midi follow the Vallée Blanche to the Pointe Adolphe Rey and cross the Géant Glacier (crevasses). Go to the left of the Grand Flambeau and via the Col des Flambeaux towards the Col du Géant. The winter hut is at the top of the second lift. You can get to it by the tunnel and the stairs from the Torino Hut or you can ski to it from the east.

⚑ 3780m   ⏱ 2$^{1/2}$hrs

↗ 200m

↘ 600m

Ref.11 ▪ Gervasutti Bivouac (2865m, AD)
Not guardianed, 8 places.

From Courmayeur take the Val Ferret road and park at Planpincieux. From the hamlet of Frébouze (starting point in spring) climb northwards through the larches to get to the glacier's alluvial cone (debris). Climb up the left bank of the glacier so you can leave the avalanche prone area as quickly as possible. Climb up the sustained steep slopes and go past the Frébouze Bivouac (possibility of serac fall as you traverse under Mont Gruetta). Head north-west in an arc to get onto the rocky headland (2833m) on which the hut sits. The hut is not guardianed and cannot be heated, but has blankets and cooking equipment.

⚑ 1560m   ⏱ 4hrs

↗ 1273m

Ref.12 ▪ Dolent or Fiorio Bivouac (2724m, PD)
Not guardianed, 12 and 6 places.

From Courmayeur take the Val Ferret road to Planpincieux (or in spring to La Vachey). Follow the road for 5km and then head left towards the Petit Col Ferret.

The slope steepens up above the moraine (30-35°/300m). As the slopes face west and are covered in grass and schist this route is exposed to avalanche. At times you will have to walk up the central headland. From the Petit Col Ferret head due west and cross steep slope under the rocks. There is a steep section under the spur that takes you onto the less sustained south-

Dolent Bivouac

west facing slopes. The two hut buildings are up and left and above the glacier. The smaller of the two can hold 4-6 and the larger, metal structure has room for 12 people.

⚑ 1560m   ◷ 4-5hrs

↗ 1164m

Ref.13 ▪ Gonella Hut (3071m, PD)
Open in summer (0165.88.51.01), winter room not guardianed (30 places).

From Courmayeur take the Val Veni road to La Visaille. Park at the roadhead and follow the path to the Combal lake. Join the right bank of the Miage Glacier and continue up the middle of the glacier to around 2600m. Cross to the left bank to go round the crevasses. From here you can see, on the west face, the track as it traverses right (path maintained and equipped with cables in summer). A steep climb up takes you to a small notch. The slopes behind this notch are not in good condition (snow slides). If the snow cover is good you can climb up the steep combe that takes you to the left of the refuge, otherwise carry on rightwards on foot and climb the easy rocky section. The hut is yellow and easy to spot.

⚑ 1650m   ◷ 5hrs

↗ 1640m

Quintino Sella Hut

Ref.14 ▪ Quintino Sella Hut (3396m, AD)

Follow ref.13 to the junction with the left-hand branch of the Mont Blanc Glacier. Climb up the right bank of the glacier (crevasses). At around 2800m climb up a combe to the north that takes you to the hut. This route is good in summer conditions. You can also get to the hut by following ref.13 to below the Gonella Hut. Climb up the couloir opposite (35-40°/300m). The right-hand branch leads to a rocky buttress next to the hut. Although this route is less direct, it is more practical in the spring even though there is the risk of rock fall in the couloir.

⊓ 1650m   ◔ 6hrs

↗ 1960m

'BELVEDERE' ROUTES

Bel.4 ▪ Mont Fortin (2758 m, PD)

⊓ 2624m (ski lift)   ◩ January-April   ⌐ 30-35°/350m

↗ 360m   ◔ 2-3hrs   ⚠ 1

↘ 300 + 1080m   ⚒ 3.1   ⊕ SP

✥ North-east

The Mont Fortin-Mont Favre chain runs parallel to the Mont Blanc Massif, from the Youla-Tête d'Arp cable-cars to the Montagnes de la Seigne. Thanks to the Chécrouit and Youla (2624m) lift this area is easily accessed from Courmayeur, and from it you get superb views of the Brenva Glacier and the Peuterey Ridge. From the top of the Youla lift traverse towards the Col de Youla and descend the west combe. At around 2320m head left and go round the ridge that comes down from Mont Favre. Traverse at this level to above the Arp Vieille Supérieure chalets (2303m) and join the bottom of the north couloir of Mont Fortin (30-35°/350m, narrow at the summit). You can ski down to the road to La Visaille.

Bel.5. ▪ Col des Chavannes (2600m, PD)

⊓ 2624 m (ski lift)   ◩ January-April   ⌐ sections of 35°

↗ 410m   ▣ 68, 69   ⚠ 1

↘ 300 + 1080m   ◔ 4-5hrs   ⊕ SP

✥ All   ⚒ 3.1

Similar to the previous route, this tour is 1 1/2 hrs longer. From the top of the north couloir of Mont Fortin, descend the south face and traverse under Mont Percé to the Col des Chavannes (50 metres of climbing with skins). Descend the north-west slope (bit steep at the start) and traverse left to get to the Col de la Seigne. You can also ski directly to the Combal lake and Val Veni.

Bel.6 ⬛ Testa Bernard (PD)

⬆	1564m (road)	🗓	January-April	⬏	sections of 35°
↗	970m	◔	3¹/² hrs	⚠	1
↘	970m	🎿	3.1	⊕	SP
✧	North/North-east				

From Entrèves drive to Planpincieux (1564m). Follow the start of the cross-coun-try ski track and cross the stream. You can now see a track as it winds up left to right past the Leuchey alpages (pastures) at 1923m to the right of the Testa Bernard (west). From the summit you can descend the north face or, via the Col Sapin, the right bank of the Entre Deux Sauts valley to Pra Sec. You can also climb up from La Vachey (4km up the valley on the cross-country ski track). Climb to the headland and access the Col d'Entre Deux Sauts via Malatra.

Testa Bernard can also be accessed from Courmayeur via Villair (1300m) by follo-wing the summer track (steep in places) that leads to the Bertone Hut (1991m). There is often transformed snow below the hut (open in summer) on the west face that can add an hour to the climb.

23   COL DE LA SEIGNE   2516m
                                                      PD

⬆	2620m (ski lift)	🗓	Winter	⬏	35°
↗	550m	📷	68, 69	⚠	1
↘	1900m	◔	7hrs	⊕	SP
✧	North-east	🎿	3.1		

From Courmayeur follow ref.6 and pass the Elisabetta Soldini Hut on your right. Carry on up the Vallon de la Lex Blanche to the col. The descent follows the same route until you come to the bridge that you cross to join the road that leads out of Val Veni. Before the chapel of Notre-Dame de la Guérison (at around 1500m) take the track to the left (not mar-ked on map) that passes next to the glacier. This is a more direct route to the car-park for the Val Veni cable-car. If you can't ski down to the valley take the Zerotta chair-lift from Lassy (1550m) to get back to the Chécrouit pistes and Courmayeur lift sys-tem.

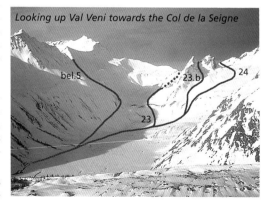

Looking up Val Veni towards the Col de la Seigne

23.a Alternative access route at the end of the

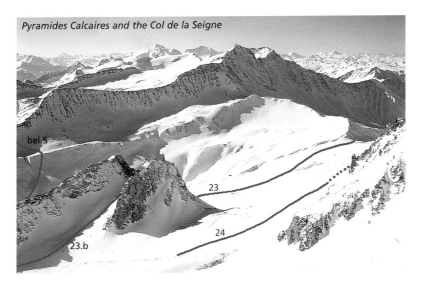

Pyramides Calcaires and the Col de la Seigne

season (PD). When the ski lifts are closed follow the Val Veni road to La Visaille (1700m) and use skins to climb up the road.

23.b   Tour of the Pyramides Calcaires (PD). There are several ways of doing this tour depending on the snow conditions. Generally, it is done from left to right by climbing up to the Col des Pyramides (2622m) and skiing the sheltered northeast face which often has powder snow in it.

24	AIGUILLE DES GLACIERS	3816m
	South-west face	AD

⚐	2620m (ski lift)	🏔	February-June	⤴	sect. of 35-40°
↗	D1+D2: 230m + 1620m	📷	53, 68, 69, 70	⚠	2
↘	D1+D2: 654m + 2530m	🕐	2 + 8hrs	⚕	SP
✣	South-west	🎿	3.3		

This is a great area for ski-tourers and there are various tours that can be done here over several days. For example: go to the Tré la Tête Hut, climb Mont Tondu and ski to the Robert Blanc Hut, ski the Col de la Scie and get back to France via the Helbronner lifts and the Vallée Blanche. This tour does not require a great deal of training as the different stages are well spaced out and the climbs up are not too long.

D1   From Courmayeur follow ref.6 to the Elisabetta Soldini Hut.

D2   Take route 23 to the Col de la Seigne and follow the north ridge (border with France) to the Montagne des Glaciers (2747m). Move onto the west/south-

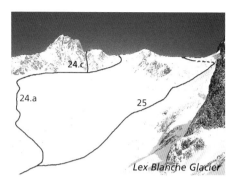

west face and traverse north-west to the passage that crosses the Rochers des Cabottes (3050m). On the Glacier des Glaciers move across the crevassed section and climb up the large north combe to the Dôme de Neige (3592m). A bit of mixed climbing up the right-hand couloir takes you to the summit of the Aiguille des Glaciers (1 1/2 hrs minimum there and back). The descent down the same route will be in the shade until the early afternoon while Val Veni will have already warmed up...

24.a   Col de la Scie (3626m, AD+). From the hut climb up the right bank of the Lex Blanche Glacier. It is quicker to climb up the south-east side of the glacier, but it is much more difficult this way - crossing heavily crevassed terrain is worse on the way up than on the way down. The final couloir is about 100m high and the slope is about 40 to 45°. You can also get to the col by following the normal route (24) to the Aiguille des Glaciers and going down its exposed north ridge. The descent of the south face and the Lex Blanche Glacier is arguably better than the classic route on the Aiguille des Glaciers. However, the snow does transform much more quickly on this side and only try this route when the weather conditions are right.

24.b   Petite Aiguille des Glaciers (3468m, AD). Follow route 24 to 3250m and climb up the south-west combe. Continue to the saddle on the summit. Descend via the same route.

On the south-west face of the Aiguilles des Glaciers, opposite Mont Tondu

24.c ▪ **Direct descent of east face under the saddle at 3690m (D).** The start of this interesting couloir often has cornices in it (45-50°/450m) and the bottom section has a big gulley in it and an exposed bergschrund.

25   COL DE LA LEX BLANCHE   3555m
South-east face   AD

⚑ 2620m (ski lift)	🏔 Februar-June	40°
↗ D1+D2: 230m + 1360m	📷 50, 70, 73	⚠ 1
↘ D1+D2: 654m + 2250m	🕐 2 + 8hrs	⊕ SP
⊕ South-west	🎿 3.3	

Until the end of the 1990s helicopters were allowed to set people down in the Dolent area of Val Ferret. Heli-drops are now permitted in three sites in the Val Veni area. Although this wild and isolated part of the Massif can certainly accommodate both skiers and ski-tourers, I have mixed feelings on the subject of heli-skiing. The pollution from these extra helicopter rides is nothing compared with the pollution generated daily by the cars and lorries that are choking our beautiful alpine valleys. All the time visitors are enchanted by these breathtaking trips and the decision-makers are able to enforce the laws regulating the heli-drops, then abuses of the system will be minimal. All the same, it can't hurt to try and convert the heli-skiers to the pleasures of exploring the area with skins on their skis...

D1 ▪ From Courmayeur go up to the Elisabetta Soldini Hut by ref.6.

D2 ▪ From the hut go to the right bank of the Lex Blanche Glacier under the Aiguille d'Estelette. At around 2500m cross to the left bank (crevasses fairly visible as they are vertical). Pass the junction with the Petit Mont Blanc Glacier on your right. Passing alongside the south buttresses of the Aiguille de Tré la Tête you get to the upper part of the glacier

On the descent of the Lex Blanche

that is less steep. Traverse due west to the Col de la Lex Blanche. The descent is by the same route. Take care on the long flat area in the valley with the Combal lake as there are often lots of holes in the soft snow. It is better to traverse along the right bank and return via the summer path.

25.a ▪ **Col de Tré la Tête (3515m, AD).** Climbing this 'the little brother' of the Col de la Lex Blanche you get good views of the north face. The access route is the same up to 3350m where you head right.

25.b   North face of the Col de la Lex Blanche (D). You can cross the Col de la Lex Blanche to access the north face of the Aiguille de la Lex Blanche. You can also cross the Col de Tré la Tête and ski down the north-west face, staying left and navigating through the seracs (AD, sometimes very exposed, 40-45°/300m).

---

26   AIGUILLES DE TRÉ LA TÊTE   3892m
South face circuit   AD

⚑	2620m (ski lift)	⛰	March-May	⤵	40°/100m
↗	D1 + D2: 230m + 1620m	📷	72, 73, 74	⚠	2
↘	D1 + D2: 654m + 2600m	🕐	2¹⁄₂ + 8hrs	⊕	SP
✥	South	🎿	4.1		

There can be a tendency to underestimate the seriousness of the descents on the highest peak in the Miage chain when it is compared with the gigantic neighbouring west face of Mont Blanc. You should plan these descents for spring even if the Chécrouit lifts are not open. The wild and isolated feel of this area (heli-drops stop in mid-May) increase not only the committing feel of these routes but also the sense of satisfaction one gets at having completed them. The snow conditions on the east face are generally good, although the couloirs can be streaked with deep central gullies.

North-east couloir of the Aiguille Centrale de Tré la Tête

D1 From Courmayeur follow ref.6 to the Elisabetta Soldini Hut.

D2 From the hut climb the length of the Petit Mont Blanc Glacier (see route 27) passing the Aiguille de l'Aigle on your right as you climb onto the steep north-east headland (3600m) of the Aiguille de Tré la Tête. Follow this ridge on foot (the north face can be icy with slabs), and you can continue to the main summit (3930m) by following the relatively exposed snowy ridge.

It is better to descend the south face from the east summit than by the normal route. This is an aesthetic tour with uniformly steep slopes and snow that gets transformed relatively early on. For this reason you should follow the start of the east ridge down for a few dozen metres (rope useful) before heading right and easily accessing the large south combe. At around 3400m keep left (towards the rocks) to avoid the hanging glacier and the rock band lower down. Rejoin the route you took up to get back to the Combal lake and your car or the ski lift system depending on what is open in the valley.

North-east side of the Aiguille de Tré la Tête

*South face
of the Lex Blanche*

26.a   North-east couloir of the Aiguille Centrale (TD). First descent by Stefano de Benedetti (15th July 1979). 50° then 45°/1100m. Rappel necessary for the serac above the couloir.

26.b   North-east couloir of the Aiguille Nord (D+). First descent by Jacky Bessat (24th June 1976). 1100m, steeper than 50° at the top then 45° and 40° lower down. Some very narrow sections.

26.c   Variant route on the left branch to the north (D+). The same as route 26.b. Join route 26.b. at the bottom (40-45°/800m).

26.d   Tête Carrée, east couloir (D+). Regular. 40-45°/900m.

27	**AIGUILLE DE L'AIGLE**	**3517m**
	Petit Mont Blanc Glacier	**PD**

2620m (ski lift)		February-June		sect. of 35°-40°	
D1 + D2: 230m + 1310m		71, 73, 74		2	
D1 + D2: 654m + 2250m		2¹/² + 6hrs		SP	
South-west		3.2			

This is often considered a subsidiary summit, but it actually makes a good objective in its own right as it is easier than the Tré la Tête and offers a great des-

From the Tré la Tête to the Bionnassay

cent (one of the heli-drop spots). The numerous crevasses on the glacier can be a bit tricky and in the middle of the Petit Mont Blanc Glacier there is quite a steep convex section (40-45°/100m).

D1 From Courmayeur go up to the Elisabetta Soldini Hut by ref.6.

D2 Follow route 25 to the right bank of the Lex Blanche Glacier. Traverse right and climb between the crevasses. Take the Petit Mont Blanc Glacier up to the base of the Aiguille de l'Aigle. Go to the col (3480m) north of the Aiguille and there is now a mixed climb (rocks, PD) to the summit. The descent is by the same route. Owing to its orientation, you must be on your way down before midday otherwise the snow can be unskiable and even dangerous at the bottom.

27.a   North/North-east couloir (TD). First descent by Stefano de Benedetti (17th July 1989). Average of 40°, sections of 45° in the central couloir. The same skier did the first descent of the north branch on 16th June 1983.

28   PETIT MONT BLANC   3424m
South face   AD

⚑	2620m (ski lift)	🏔	February-June	⇅	45°/50m
↗	D1 + D2: 1450m + 370m	📷	71, 73, 74, 75	⚠	1
↘	D1+D2: 654m + 2530m	🕐	4 + 3½ hrs	⊕	SP
✣	South	🎿	3.2		

For the purposes of this guide I skied the north-east couloir of the Petit Mont Blanc in June 2001 starting from La Visaille at 5:30 in the morning. The climb up the south face was in powder snow while the ski down the north-east couloir was in wind-blown snow and ice. I managed to do the tour in 6 1/2 hours and some judicious slide-slipping was required…

D1   From Courmayeur follow ref.7 to the Petit Mont Blanc (Giovane Montagna) Hut.

D2   The climb to the Petit Mont Blanc takes 1hr. Walk the last few metres on the easy rock ridge. The descent down the same route is not very interesting and it is better to take the combe immediately to the south that avoids the hut but does require a long traverse lower down. Climb up a little way to get onto the glacier and follow route 27 out.

28.a   Via the Petit Mont Blanc Glacier (AD). From the summit cross the south crest and access the glacier via a short, steep west-facing slope (40°/50m). Go round the crevasses in the middle on the

North-east couloir of Petit Mont Blanc

28.b

right. At around 2800m traverse right (crevassed area) to pick up the route you took up and off the glacier (at 2600m).

28.b   North-east couloir (TD). Accessing the summit from the hut gets you to the top early and is not too tiring. Start to the left of the cornice on the summit. The snowy middle spur is skiable when you access it from the right couloir (similar to the left couloir but wider). After the top 250m (nearly 55°) the two couloirs

At the top of the right couloir

meet up around a deep gully that becomes deeper and deeper. The slope gets less steep at the bottom (from 45° to 40°). When it is cold you can climb up the couloir from the bottom, but it is a long and monotonous 1100m, and there are likely to be rock falls from the left side even in the morning. This is, nevertheless, a very aesthetic couloir and it is the first 250m that are the most serious, especially in hard snow.

29 COL DE MIAGE   3367m
South face   AD

⚑	2620m (ski lift)	🏔	March-June	⌐	40°m
↗	1400m	📷	76	⚠	2
↘	654m + 2077m	◐	7hrs	⌂	SP
⊕	south-east	🎿	3.3		

This is a great tour to do in a day, but you have to set off really early to safely descend the south face of the Col de Miage. I suggest you make use of the Durier Hut, newly renovated by a group of Saint-Gervais guides and the CAF, and combine it with other routes in the area: traverse to the Conscrits Hut via the Miage chain, Col de la Seigne via Mont Tondu, the Armancette Glacier, return via the Tré la Tête Hut…

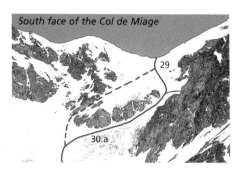
South face of the Col de Miage

Moreover, the sense of isolation and serenity you get from a night in the Durier Hut is an unforgettable experience.

Follow ref.6 to the bridge just below the Combal lake (1950m). Climb north-west to get to the right bank of the Miage Glacier and move to the middle of the glacier (crevasses). About 6km of relatively shallow climbing takes you to the bottom of the Col de Miage. At the junction with the Bionnassay Glacier, climb to the left bank of the suspended glacier. Move up diagonally on quite a sustained slope until you get to the final wide combe that leads to the col. The descent follows the route you took up. Some years you can ski down the right bank of the suspended glacier (steeper and gets the sun a lot earlier).

29.a East face of the Col Infranchissable (D+). This route is not often skied as it is quite exposed (seracs, crevasses) and you should avoid climbing up it. On the way down the maximum slope is never greater than 45°/200m (steep steps at the top), but it is rarely in condition and there is an ice cornice at the col and the slope itself is often icy.

Returning to the Gonella Hut

30   MONT BLANC   4810m
Aiguilles Grises   D

⚑ 1660m (road)	🏔 April-June	↳ 40°
↗ D1+D2: 1410m + 1740m	📷 74, 76, 79	⚠ 3
↘ D1+D2: 0m + 3150m	☁ 4 + 11hrs	⊕ HP
✧ West	⚔ 4.3	

Any mountaineer will tell you that the west face of Mont Blanc is 'Himalayan'. They are drawn to it by its isolation, steep glaciated faces and sheer size.

The guide and teacher at ENSA, Yves Pollet-Villard, climbed all over the world and one of his passions was taking clients to discover new routes. He was with René Desmaison on the first ascent of the Freney Pillar and on Jannu, but he was always very modest about his impressive achievements. The mayor of La Clusaz, always respectful of the mountains and their inhabitants, his career ended in a deep crevasse on the Dôme Glacier. He had set out to traverse Mont Blanc with five clients and his friend Joël Collomb-Paton, also a guide from La Clusaz, but they had changed their minds because it was too hot. While climbing down Yves was swept into a 35-metre crevasse, and covered by, a slab of wet snow. He will always remain a great example to all those who knew him. It was he who set up the training scheme in Nepal for Nepalese and Sherpa people wanting to become guides. He thought that the mountain people of Nepal should have access to a high standard of technical training to become responsible guides in the mountains. A great deal of his numerous expeditions were organised with the aim of training the local guides in the local mountain ranges.

D1 ▪ From Courmayeur take the Val Veni road to the Cantine de la Visaille and then follow the track to the Combal lake. Now move up to the Gonella Hut following ref.13.

D2 ▪ Traverse 100m across a steep slope to get to the Dôme Glacier. I strongly recommend you check out this route, and even cut steps, the day before. Head north and leftwards up the combe and then round the Calotte des Aiguilles Grises and continue right to join the left bank of a second sloping plateau. Climb up the left side to the Col des Aiguilles Grises (3810m), and go ridge and round the rocks towards the Piton des Italiens (4002m). If the snow is good you can climb straight up the middle of the combe to the Piton des Italiens. Asteep couloir (40°/250m and used on the descent) takes you to the ridge on the right of the Piton des Italiens. The climb towards the Dôme du Goûter is relatively straightforward, but watch out for the underlying layers of ice and the cornices on the left (very exposed to the wind). Join the Col du Dôme just below the summit and follow route 134 to Mont Blanc. On the descent there are some steep sections on the west ridge of the Dôme du Goûter and the slope gets increasingly exposed until you reach the Piton des Italiens. Luckily the snow is often good here in the morning. It is nevertheless very important that you keep on schedule at each stage so that you reach the Dôme Glacier early enough. If the snow is good you can miss out the section past the Gonella Hut, but you must check out the route the day befo-re. Note: the south face direct of the Dôme du Goûter is often skiable (D, 40°/500m, exposed sections, bergschrund, crevasses on the Dôme Glacier).

30.a   Col de Bionnassay (D). The descent of the Italian Bionnassay Glacier is superb and can be done after having climbed to the Piton des Italiens. However, at around 3400m there is a huge crevasse that blocks the route and can be very difficult to cross. I don't really recommend this route for this reason unless you have been able to see the route beforehand (the slopes on the left side of the combe might be more skiable). Be prepared for abseils and setting up snow anchors.

30.b   South-west face of the Bosses Ridge (TD). A select few, 'connaisseurs', descend this long face, but it is rarely in condition because of the wind (ice). 40-45°/350m, sections of 50°. Check out the section where you have cross the seracs (at around 3800m) beforehand to see if it is practicable.

31	**MONT BLANC**	**4810m**
	West face	TD+

⚑	1660m (road)	🏔	May-June		45°-50°/900m
↗	D1+D2: 1960m + 1414m	📷	79	⚠	3
↘	D1+D2: 0m + 3374m	◔	4 + 11hrs		HP
✦	West	⚔	5.1		

The routes on Mont Blanc's 'Himalayan' face are complex and committing. Its isolation and height (more than 2000m) means that this face is rarely skied and then only by highly experienced and capable ski-mountaineers. It is diffi-cult to get a good look at this face apart from the top of the Miage or Tré la Tête peaks and attempts to ski it are becoming more and more rare. If it were mere-ly a question of descending a simple couloir, accessing this area from the nor-mal route on Mont Blanc would be quite straightforward. However, the seracs, risk of slab avalanches, and route finding itself make this a very risky and fran-kly hypothetical solution. A few skiers have been dropped at the top by helicopter and have checked out the descent during the ride up. This is an expensive option and is rarely used except for first descents. For all of these descents the access routes like the descents themselves are both exposed and committing.

D1 ■ Follow ref.14 to the Quintino Sella Hut.

D2 ■ A traverse up and to the east brings you to a sustained slope. After a wide headland descend slightly towards the glaciated face of Mont Blanc to the right of the lower rock spur. Climbs on the west face start on this sloping plateau, and for the most direct route, the Tournette, you head a little to the left and take the huge face/couloir (crevasses, bergschrunds). Move right to go round the section of mixed climbing. The slope steepens up to 50° and the couloir gets narrow. The top section may be skiable, but is rarely has enough snow. The best route heads right at about 4500m to cross the spur as soon as possible. Traversing right takes you round the rocky outcrop under the summit ridge using the top of the suspended glacier. You can also climb straight up the couloir to above La Tournette and to the summit of Mont Blanc (55°/300m).

On the descent the initial slopes on the south face steepen up from 40° to 45°. Keeping close to the rocks, take a long traverse to the right to get to the Tournette couloir. The first descent was by Sylvain Saudan on 25 June 1973. Owing to its westerly aspect this face can be skied after midday, but the lower section becomes dangerous in the afternoon.

Mont Blanc's huge west face

31.a   South face direct (TD+). From the summit follow Saudan's route (number 31) and go round the first spur. Get onto the even slope with the band of seracs to the left. At this point the route gets more difficult and steeper and the slope is more than 50° (possible abseil). Lower down the slope gets wider but is still very serious up to the first bergschrund. First descent by Stefano de Benedetti in September 1980.

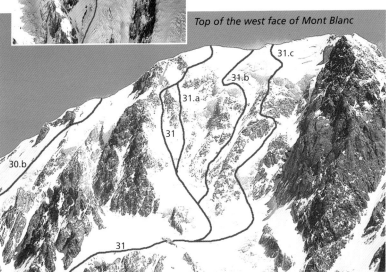

Top of the west face of Mont Blanc

31.b **Domenech-Jaccoux Route (ED).** Scarcely had this climbing route been done for the first time, than it was being skied for the first time by the Genevan Dominique Neuenschwander (15th June 1986). It is a logical route to take although it is exposed to serac fall (950m at average of 45°).

31.c **Central buttress (TD+).** Less exposed to serac fall than the previous route, this line (1000m, 45-50°) was spotted and first skied by Pierre Tardivel in July 1993. The section between the rocks is often narrow and difficult to spot. It is essential that you climb the route first before trying to ski it.

32   MONT BLANC DE COURMAYEUR   4704m
arête de Peuterey   TD+

3460m (cable-car)		May-June		45°/800m, 55°/300m	
D1+D2: 400m + 1850m		80, 81, 83		3	
D1+D2: 160m + 1850m		4 + 11hrs		HP	
East		5.3			

Pierre Tardivel's descent of the Grand Pilier d'Angle cemented his reputation as one of the world's most talented extreme skiers. Since that time he has dedicated himself to his all-consuming passion for skiing and has successfully skied numerous routes in the Northern French Alps, Switzerland and Nepal including a descent of Everest from 8750m. Everest has subsequently been skied all the way from its summit by the Slovenian Karnicar in the autumn of 2000, on the Nepalese side. In spring 2001 the young Chamoniard Marco Siffredi became the first person to snowboard Everest from its summit, via the Norton Couloir on the Tibetan side.

Peuterey Ridge

D1 Take the lifts to the Pointe Helbronner and follow ref.8 to the Bivouac de la Fourche.

D2 Descend the short steep slope on the south-west face that takes you onto the upper plateau of the Brenva Glacier. Cross the glacier heading south to get to the Col Moore (3500m) and descend the other side using crampons (at night). This passage is steep and can be difficult (narrow sections, probably bergschrunds and risk of serac avalanches on the plateau). Traverse south-west towards the Col de Peuterey. The slope gets steeper as you pass under the Grand Pilier d'Angle. There are now two or three crevasses and bergschrunds

Patrick Vallençant on the Blanche de Peuterey

before you get to the 300m steep slope that takes you a little to the left of the col (3934m). Head right and cross the bergschrund quite early on, at the back of the small cirque, to reach the start of the Eccles Couloir (not obvious). A series of rock and ice steps lead to the summit slope which gets slightly less steep before the Peuterey Ridge. For about 200m the climbing on the crest is relatively easy before the slope steepens up again. The last 300m of the right side of the face (that you take to go round a rock) reaches 55°.

On the descent, be prepared to set up a short abseil (snow anchor or stake) just under the summit as the cornices can be very high. The section at the start is very delicate and you simply must not fall. The section of the ridge that leads to the Eccles Couloir is less steep, but it has the same aspect of slope and I remember the snow breaking into small slabs under us when we descended it in 1977. The Eccles Couloir itself has convex sections of over 55°.

The slope under the Col de Peuterey faces north and the skiing is easy to the Brenva Glacier. Getting back up the Col Moore (80m) and on to the Col du Trident or the Col de la Fourche and back to the Aiguille du Midi/Pointe Helbronner is less pleasant. Some years the Vallée Blanche can be skied up to the end of May.

Note: The climbers' line on the Innominata Ridge was skied by Stefano de Benedetti on 11 June 1986.

32.a   Grand Pilier d'Angle (ED+).

When it was first climbed in 1962 by Bonatti and Zapelli, this route was extremely technical and challenging. Front-pointing was in its infancy, and their ice-axes were designed less for climbing than for cutting steps. This face rarely has snow to the right of the serac and Pierre Tardivel closely observed it during the summer of 1988. His observations were confirmed during a helicopter ride, and he was dropped off at the top of the route (4200m). With several abseils he was able to pull off quite a remarkable descent given its incomplete snow cover. This 900m face includes 500m of sustained 55° slopes.

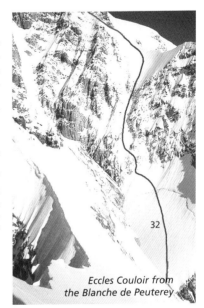

32

Eccles Couloir from the Blanche de Peuterey

33   AIGUILLE BLANCHE DE PEUTEREY   4112m
North face   ED

🏳	3460m (cable-car)	📷	May	⌐	55°/150m
↗	D1 + D2: 400m + 1400m	📷	83	⚠	3
↘	D1 + D2: 160m + 1850m	◔	2$^{1/2}$ + 11hrs	⚐	HP
⊕	East	⚒	5.3		

I first developed the idea of skiing the Peuterey Ridge after having spotted an unbroken line that used the Eccles Couloir. I also wanted to film a first descent with Patrick Vallençant. Patrick was developing his own extreme skiing technique and was interested in making films, and having two of us meant we could actually film each other on the descent. Our first attempt in mid-May (1977) failed: too much snow and bad weather. At the end May we were back at the hut with the film crew, and we were ready to try the new line on the Aiguille Blanche de Peuterey that had looked so enticing from the Ghiglione Hut. I have some very special memories of setting off at night as the snow crystals sparkled in the moonlight. We didn't need head torches to ski through the powder snow that had fallen the day before and our spirits were high as

Setting off below the summit with the Col de Peuterey in the background

we reached the Blanche de Peuterey and set off along the ridge to the summit. The weight of our rucksacks (cameras, radios etc) made the climb very tiring and it actually took us two hours to ski the descent as we had to keep stopping to film each other. The Peuterey Ridge is a physically demanding route, which makes it also very committing. The majority of the other descents on this side of Mont Blanc have been done from helicopter drops (with the exception of the Brenva Spur skied by Heini Holzer, the Sentinelle Rouge by Jacky Bessat and Emmanuel Ballot's routes).

D1   From the Helbronner lift follow ref.8 to the Bivouac de la Fourche. You can also get to the bivouac hut from the Aiguille du Midi (see route 112, Géant section).

D2   From the hut follow route 32 to the Brenva Glacier in the direction of the Col de Peuterey. Under the col head left and cross another bergschrund to get to the bottom of the north face of

Climbing up the face

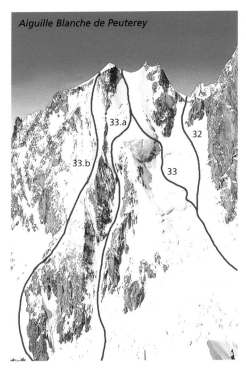

Aiguille Blanche de Peuterey

the Aiguille Blanche. When we did the first descent we crossed an ice wall to get to the suspended glacier (5-10m of seracs likely). You can avoid this by climbing up the couloir that runs alongside it (55°/200m). The upper section has another bergschrund and leads to the final slope between the two summits. If the conditions are the same as they were for our first descent, powder snow that has bonded well to the slope, you can ski the whole face and jump the serac at its lowest point. As the slope is rarely in these conditions, take gear to abseil round the serac. The direct couloir on the left bank rarely has snow.

33.a   Direct descent of the north-east couloir (ED+). The start of this direct descent down the north face goes right of the serac. The Italian Stefano de Benedetti used the deep east couloir and skied an exposed direct line that goes under the seracs (14th September 1980). The average gradient of the slope is 45-50°/900m. You need a lot of snow to be able to climb up under the north face of the Blanche and back to the Col Moore. In exceptional cases you can follow the right bank of the Brenva Glacier (see route 37), otherwise you'll need a helicopter!

33.b   East face (ED+). Also skied by de Benedetti (14 June 1984). Complex and very exposed route that slaloms between the rocks with several sections of 55° over the 800m of the total descent.

34	**MONT BLANC**	**4810m**
	Sentinelle Rouge	**ED**

⌐	3460m (cable-car)	🏔	May-September		50°-55°/1400m
↗	D1+D2: 400m + 500m	📷	85	⚠	3
↘	D1+D2: 160m + 2600m	🕐	2½ + 9hrs	⊕	HP
✦	South-east	🎿	5.4		

Many ski-mountaineers dream of skiing the towering faces on the Italian side of Mont Blanc, but only the most audacious and dedicated among them have managed it. Despite an atmosphere of competition French and Italian skiers have bided their time, waiting patiently for the conditions to be right, and have skied some remarkable first descents. For some the whole point of skiing these routes is to do the first descent, so when it comes to repeating a line that has already been skied they lose their motivation. Moreover, the difficult and committing routes to access and leave these descents are also very important considerations. You also have to have a safety margin, and they may be extreme but these skiers are not mad...! I have chosen to start with the Sentinelle Rouge in honour of my friend Jacky Bessat, a talented extreme skier and roofer by trade.

On the Brenva Spur

D1 From Entrèves and the Pointe Helbronner lifts, follow ref. 8 to the Bivouac de la Fourche.

D2 Climbing the difficult routes on this face is in itself very committing, and the usual access route starts from the normal route on Mont Blanc (by the Mont Blanc du Tacul in the case of Jacky's descent) or by helicopter. The Sentinelle Rouge appears in the climbing guide for the Massif. Jacky Bessat skied the route on 17 July 1977 passing via the bands of snow on the Sentinelle Rouge spur. You may have to rappel past several sections. Now take the large couloir on the left to avoid the last gully and to get to the bottom of the Brenva face.

34.a   Major route (ED+). First skied by Stefano de Benedetti on 7 September 1979 (50-55°/1400m). Very exposed and technical route requiring three rappels and includes rocky sections.

34.b   Grand Couloir de la Brenva (ED+). First done by Tony Valeruz in April 1977 (heli-drop), 50-55°/1400m, very exposed to serac avalanches.

35	**MONT BLANC** Brenva Spur		**4810m** TD
⌐ 3460 m (cable-car)	may-June	40°-45°/1000m	
D1+D2: 400m + 1400m	85, 86	⚠ 3	
D1+D2: 160m + 1610m	2¹ᐟ² + 9hrs	HP	
East	5.1		

The South Tyrolean ski-mountaineer, Heini Holzer, did the first descent of the Brenva Spur on 30 June 1973. He started at the rocks at around 4350m and that year there was good snow cover, which is rare. The same year Patrick Vallençant and I skied the Couturier and Whymper couloirs on the Aiguille Verte and made two attempts on the Cordier and Y couloirs (also on the Verte). You have to be pretty motivated and sure that you know what you are doing if you are going to try to ski things like that with 2.07m skis and boots that only just come over your ankles! Modern ski-touring boots are much better suited to skiing steep slopes all the more so since these days people tend to ski steep slopes in soft snow.

Here comes the sun!

35

D1 From Entrèves and the Pointe Helbronner lifts, follow ref. 8 to the Bivouac de la Fourche.

D2 From the Col de la Fourche descend the short steep slope that leads to the Brenva Glacier and then go to the Col Moore. From here there is some mixed climbing on the left that takes you up the classic route on the Brenva Spur. Now rejoin the central ridge that disappears in the steep face beneath the upper rock spur (4250m). The section that takes you up to the Col de la Brenva can be difficult, but it changes from year to year. Go right and cross the seracs and crevasses. From here you have more

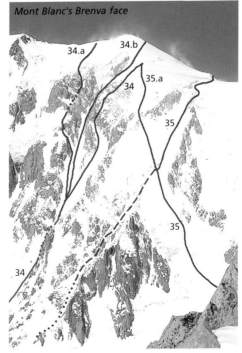

Mont Blanc's Brenva face

34.a   34.b

34   35.a

35

35

34

than an hour's climb up to the summit of Mont Blanc (500m higher up). The snow on the descent from the top of the face can be hard or wind-blown. Lower down, on the less steep ridge, it is better to take the north facing Güssfeld Couloir. However, this section can be exposed to serac fall some years (more direct route on the climb up!). The return route is easier via the Ghiglione Hut.

35.a   Direct descent from the summit (TD+). By crossing the upper seracs nearer the summit, Stefano de Benedetti was able to ski from the top of Mont Blanc. Then he had a long diagonal descent to the Brenva Spur and he traversed left to go to the north and round the round the seracs. The total descent is 1300m and 500m of that was at over 50°.

35.b   Col de la Brenva (TD). Skied by Pierre Tardivel on 10th July 1988 after a heli-drop (40-50°/700m). The lower section is not too steep, but can be quite hit and miss owing to the seracs. The bottom of the face, on the other hand, is more sustained and still exposed.

36   Mont Maudit   4465m
East face   TD+

⚐	3460m (cable-car)	⛰	May-June	⌐	50°-55°/600m
↗	D1+D2: 0m + 1300m	📷	86	⚠	3
↘	D1+D2: 0m + 1300m	⊘	8hrs	⊕	HP
✦	South-east	⚔	5.3		

All the descents on the east face of Mont Maudit are very exposed and extremely committing. The Kuffner Ridge is a technical mountaineering route, and that is why I only mention it as a variant route. I should imagine that those skiers planning to ski the Arête Kuffner probably don't need a precise technical description of the route unless it may serve to dissuade them from doing it…
The main route was first climbed by Gérard Decorps and Richard Baumont on 3rd July 1977, and it was first skied by Stéphane Dan (known as Fanfan).

East face of Mont Maudit

D1   From Entrèves take the Helbronner lifts up and go to the old Torino Hut (3322m).

D2   From the hut follow route 37 (below) to cross the Col du Trident (3679m) that takes you onto the Brenva Glacier (3500m). From there climb to the foot of Mont Maudit and climb 150m up the large east couloir. Follow a passage left to get to the snowy section under the secondary east ridge. Head diagonally left (steep, likely to have snowy gullies) up to a very steep section beneath the second snow ridge. Via the south face you can now reach the secondary summit of Mont Maudit marked 4361m on the map (south of the main summit which is defended by an enormous cornice). On the descent (first skied by the Italian Stefano de Benedetti in June 1983) the slopes are very sustained and very committing, especially above the rock bands. At the top, under the cornice, the snow is often hard as it gets the sun. The Grand Pan de Rideau section (snow slope) and the part where you access the east couloir are very steep.

36.a   Large east couloir (TD). This was first descended from the cornice at the top in 1983 by Jean-Marc Boivin and a companion. The gradient of this 650m slope varies from 45° to 50°, and the couloir is steep-sided and exposed to an enormous serac at the top. It was this 'sword of Damocles' hanging over my head and not being able to escape anywhere that made me abandon my first attempt on this route in spring 1978 after having climb two thirds of the way up.

36.b   Kuffner Ridge (TD+). First descended by Jean-Marc Boivin and Eric Bellin with two rappels (sections of 50-55°). Start at the summit of Mont Maudit.

37   COL DU TRIDENT   3679m
Brenva Glacier   D

3460m (cable-car)	Februray-April	40°
350m	4hrs	2
2300m	4.1	HP
All		

This is undoubtedly one of the nicest descents on the Italian side of the Massif. If the winter brings lots of snow and wind (to fill in the crevasses), this can be skied from February onwards. You can also access the glacier from the often icy north slope of the Col de la Tour Ronde marked 3627m on the map (50-55°/120m). Harder on the climb up, this route is more direct and more comfortable on the descent to the Brenva Glacier (see alternative access route 113.a, Géant section). The Brenva Glacier had noticeably receded in the 1990s and in 1994 a huge avalanche swept down the south face of Mont Blanc, taking thousand of trees with it, crossed Val Veni and came to rest on the north face of Mont Chétif.

From Entrèves take the Helbronner lifts to get to the Col des Flambeaux. Go round the north face of the Aiguille de Toule and get to the foot of the Tour

Ronde. Climb up the Combe Maudite moving away from the Brenva Ridge (also known as the Frontier Ridge). Now climb up the slope that leads to the glacial dome (calotte) that is clearly visible. The bergschrund may be quite high and difficult to cross. The gradient of the north-facing slope of the Col du Trident gets up to 45°/100m near the rocks on the left (old rope to access to Ghiglione Hut). The final section of the slope that accesses the col is easy towards the right (see route 114, Géant section). From the col traverse left as soon as the rocks allow and stay high so that you can get to the snowy saddle with as little climbing as possible (crossing crevasses and a bergschrund!). From the saddle go left again to go round behind the snow ridge. Now continue along a short and steep slope to get to the large combe

Crossing the Brenva Glacier

that comes down from the Tour Ronde. Cross the combe to get to the sustained slope under the Aiguille de la Brenva and then the Brenva Glacier (2700m). I recommend that you stay on the moraines on the left bank of the glacier at the beginning of the season, and then move towards the Rochers de la Brenva and follow the base of these on their west face. Traverse hard left between the two

Brenva Glacier and the Aiguille de la Brenva

rock bands (exposed section of hard snow, risk of snow slips coming from above when snow is soft). When you get to the larches stay left to find the first couloir that leads to a second, wider one and then the moraine. From there descend down the left of the glacier to get back to Entrèves. From the end of February and when there is lots of snow you can use the right bank of the glacier. To do that, cross the glacier at around 2700m: several crevasses, sloping plateau and section below the rocks of the Aiguille Noire de Peuterey. There is a steep slope (40°/200m) at the exit of the glacier that is sometimes icy. Lower down, you can return via the moraine on the right bank of the Brenva Glacier then on the path down to the Mont Blanc Tunnel.

37.a   Brenva Glacier via the Tour Ronde (D). The best way to access the Brenva Glacier is undoubtedly via the normal route on the Tour Ronde. Although the east couloir can be difficult, you are soon on the summit ridge. The start of the south-west couloir is about 100m before the summit. There is about 40°/300m. Once on the glacier, descend the right bank or in the middle of the glacier until you are below the rocks at around 2700m. Now follow route 37. Warning: The snow in the south-west couloir can be hard or difficult so be ready to belay each other for several dozen metres.

38   COL D'ENTRÈVES   3527m
Traverse   AD

⚑	3460m (cable-car)	📐	January-May	⤿	35°-40°/250m
↗	220m	📷	90	⚠	1
↘	1640m	⏱	4hrs	⊕	SP
✥	South/South-east	⚡	4.1		

Although there is more climbing for this route, the technical section at the top of this descent and its overall beauty make it more popular than the descent under the Aiguilles Marbrées (route 40).

From Entrèves take the cable-cars up to the Pointe Helbronner and follow route 37 to the north combe of the Aiguille d'Entrèves and climb to the Col d'Entrèves. From the cornice, which can be quite high, check out the descent. A rock spur on the left gives relatively easy access to the south-east slope. Traverse right across the small rocks and the tops of the couloirs. Follow these outcrops and couloirs to cross the large steep combe of the Entrèves Glacier. Avalanches are constantly changing the terrain on this face. Lower down, at the foot of the Aiguille de la Brenva and the Père Eternel, the glacier becomes convex (one or two dangerous crevasses). You might want to be roped up as you cross this area. Go round the spur on the left and there is now a long traverse beneath the Toule Glacier to get back to the Pavillon lift station (2174m). This traverse can be risky if the snow is soft as the smooth moraine slopes can be avalanche-prone. The south face above the Mont Blanc tunnel is rarely descended, except when the snow has refrozen in the spring (extra 700m of descent). It is quite possible that you will not be allowed to ski in this area as there is a risk of ava-lanches reaching the car-parks below.

39   TOULE GLACIER   3411m
South face   PD

⌐	3460m (cable-car)	⛏	December-May	⌐	40°
↗	20m	◷	2hrs	⚠	1
↘	2000m	⚲	3.1	⊕	DP
✦	South				

Thanks to the cable-cars and the fact that there is no walk up to this route, this is considered an exceptionally fine off-piste route. In fact, in good winters, you can ski this route several times in one day.

From Entrèves take the cable-cars up to the Pointe Helbronner. There is now an easy descent north-west to the Col des Flambeaux from where you head south-west (at the same height) to the Col Oriental de Toule (east col). Cross the wall of snow built up by the wind to get to the metal staircase that gives access to the south face. At the foot of the stairs go straight down the glacier or a little to the left (crevasses in the middle, lower down). Exit left, after the steepest section between the seracs, and cross the moraine to get back to the Pavillon lift station (Mont Fréty, 2174m). From here you can follow the standard route back to La Palud. The risk of avalanche can make the lower section dangerous, and the various variant routes should only be followed in good conditions. Risks can be increased by sudden changes of snow quality.

39.a   Tunnel variants (PD). There are variants routes under the glacier that take you to the entrance of the Mont Blanc tunnel. Take care as these routes follow steep ravines or grassy slopes that are prone to avalanche. You may not be allowed into this area as avalanches set off by skiers can endanger the tunnel area.

Toule Glacier

40   COL DE ROCHEFORT   3389m
Under the Aiguilles Marbrées   AD

3460m (cable-car)	January-April	45°/50m
60m	91	1
2150m	3hrs	SP
South-east	4.2	

Although this is a popular descent and is frequently skied, it remains a high mountain route across a glacier. Access to the top slope is quite exposed and any slip could have very serious consequences...

You can also climb up the Y couloir on the Aiguilles Marbrées and join the classic south-east slope from higher up on the steep east face (start at 3450m). This approach route is less recommended, and you should be sure that there is sufficient snow cover before starting on it (take a rope).

From Entrèves go to the Pointe Helbronner. Go round the Aiguilles Marbrées (3310m) and climb for 30 minutes on the north side of the huge Col de Rochefort (rocks lightly covered by snow) and get to the right side of the col. You now have to traverse right for about 60m to get on to the large south face. This section often has hard snow or even ice and is exposed (hand rail advisable). Side-slip this 45° slope. Once you have passed the large pointed rock the slope eases up a little on the right. Depending on the snow conditions (wind-packed, powder, or hardened by the snow slides), pick the best route to the middle funnel-shaped gully. Join the glacier and ski down the middle at first and after the sloping plateau keep to the right bank to avoid the final bulge. Now head left and cross the large couloir to get to the left bank of the small valley at around 2200m. Cross the west bank once again and go through the first groups of larch trees. Lower down you reach some chalets and a track and finally the road between Planpincieux and Entrèves.

40.a   Jétoula (AD). Follow route 40 to 2200m and check out a route on the right bank. Ski to the foot of the Arête de Jétoula via a series of small valleys and a small couloir between rocks. There is now a long traverse to the moraine (larches) and a steep couloir takes you to the bottom of the well used section that comes down from the Pavillon cable-car station.

40.b   Dent du Géant (D+). Some of the Courmayeur guides (notably the mountain guide and extreme skier Giorgio Passino) ski the south/south-west face from the foot of the Dent du Géant. This extremely aesthetic route is a bit rocky at first and then turns in to a huge slope that narrows at the bottom and becomes a couloir/gully. You have to know what the conditions are like on the face before starting this descent.

On the Marbrées

41   GRANDES JORASSES   4208m
South face   D+

⚑ 1600m	📷 may-June	⌣ 45-50°/200m
↗ D1+D2: 1200m + 1400m	📷 92, 204	⚠ 3 (seracs)
↘ D1+D2: 0m + 2600m	☉ 3 + 12hrs	⊕ HP
✦ South	🎿 4.3	

The best time to ski this descent is either in the spring, and it has to be very cold, or in the summer when you have to carry your skis a lot. It was first skied, after a heli-drop on the summit, by the Swiss skier Sylvain Saudan in April 1971.

D1   From Planpincieux, 3km up the valley from Entrèves, follow the path to the Boccalatte Hut (ref.9).

D2   Climb a few metres up from the hut and put on your skis. Head straight up first on a headland and then at the back of the combe that is next to the spur on the right (Rognon de la Bouteille, 3301m). Continue in the direction of the Rocher du Reposoir that you climb (crevasses, sections of III, pitons, mixed climbing along ridge for 250m, 1 to 1 1/2 hrs). There may be a snow and ice wall to cross on the exposed traverse (crevasses) of the Whymper Couloir. Join the spur that comes down from the Pointe Whymper. 50-80m of mixed climbing (III), followed by a short ridge gives access to glaciated plateau at around 3850m. From here, traverse under the seracs and follow the normal route to the summit (easy mixed climbing to the right) or climb straight up the slope after the seracs (40-45°/150m). You can sometimes also climb up between the Whymper Spur and the seracs on the right to get to the final sloping plateau. This route is quicker, but is steeper and is sheltered from the menacing upper glacier. I tried this route myself in July 1980 (both ascent and descent done on skis). Descend via the

South face of the Grandes Jorasses

41

At the bottom of the Whymper Couloir

route you have picked out on the way up. After having checked it out from the Rocher du Reposoir on the way up, you may also want to ski in the glaciated valley under this spur. The Reposoir Spur is a safer but more difficult access route (on the way up) than crossing the glacier, which is a continuation of the glaciated valley between the Pointe Croz and the Pointe Whymper. Finally, although it is not very difficult this route is complex, long and very physically demanding.

42   MONT GRUETTA   3684m
South face   D

⚑	1480m or 1530m (road)	🏔	March-June	⤴	40-45°/400m
↗	D1+D2: 1300m + 900m	📷	94	⚠	2
↘	D1+D2: 0m + 2270m	☻	3-4 + 10hrs	⊕	HP
✤	South	🎿	4.3		

During the 70s and 80s, when helicopter drops where allowed in this area, numerous descents were made fairly easily on this steep face of Val Ferret. Nowadays, it is better to plan your descents here for spring, but watch out for warm periods (especially when the fœhn is blowing). Nevertheless, its beauty and its committing and technical nature make Mont Gruetta one of the best descents in the Massif.

Note: On rare occasions the Triolet Glacier, at the foot of Mont Gruetta, is also skied although it is heavily crevassed. Access from the Dalmazzi Hut, however, is not recommended as it is very exposed to avalanche. This is a pity because the east couloir of the Col de Leschaux (40°/500m and 52° at the summit) is a great descent. I don't recommend this route even as a variant.

Mont Gruetta

D1 ▪ From Planpincieux go the hamlet of Frébouze and then the Gervasutti Hut (ref.11).

D2 ▪ From the hut descend 200m to go round the bottom of the south spur. Climb up the left side of the steep glacier that drops down from Mont Gruetta until you get to the middle plateau. Now traverse to

Mont Gruetta (centre) and Mont Dolent (right)

avoid the crevasses and seracs and climb up under Mont Gruetta and then get on to a second sloping plateau. The top part is a little less steep apart from the section of a few metres under the ridge. From there you can get to just left of the point marked 3654m on the map. This is not a true summit and the round trip eastwards along the ridge takes at least an hour (not very interesting). There is sustained skiing on the descent by the same route and there are some very deep crevasses that sometimes point in the same direction as your skis...

42.a   Col des Hirondelles (3480m, D). From the hut head due west and go over the convexity in the glacier on the left side. Now go above it to get to the upper section below the col. Join this section from the left and after a steep section. It is better to ski the route when the snow cover is good as there are numerous and deep crevasses. The Col des Hirondelles offers a unique viewpoint over the French side of the Massif.

43 MONT DOLENT		3823m
South face		AD

⚑	1600m (road)	🏔	February-May	⛰	40°/150m
↗	D1+D2: 1120 + 1100m	📷	94, 96	⚠	2
↘	D1+D2: 0 m + 2200m	☽	4 + 6hrs	⊕	HP
✦	South	🎿	4.1		

Three countries meet at Mont Dolent, and it is one of the few 'pyramidal' mountains to offer a relatively regular descent route. Most ski-tourers do the final round trip to and from the summit on foot. One day in May 1980, I set off from

Chamonix at 2 o'clock in the morning with two young clients from Paris. We climbed up with head torches and the snow was firm as it was night-time. Despite having passed the hut after daybreak, we were still on the summit by 11am and we got back to Chamonix that afternoon. I only mention this to prove that this trip can be done in a day. We opted to do it in a day because the Dolent Hut is small and often full, and bivouac equipment and tents being heavy it would have hampered a great ski. To avoid the long and tedious walk up Val Ferret, you can also camp at the site of the old Elena Hut (2060m), or even go up from La Fouly in Swiss Val Ferret (with a very early start).

D1 From Courmayeur, go to Planpincieux and follow ref.12 to the Dolent Hut (2724m).

D2 From the hut there is an ascending tra-
verse under the south-west slopes of the Pointe Allobrogia before you get to the Pré de Bar Glacier. Climb up the right branch of the glacier below Mont Grépillon and join the ridge at the Col du Grépillon (3500m) via a steep hump. Continue under the south-east ridge and then climb up the couloir to the left. You get to the summit after 150m at nearly 40°. The descent from the summit is exposed above the rock band. Your descent route follows more or less the route you took up, but keep left as the slopes are better to ski on this side.

*On the start below
the summit*

On the Pré de Bar Glacier

44   TÊTE DE FERRET   2713m
West face   PD

1560m (road)	January-May	35° max.
1150m	6hrs	1
1150m	2.3	SP
West		

The traverse into Switzerland is part of the famous Tour of Mont Blanc. It can also be done with snow-shoes (10hrs). However, although crossing Petit Col Ferret is easy on the Swiss side it is steep on the Italian side.

Mont Dolent and Col Ferret

From Planpincieux follow route 43 to get to the end of Val Ferret (10km!) and the (Refuge de) Pré de Bar Hut (2060m). From here climb up the headland to the left of the mountain stream that comes down from the Pointe de la Combette. At about 2450m traverse north in the direction of Grand Col Ferret (2537m) and follow the frontier ridge to the summit (snow often hard and wind blown). Descend via the same route before it gets too hot!

44.a   Traverse into Switzerland (PD). From the Grand Col Ferret traverse northwards to get to the Arête des Planfins which you follow to the mountain known as La Dotse (2492m). Ski to the bottom of the valley via the headland alongside the Ravine de la Peule. Follow the road to La Fouly watching out for the numerous avalanches on the south-west side. You can pick up taxis and buses in the village.

SWISS VAL FERRET

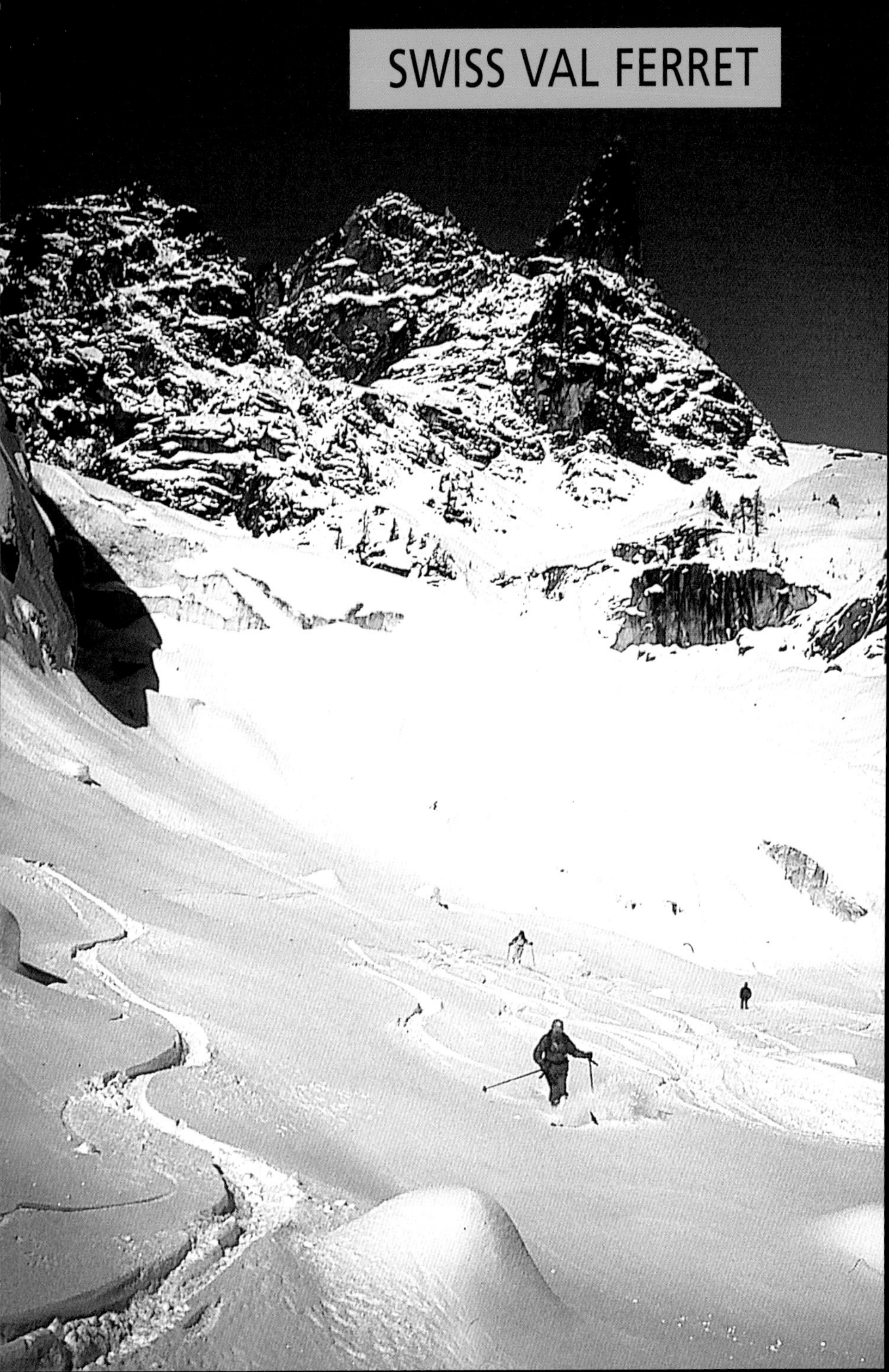

PRACTICAL INFORMATION

International dialling code: 00 41
CAS (Swiss Alpine Club) hut information: (0)21 320 70 70
Mountain rescue: 1414 or 144
Rescue radio frequency: channel K 158 625 and channel E 161 300
Champex Tourist Office: (027) 783 12 27
La Fouly Tourist Office: (027) 783 27 17
La Fouly Guides Office: (027) 783 27 17
Swiss weather forecast: 157 126 248 / www.meteosuisse.ch
Snow report: 187
Post bus: (027) 783 11 05
Taxi Le Châble: (027) 771 72 73

SKI LIFTS

Vichères-Bavon: (027) 783 17 07
La Breya (Champex): (027) 783 13 44

ROAD ACCESS

From Chamonix, via the Col des Montets, go to the Swiss border at Le Châtelard. Continue to Martigny via Trient and the Col de la Forclaz. Now follow directions to the Col du Grand Saint Bernard until you get to Sembrancher and then go to Orsières.

■ **La Fouly** – From Orsières follow the La Fouly-Val Ferret road for about 13km. Leave your car in the La Fouly lift station car-park or continue up the road to Le Clou (1614m) as far as you can go.

■ **Orsières or Praz de Fort** – Follow directions above to get to Orsières. For Praz de Fort, from Orsières follow the La Fouly road for about 6km.

■ **Champex** – Follow Sembrancher-Orsières directions and take the Champex turning in Orsières. Alternatively, on the road to Sembrancher from Martigny there is a turning for Champex in 'Les Valettes' (4km after the exit from Martigny). Park at the La Breya chairlift. Climb to the Val d'Arpette using skins or take the chairlift to Les Grands Plans (2188m).

■ **Col de la Forclaz** – After the border (Le Châtelard) and Trient, on the way to Martigny, is the Col de la Forclaz. Depending on which route you plan to ski you can either park in the car-park on the col or at a place called 'La Caffe' (1235m) on the right-hand side of the road two bends below the col (Martigny side).

■ **Ravoire** – From Chamonix go to the Col de la Forclaz. On the road down to Martigny, after the hairpin bends, the Ravoire turning is on the left at 'Chanton d'en Bas', 908m. Follow directions to Les Repperins then turn left

Previous page: Leaving the Saleina Glacier below the Petit Clocher du Portalet.

towards 'Chez Pillet'. Park at the end of the road, below the hamlet in the forest, or a little higher up.

■ **Trient village** – On the road to the Col de la Forclaz from Chamonix, take the southerly exit for Trient and park at 'Le Praillon' or 'Le Peuty'.

■ **Bovine** – 7km from Martigny, on the Grand Saint Bernard road, turn right in the hamlet called Le Bourgeaud and follow the road to Bovine. The first car-park (900m) is used in winter. In spring you can continue by car along the track towards Les Assets (1290m).

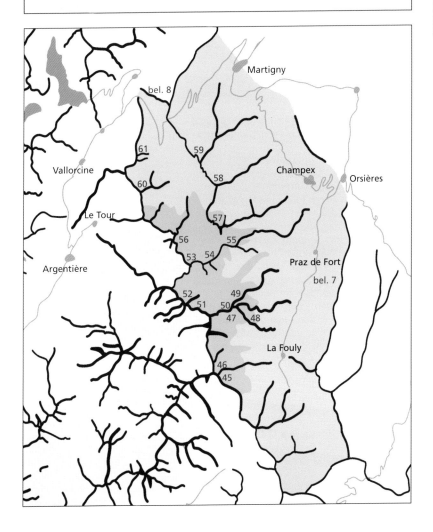

Swiss Val Ferret offers a very special collection of ski descents and tours. The numerous heli-drops of skiers in the winter have little affect on the ski-tourers in the area as the classic tours, such as the Three Cols, and the start of the Chamonix-Zermatt Haute Route don't really get skied until the spring. There are three big huts that are convenient for early morning starts. A fourth hut (smaller and in a wonderful location) is also used by skiers, although it was built with summer climbers and mountaineers in mind and is similar to the La Maye Bivouac on Mont Dolent.

Given the long traverses over cols, the long climbs up mountains and their technical descent routes, access to the highest areas in this sector is more often from the French side of the Massif. The height gains and losses from the Trient Hut in particular are quite substantial. There is also the foehn to contend with. This warm wind is particularly strong as it blows in from Italy and can drastically change the snow conditions. Thankfully, the Swiss weather forecasting service is pretty good at predicting its arrival.

MOUNTAIN HUTS

Ref.15 ■ La Maye Bivouac (2667m, PD)
12-15 places, not guardianed, gas (not guaranteed).

From La Fouly go up to the Crêtet de la Gouille (2078m) via the Léchère alpages (pastures). At around 2100m join and cross the Combe des Fonds (owing to the high risk of avalanche and the debris they leave behind, it is not recommended that you attempt to climb straight up the Combe). Now, on the slope opposite, there is an ascending traverse that takes you to the foot of the Dolent Glacier. Climb alongside the glacier. Watch out for the serac falls - although infrequent, they can set off enormous avalanches! Now head towards the pronounced notch in the east ridge (Arête Gallet). The Maye Bivouac is on a promontory at the foot of this ridge.

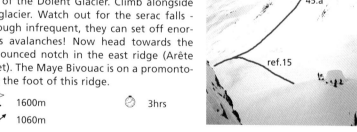

Maye Bivouac

45.a

ref.15

⌐ 1600m   ◔ 3hrs

↗ 1060m

Ref.16 ■ A Neuve Hut (2735m, PD)
CAS, guardianed in spring, winter room unguardianed, 30 places, tel: (027) 783 24 24 or (027) 783 21 11.

Starting in La Fouly go past the A Neuve chalets and climb up the large north-west combe to the glacier. The summer path follows the rocky moraine on the right,

when on skis I prefer to climb up the centre of the combe (watch out for the mountain stream under the snow). Get on to the glacier and leave it at around 2200m where you cross the first line of moraine to get onto the south face of Les Essettes. Now climb north/north-east to the rock band that the A Neuve Hut sits on and go left to access it.
If you are going to climb up in the afternoon sun watch out for avalanches!

A Neuve Hut

⚑ 1600m   🕐 3hrs

↗ 1130m

Ref.17 ▪ Saleina Hut (2691m, AD) via the Col des Planereuses –
Open but not guardianed in the spring, 20 places,
tel: (027) 783 17 00 (summer) or (032) 835 23 91.

Follow route 48 (this chapter) to the Col des Planereuses and descend the Saleina face from the col heading right at the base of the spur on the Grande Pointe des Planereuses. Ski along a slight north-facing headland to the hut.

⚑ 1600m   🕐 5-6hrs

↗ 1630m

Ref.17.a ▪ Saleina Hut (2691m, AD) via Praz de Fort

From Praz de Fort climb up the left bank of the Vallon d'Arpette de Saleina, if possible to the end of the road (1500m). When it is hot, watch out for the numerous avalanches that come down from the Ravines Rousses face. Despite this risk of avalanche (taking this route when it is cold reduces this risk), this is less hazardous than following the summer path (right bank, ladders and cables) that can be tricky and even dangerous in winter and in spring. Follow the approach route for 48 to the slopes beneath the Pointe des Planereuses. At around 2100m climb up and traverse left to reach the hut which is hidden behind the top section of the moraine. The significant height gain and dangerous nature of this route make this variant less well used. Moreover, the access from the French side is also much more straightforward and there are a greater number of routes that can be done from the Grands Montets.

⚑ 1500m   🕐 3-4hrs

↗ 1200m

Ref.18 ▪ Trient Hut (3170m, PD)
Guardianed from mid-March to May, open out of season, 140 places,
tel: (027) 783 14 38 or (027) 722 91 58.

Leave your car at the La Breya chairlift in Champex and climb up the Val d'Arpette
to the Col des Écandies (2796m). Now follow the rock bars under the Petite Pointe
d'Orny and the Pointe d'Orny to get to the Trient Hut (3170m) via a bank to the
left of a last rock (normal descent on Chamonix-Zermatt Haute Route). In winter
start at the top of the La Breya chairlift.

| ⌐ 1500m | ↗ 1700m | ⏱ 5hrs |

Ref.19 ▪ Orny Hut (2811m, PD)
Open but not guardianed in the ski season, 80 places, tel: (027) 783 18 87
(summer) or (027) 207 13 48.

There are several access routes to the Orny Hut. The safest and longest route follows the Val d'Arpette from Champex (ref.18) to below the Trient Hut and then
descends the left bank of the Orny Glacier to the hut. You can also start in Praz
de Fort and climb up the left bank of the Vallon d'Arpette de Saleina which is
shorter but is often exposed to avalanches. Access via the La Breya (Champex)
chairlift is not recommended as it is rarely safe and is very exposed to avalanches
(long traverse along steep slopes).

⌐ 1500m	⏱ 6¹ᐟ²hrs
↗ 1610m	
↘ 200m	

'BELVEDERE' ROUTES

Bel.7 ▪ Tour de Bavon – Bec Rond (2540m, F)

⌐ 1400m	🗓 December-March	⮦ Sections of 35°
↗ 280m	⏱ 3hrs	⚠ 1
↘ 1200m	⚒ 1.3	⊕ DP
✳ All		

From this half-day tour you get great views of the three Swiss glaciers at the east
end of the Massif. This is a pleasant, easy tour for the beginning of the season,
and the north faces of the Bec Rond and the Tour de Bavon often have good powder snow. The lifts at Vichères-Bavon make it easy to access the start of the tour
at 2200m. From Martigny follow directions to Col du Grand Saint Bernard and at
Liddes take the turning on the right to Vichères. From the top of the chairlift
climb south along the crest. Descend to the col and follow a wide dome that finishes in a steep ridge (Bec Rond, 1hr). Several descent routes are possible on the
east, north and north-west faces.

Val Ferret from Bec Rond

Bel.8 ■ L' Arpille (2085m, F)

⚐ 1270m (road)	🏔 January-March	⌐ 30°
↗ 815m	☉ 3-4hrs	⚠ 1
↘ 815m	🎿 1.3	⊕ DP
⊕ East/North-east		

Although in an area that forms a natural border between France and Switzerland, this route is entirely in Switzerland. This pretty route can be done at the beginning of winter even if the snow cover is not great, as the soft grass of the high pastures won't ruin your skis. From the summit you get good views of the numerous tours in the area. To the north are the routes starting in Les Marécottes, les Dents du Midi and La Tour Salière; while to the south are the slopes below the Col de Balme and Les Grandes Autannes (spelt Otanes on Swiss maps), the Pointe Ronde, and finally the great white expanse of the Trient pla-

teau. On the road to Martigny from Chamonix, after the Col de la Forclaz, take the turning to Ravoire (on the left, 908m). After the second hairpin bend turn left towards Les Raperrins. At the end of the road, follow the forest track (heads south-west) that leads to the chalets of the Arpille summer pastures (1816m). Climb the north-east slope and then follow the easy

L'Arpille

ridge to the summit (3 1/2 hrs). There is a short, pretty descent down the east
face in the spring or if the snow is stable or powdery. However, you then have to
traverse across the bottom of the hill to get back to the chalets (very popular
snow-shoe route).

45   MONT DOLENT   3823m
Gallet Ridge   AD+

⌐ 1600m	🗺 February-May	⌐ 40°-45°/350m
↗ D1+D2: 1120m + 1100m	📷 104, 106	⚠ 2
↘ D1+D2: 0m + 2220m	⏱ D1 + D2: 4 + 6hrs	⊕ HP
⊕ East	⚒ 5.1	

This high corner of Val Ferret is what you imagine a high mountain valley
should look like. A small village nestles at the end of the road and is home to a
number of world-class mountaineers. Here nature can be wild and harsh, and
yet beautiful. With the autumn comes violent southerly winds, and the paraly-
sing winter snows lead to avalanches that sweep woodland and houses before
them. The 'montagnards' (mountain dwellers), however, have learnt to live with
catastrophe and their respect for nature's laws remains constant. Among those
who call this high valley home are the guide Xavier Kalt, known across the Alps
as the co-founder (with Roger Frison-Roche) of the International Union of
Mountain Guides, Michel Darbellay (first solo ascent of the Eiger), and the
Troillet brothers, Jean and Daniel, who are also both guides. This area is far from
the Chamonix 'circus' and is not some kind of Disneyland, and deserves our
respect. Try not to disturb this peaceful and gentle corner of the Alps!

Mont Dolent, Swiss side

On the Gallet Ridge

D1 From La Fouly follow ref.15 to the Maye Bivouac.

D2 From the hut climb up the left bank of the Dolent Glacier between 2900m and 3300m (watch out for the crevasses). Depending on the season, it is sometimes better to climb up the centre of the glacier and to follow a kind of large headland (seracs and crevasses) and go right of the point marked 3208m on the map. Cross the bergschrund as high as possible and join the ridge via a steep slope (40°) that you climb on its north face (cornices higher up). Follow the ridge to the summit with crampons because this last section is quite exposed and atmospheric. Follow the same route on the descent (or move to the centre of the glacier at around 2900m) then descend to the Combe des Fonds. The complete descent of the north face is sustained and you should have a good look at the face and choose your route before setting off (start below the point marked 3188m on the map). Note: The north face, from below the Gallet Ridge to La Fouly, is sometimes skied (more committing).

45.a North face of the Pointe Allobrogia (3177m, D+). Start as if for route 45. As you reach the foot of the Dolent Glacier (at around 2320m), head towards the east combe that leads to the north-east face of the Pointe Allobrogia. This steep, shaded face has a gradient of around 50°/400m with steep slabs of rock. It doesn't take long to get to the route and you can see it from the Grande Lui. It can even be done, there and back, in a day (1600m height gain and loss!). First descent of the East face by Rémy Lécluse and Jérôme Aubert on 3 Feb. 2004 (between 45 and 55°/700m).

45.b Notch to the north of the Maye Bivouac Hut (D-). 20 mins from the hut there is a deep couloir from where you can ski directly on to the A Neuve face. Keep well left from 2450m (50°/150m) and continue to La Fouly (you need lots of snow!).

46	**MONT DOLENT** North face	**3823m** TD

⚑	1600m	🏔	March-Mat	⤴	45°-55°/300m
↗	D1+D2: 1130m + 1090m	📷	106, 107	⚠	3
↘	D1+D2: 0m + 2220m	🕐	D1 + D2: 3 + 7hrs	⚐	HP (rappel)
✥	North	⚔	5.2		

Skiing the north face of Mont Dolent is both commendable and audacious given the number of objective dangers that this face presents. The steep slope at the summit sits on top of an ever-present band of seracs, and the A Neuve Glacier can become a labyrinth of crevasses and seracs which is hardly appealing. Therefore, it is better to access the route from the east ridge (route 45) or via the normal route (43). You could, of course, also use a helicopter to access the summit, but it is certainly not something I would recommend. It ridicules the whole ethic of steep skiing, and in this particular case, isn't a very honest way of achieving one's goal. This unfair advantage means finance will win the day every time – hardly a very respectable tactic! The public does not understand the fact that the second or the nth descent may be more technically demanding than the first one. Nevertheless, it often the first descent that sticks in the memory and about which one talks... Tracks are ephemeral, words are not...

D1 From La Fouly go to the A Neuve Hut (ref.16). You can see the north face of Mont Dolent from here and you can pick out best line between the crevasses to get to the first slope that is less steep under the Aiguille de l'Amône.

North face of the Dolent

D2 From the hut join and cross the A Neuve Glacier, more or less following the contour lines (2650-2700m) to the bottom of the rocks of the Aiguille de l'Amône (watch out for the crevasses that point in the direction you are moving!). Now climb up the steep glaciated combe broken by seracs and crevasses. Higher up the route becomes very exposed and is enough to put off the more opportunistic climbers. In fact, this face is rarely climbed because of the numerous dangers it presents. The slope at the summit is between 45° to 50° of roughly 250m. You should take gear for setting up quite a long rappel on the descent. First descent by Pierre Tardivel on 25th June 1990.

Aiguille de l'Amône

46.a   North-east face of the Aiguille de l'Amône (3584m, TD). Follow the approach route for the north face of the Dolent. Pass the spur that comes down from the Col d'Argentière (point marked 2661m on map) and go to the right of the numerous crevasses. A basin below the Aiguilles Rouges du Dolent leads to the bergschrund at around 3100m. The north face is very steep at the top (55°). Cross the crest on to the north-east face (less steep but more exposed above the rock band). This impressive line is very aesthetic, but is also quite risky and is not often skied. The first descent was probably by Olivier Roduit, a guide from Verbier, in 1990 (45-55°/800m).

46.b   Col d'Argentière, south-east face (D). This face gets the sun early and gullies quickly form on it. This route is the quickest route to get to La Fouly from the French side of the massif. The slope is 45°/600m. It is easier to access this route from the French side because the crevasses and bergschrunds on the Swiss side (A Neuve Glacier) make it difficult and dangerous ground to cross.

47	**GRANDE LUI**	**3509m**
	South face	**PD**

⚑	1600m	🗓 February-March	⌐	35°/150m
↗	D1+D2: 1130m + 780m	📷 107, 108	⚠	1
↘	D1+D2: 0m + 1910m	⊘ D1 + D2: 4 + 5hrs	⊕	SP
✦	South	✗ 3.1		

The south-east face of the Grande Lui is excellent to ski when the snow is just starting to be warmed by the sun. The ideal time, between 7am and 9am, makes for good and safe skiing right to the bottom. However, after 10am the sun, sometimes helped by the fœhn, can be so destructive that you'll wish you'd never gone there in the

A Neuve face of Grande Lui

first place! Having said that, most of the descents are done at this time and not only is it more dangerous but deep ruts start to form that can be difficult for the early morning skiers. There are various routes that can be done from the Saleina and Argentière huts, but a late start on this south-east facing slope will probably mean skiing in very soft snow (unless it's the middle of winter).

D1 From La Fouly go to the A Neuve Hut (ref.16).

D2 From the hut go to the left of the rock band and climb directly up the fairly steep glacier for 200m. Head left and pass beneath the crests (Col de Saleina) and up to the rocks near the summit (on foot, snow-covered rocks). The descent should be done relatively early as the sun, often aided by the southerly wind, quickly transforms the snow on this side

47.a　Col de l'A Neuve (3406m, AD). From the hut follow the access route for 47 to the Col de Saleina at around 3250m. Now traverse left and descend below a rock spur (steep slope) and climb up the east-facing slope (steep section) to the col. Descend the A Neuve Glacier towards the left bank. You should try and get a look at the descent route from the hut, as you need to take care on the top section of the glacier which is heavily crevassed. At around 2500m rejoin the route you took on the climb up.

47.b　Col Supérieur du Tour Noir (3690m, D). Follow 47.a to below the Aiguille de l'A Neuve. Head left under the Col Supérieur. After the bergschrund the slope slowly steepens up and is 45° below the central headland that you cross at about 3600m. There is now a diagonal traverse to your left (150m) to the col. Either ski back down the same way or ski the steep couloir on the French side and the Améthystes Glacier (route 76.c, Argentière section). The col is rarely accessed from the Swiss side and I much prefer the French access route.

48　THREE SWISS COLS　　3160m
Essettes, Crête Sèche, Planereuses　　AD

⌐ 1600m	🏔 February-may	⌐ 35°-40°
↗ D1+D2: 1130m + 500m	📷 103, 107, 108, 109, 110, 111	⚠ 1
↘ D1+D2: 0m + 2100m	🕐 D1 + D2: 4 + 4¹/² hrs	⊕ AD
✦ All	🎿 3.2	

There are some exceptionally good routes in this area and various access and exit routes are used. Bearing in mind the faces to ski in the shade and in the sun, there are numerous possible traverses to do from France or from Switzerland.

Tour Noir and Grande Lui

In one day, starting at Les Grands Montets, we crossed the Col du Chardonnet, then the Col de Tita Neire and the Col des Planereuses (48.c) and spent the night in La Fouly. The cold weather meant we had good powder snow. You should, however, take care on the descent of the long east face if it gets warmer because it is very avalanche prone. Via route 49 and the new Saleina (winter room, 20 places, gas) or from the Aiguilles Dorées Bivouac (12 places), the tour from La Fouly is a high quality trip that has some athletic climbs! To get the best of the descents you should stick to the timetable for the south-east facing areas even if this means finishing a route at around 10am.

Les Planereuses

D1   From La Fouly climb to the A Neuve Hut (ref.16).

D2   Climb up the glacier below the Pointes des Essettes and at around 2900m you should spot the Couloir des Essettes above a large snow cone. Climb to the col (3113m, 45°/50m) and cross the gully from the right. Cross the Treutse Bô Glacier at around 3000m and go to the snowy saddle of the Crête Sèche (3024m) – not to be confused with the Col de Crête Sèche, 100m lower and which we don't cross. Take a couloir (north face) to get into the first basin of the Planereuses Glacier (2900m, see 48.c). Continue north/north-west down a short steep slope to the Col des Planereuses (3030m). For those who want some more climbing, you can always add the round-trip to the Grand Darrey (+2hrs). From the Col des Planereuses descend the Saleina face (a few rocks). Traverse right towards the spur that comes down from the Pointe des Planereuses and join the Saleina Glacier. Cross the glacier (crevassed area) to its left bank. Pass under the small valley of the Ravines Rousses and join the Vallon d'Arpette de Saleina that leads to the road to Praz de Fort. There won't necessarily be snow below 1300m after April.

48.a   Col de Tita Neire (3157m, AD). After the col at the Crête Sèche descend to the Glacier des Planereuses and head west, below the Darrey Glacier, to the Col de Tita Neire (20m of steep climbing below the col). The descent is due north and on the right of the valley that joins the Saleina Glacier. Now follow route 48 (+1hr).

48.b   Col de Saleina (3419m, AD). Same start as 48.a. After the Col de Tita Neire climb to the Col de Saleina, passing below the Petit Darrey, and ski down to

La Fouly via the route up to the A Neuve Hut. Alternatively, from the shoulder north-west of the Petit Darrey (3240m) you can also descend on the left of the glacier to easily join the Saleina Glacier and follow the other variants out.

48.c   Planereuses (AD). After the col at the Crête Sèche (after the Essettes col), the Planereuses face has 1800m of virtually direct descent on the right bank of the mountain stream. You need safe snow conditions as some of the slopes that exceed 30° are avalanche prone. The final gully is barely skiable (even dangerous). Avoid it by heading right and choose between the avalanche couloirs (not obvious tree skiing with steep slopes and rock bands, but protected). Rejoin the road near Branche d'en haut, and then Praz de Fort.

49   TOUR OF THE 'DARREY'   3419m
Via Saleina Glacier (west face)   AD

⌶	1600m	⬛	February-May	⌐	35°
↗	D1+D2: 1730m + 730m	📷	110, 111	⚠	1
↘	D1+D2: 640m + 1820m	◔	D1 + D2: $6^{8/2}$ + 4hrs	⊕	SP
✦	All	⚡	3.2		

This route takes you down the Grande Lui in good conditions in the morning. I am always surprised to see that the ski route marked on the IGN TOP 25 map shows the traverse of the Col de la Grande Lui. While the climb up its north face is straightforward, the descent down the other side, the south-east face, is

The magnificent Saleina cirque

nothing of the sort. It is steep (40°), steep-sided, and above all it collects and channels all the snow that starts to slide with the arrival of the first rays of sun. You should therefore avoid it. Despite the 120m of climbing to the north of the Col de Saleina (3419m) and the bergschrund, I think the route described here is better and behind the crest are the snowfields of the Grande Lui (route 47). Stick to the time given for the descent and ski it well before midday, as the snow quickly becomes unskiable and dangerous.

D1 From La Fouly go to the Saleina Hut (ref.17) after having crossed the cols at the Essettes, the Crête Sèche and the Planereuses.

D2 From the hut descend west and join and climb up the Saleina Glacier (2650m). Go round the large central rognon to join the north combe of the Grande Lui. Climb up the left bank of the combe at first and then the centre. Don't go to the Col de la Grande Lui, instead, go back right and climb the steep north couloir (40°/100m) of the Col de Saleina. Descend via route 47.

49.a Three Swiss cols 'backwards' (AD). The Planereuses-Treutse Bô-Essettes direction. Descent to La Fouly or return via the Col de Saleina (short steep descent, 40°/100m on the north face).

49.b Évole Glacier (PD). Great descent from the south shoulder of the Petite Pointe des Planereuses (2950m), in cold snow. Join the Saleina Glacier via a fault line at around 2400m at the area known as 'La Gare'. Easy access from the Saleina Hut.

Saleina face of the Grand Darrey and Grande Lui

50   GRANDE LUI   3509m
West face   D–

⚑	1500m	🏔	February-May	⌐	40°-45°/250m
↗	D1 + D2: 1200m + 900m	📷	111, 113	⚠	1
↘	D1 + D2: 0m + 2100m	⏱	D1 + D2: 4 + 6hrs	⊕	SP
✦	West	⚒	4.3		

As well as the beautiful descent of the south face, there are several routes up the Grande Lui that are of interest. Two clients and I were able to descend the north-east face of the Col du Tour, climb (from the small col, 3255m on map) the north/north-east face of Grande Lui to its summit, spend the night at the A Neuve Hut and do the five cols (Three Swiss Cols in reverse together with the

Fenêtre de Saleina and the Col du Tour) the following day. Accessing the Grande Lui/Darrey group is easier from the French side of the Massif (via Col du Chardonnet or the Albert 1er Hut). You can have quite a long approach to this face of the Grande Lui, as it faces west and can still be skied by the middle of the day. The same is true of the glaciers on the French side on the way back. Sat between the Saleina, Trient and A Neuve glaciers, Grande Lui is a great viewpoint and you can't miss it if you are skiing in the area. I have not included the alternative access route via the west face of the Col de l'A Neuve as I have never seen it in condition (high bergschrund, slabs of ice…). Another less steep central couloir can also be skied (40°/200m, a little steeper at the top), but is generally used on the way down.

_____

D1 Follow ref.17 to the Saleina Hut.

D2 From the hut join the south branch of the Saleina Glacier. Go round Grande Lui and get on to the west face (3200m). Climb the obvious couloir on the left to the summit. The narrow slope at the bottom is a regular gradient and the descent is by the same route. Watch out for the rocks that sometimes appear through the snow and the gullies that generally appear in the spring.
Note: If, on the climb up, the west face is not in good condition for skiing, climb to the summit and via the south face join the A Neuve plateau. The simplest way to get back to the Saleina Glacier is to cross the Col de Saleina (10mins of climbing and 40°/100m on the descent of the north face). Now follow routes 48 or 49. The most popular access routes are from the Trient, Argentière and Albert 1er huts.

51   AIGUILLE D'ARGENTIÈRE   3900m
Barbey Couloir   D

⚐	1500m	🏔	February-May	⛏	45°/400m
↗	D1+D2: 1200m + 1300m	📷	113	⚠	2
↘	D1+D2: 0m + 2500m	⏱	D1 + D2: 4 + 6hrs	⊕	HP
✦	East	⚔	5.1		

The descents on the Swiss side of the Aiguille d'Argentière are generally accessed from France and the Grands Montets. There are no cable-cars on the Swiss side and the area has a more 'wild' feel to it. However, as I have already mentioned the climb to the Saleina Hut is a long and dangerous one. It is also possible to access this area from the Albert 1er Hut via the Fenêtre du Tour, but it is a long route both on the way there and the way back.
The descent of the Barbey Couloir is long and serious which makes for a great day out! Daniel Chauchefoin was probably the first person to ski this route on 28 May 1978. Several guides (including myself and the Stages Vallençant guides) started taking clients to ski this face in the 1980s. This face gets the sun very early, and if the snow is good it can be skied by good and not necessarily 'extreme' skiers even though officially the slope is given 47°/400m. In fact, if you stay

right there are even some sections of 50° and 55°.

Earn your turns!

D1 From Praz de Fort follow ref. 17.a to the Saleina Hut.

D2 From the hut follow route 50 to 3000m. Now head towards the basin to the left of the north-east spur of the Aiguille d'Argentière. Make a detour left to avoid the crevasses and join the foot of the face and climb up it. At the top there is a final shoulder that overlooks the north face. From here you can see the cornice on the summit ridge that is usually on the left towards the secondary north-east summit.

On the way down, the right-hand sections (almost north-facing) generally have better snow. Although this looks like quite an even face, there are often quite deep gullies and rock spurs on this face. All the lines down this face lead to a final funnel shaped section that you avoid by taking the small east-facing slope (see also route 74.a).

On the way up to the Col de Saleina

52   AIGUILLE D'ARGENTIÈRE   3900m
North face   TD

P 1500m	🏔 may-June	50°/350m, sect. of 55°
↗ D1 + D2: 1200m + 1300m	📷 114	⚠ 3
↘ D1+D2: 0m + 2500m	🕐 D1 + D2: 4 + 7hrs	⊕ HP
✧ North	🎿 5.3	

A true ski-mountaineer and a climbing partner of Messner, the Italian Heini Holzer was passionate about skiing beautiful mountains. From the Couloir de Lourousa in the Argentera to the steep peaks of the Tyrol, not forgetting the first descent of the Brenva Spur, Holzer was one of the pioneers of extreme skiing at the beginning of the 1970s. The technique he developed for turning that was based on a hard push on both poles is probably what led to his fatal error on the north face of the Piz Roseg. He will be remembered for, among other things, his first descent of the north face of the Aiguille d'Argentière after having climbed up the same route in crampons. The face is rarely in condition these days (not enough snow), unlike the 1940s when it was a great regular expanse of snow that didn't even have any seracs. This route is only very rarely repeated.

Alternative access routes: From the Trient Hut via the Fenêtre de Saleina; from the Albert 1er Hut via the Fenêtre or Col du Tour; or from the Argentière Hut having first got some idea of the conditions on the north face.

D1 From Praz de Fort follow ref.17.a to the Saleina Hut.

North face of the Aiguille d'Argentière

52.a

73

52

D2 From the hut follow ref.17.a (in reverse) in the direction of the Col du Chardonnet (72) to the foot of the north face. Climb straight up the slope to the left of the first suspended glacier. Generally, the glaciated slope on the left offers a uniform and wide slope that can be skied. You can also go right and head left again once you are above the seracs. However, the steepness of the slope means that the snow doesn't stick well to this slope (gradient reaches 55°).

52.a   Right bank of the north face (TD). First descended by Daniel Chauchefoin on 1st March 1978. The section between the serac bands varies from year to year. The lower section is over 50°.

53	**TÊTE BLANCHE** North face	**3429m** AD

1500m		March-May		50°/80m			
D1 + D2: 1700m + 350m		113, 119, 121, 138		1			
D1 + D2: 0m + 2000m		D1 + D2: 6 + 5hrs		HP			
North		4.3					

The descent of the north face of the Tête Blanche is a great route to ski to get a feel for steep skiing without any real danger (apart from the instability of the snow!). The trick to skiing in the enormous Trient sector is to get around quickly and make use of the long descents on the French and Swiss sides of the Massif. As the approach route to the hut is quite long, it would be a shame not to stay a little while and try out the various routes that are within skiing distance of the hut.

D1 Follow ref.18 to the Trient Hut (3170m).

D2 From the hut traverse south-west (descending at first) and then go to the foot of the north face. The climb up is pretty straightforward. The descent is 40° at first under the summit and steepens up to 50° (a little steeper if you ski on the left). If the face is icy you can ski the Col Blanc (under the Petite Fourche, 3405m). Watch out for the enormous permanent cornice that guards the access to the col.

53.a   East couloir of the Col des Fourches (3433m, D). Climb to the Col Blanc and follow the ridge to the Col des Fourches (south of the Petite Fourche). There is a cornice at the top of the 220m couloir (45°/120m) that leads to the Saleina Glacier (descend to La Fouly via route 50 or return via the Fenêtre de Saleina via route 68).

53.b   Right bank of the Trient Glacier (AD). Under the Trient Hut pass below the Pointe d'Orny and the Col des Écandies on the right bank of the glacier. Ski the north face of the Chaux de Vésevey on the right bank of the glacier. At around 2000m join the end of the glacier (can be skied at the end of winter) to avoid the small ravines on the right that are full of shrubs and bushes, rocks and avalanche couloirs. From the bridge onwards (gite, 1583m), follow the left bank of the mountain stream to get to Trient. Avoid the path that leads to the Col de la Forclaz (long and gets cleared of snow early on). The glacier, like many others, is retreating and its snout is becoming more and more steep and exposed.

53.c **Fenêtre des Chamois (2985m, AD).** Follow the route you took up and shortly after the Petite Pointe d'Orny you get to the Fenêtre des Chamois (at the foot of the west shoulder). The couloir is narrow and you will have to side-slip some of the way down. It leads to the top of the Val d'Arpette (below the Col des Écandies), 40°/100m.

54   AIGUILLES DORÉES   3410m
Copt Couloir   D+

⌐	1500m	⬟	March-May	∟	50°-55°/200m
↗	D1+D2: 1700m + 310m	📷	116, 118	⚠	2
↘	D1+D2: 0m + 2100m	⏱	D1 + D2: 6 + 5hrs	⊕	HP
✦	North	🎿	5.2		

The Copt Couloir is nice and short and is a good place to consolidate a taste for steep skiing. If the snow is hard your first turns will be quite hesitant. Stay in balance and control and link your turns with the help of judicious side-slipping. The start of this route is quite comfortable and not too intimidating.

D1   From Champex go to the Trient Hut via ref. 18.

D2   From the hut (3170m) descend to the Col d'Orny (3098m) and traverse due south across the Trient plateau to the foot of the north couloir of the Col Copt. Climb up the couloir to the snowy saddle uphill of the col. On the descent the slope is steeper on the left bank. You can descend via the Orny Glacier and this is a great ski on easy slopes. Go back to the Orny Hut and, still keeping well to the

Aiguilles Dorées and the Copt Couloir

left, join the Combe d'Orny. Stay on the right bank of the mountain stream as you make your way through the bands of rock or go to the right of them and ski the north face. Continue to the small narrow valley, cross the stream (point marked 1490m on the map) and follow the forest path that traverses left. The descent of the Vallon d'Arpette de Saleina (from the Orny

Combe d'Orny

Hut) is not recommended as the snow is not often in condition and there is a risk of snow slides, unless in the morning.

54.a Col des Plines (3246m, PD). Ski along the base of the Aiguilles Dorées until you get to the Col Droit below the Roc des Plines. You join the Plines Glacier (Dorées Bivouac) and the left bank of the Saleina Glacier after a short sustained slope (risk of slab avalanches). You can also descend directly down the Ravines Rousses Glacier (30-35°/250m) and the Saleina Glacier. This is one of the best descents in the area. Finish in Praz de Fort.

54.b Combe d'Orny – Le Châtelet (PD). Follow route 54 on the left bank of the Orny Glacier, then along the moraine (point marked 2630m on map). Follow the northerly base of the Pointes des Chevrettes and climb up the Combe du Châtelet to the col (2441m). You can ski from the col back in to the Combe d'Orny and follow the last section of route 54. Alternatively, you can also traverse the top of Le Châtelet and descend a north-facing couloir behind the first secondary summit to the bottom of the valley and then next to the stream. Pick up the road that goes to Issert.

55	**LE PORTALET**	**3344m**
	North face	**D**

⚐	1500m	🏔	May-June	⤵	40°-45°/300m
↗	D1+D2: 1700m + 350m	📷	118	⚠	1
↘	D1+D2: 0m + 2010m	🕐	D1 + D2: 6 + 4hrs	🏠	SP
🧭	North-east	🎿	4.3		

This area has been skied a great deal as a result of heli-drops and a whole range of route combinations have been tried. Access to Le Portalet has been made easier by the heli-drops even if just recently they have been restricted to one area: the Col des Plines. The climb up the west face of the Portalet in firm snow and the descent of the couloir does not take too long and as recompense you get about 2000m of skiing. The west face of the Portalet (overlooking the Ravines

Rousses Glacier) is equally skiable and is descended quite regularly by local skiers, especially after having being dropped on the summit by helicopter.

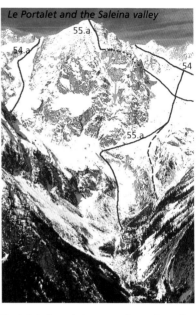

Le Portalet and the Saleina valley

D1 Follow ref.18 from Champex to the Trient Hut.

D2 From the hut descend to the col then head south-east to the foot of the north face. There is now a long diagonal climb up and to the left. A system of rock ridges and gullies take you to the summit crest. The descent of this face does not always have a good covering of snow, but it is quite aesthetic. At the bottom of the face you can choose one of the descents of the Orny Glacier (see route 54).

55.a   East couloir (D+). Seen from the valley there appears to be a narrow but particularly aesthetic line on the Portalet. A couloir comes down from the summit and cuts across the east face that is made even more impressive by the vertical wall of the Petit Clocher next to it. While the upper section of this face is very skiable, the narrowness of the lower section makes it more difficult. Luckily, as a conciliatory gesture, nature has sculpted a nice and steep shaded combe to the north-east that steers you away from the narrow section after about a third of the way down. After this you can now head back right and go round the Clochers du Portalet and find the best snow. The final section of the descent is down the right bank of the Torrent de l'Affe. After skiing through the lines of moraine you get to the bottom of the Vallon d'Arpette de Saleina (40-45°/200m). Local skiers, and notably guides, ski this spectacular and atmospheric east face in cold winter periods, but they climb up the west face from the Col des Plines.

56	**AIGUILLE DU TOUR**	**3542m**
	Normal route on the Swiss side	**F**

⊓	1500m	🏔	February-May	⤵	sect. of 35-40°
↗	D1+D2: 1700m + 480m	📷	119	⚠	1
↘	D1+D2: 0m + 2100m	☉	D1 + D2: 6 + 4h	🕑	SP
⊕	All	🎿	2.3		

The numerous descents in this area are well known by guides who frequently take clients heli-skiing. Thus the numerous variant routes spotted on the flight up can be tested on the way down, a luxury not open to ski-tourers who may not

The Trient Massif

be able ski the route if they have not seen the it on the climb up. This advantage is even more important in this, the Glacier des Grands area. The terrain here can be change greatly from one year to another and depending on the snow cover the glacier can at times be virtually unskiable (crevasses, avalanches…).

D1 From Champex follow ref.18 to the Trient Hut.

D2 From the hut follow route 53 and, after having made a wide turn (crevasses at the beginning), you reach the large sunny slopes of the Aiguille du Tour. Climb in the direction of the summit until you meet up with the tracks coming up from France. The slope steepens up above the bergschrund and you quite often have to leave your skis and carry on to summit on foot (1hr there and back, grade III rock climbing).

You can descend via the same route, but I prefer the descent on the Glacier des Grands side. To ski this route, go round the Aiguilles du Tour cross the col to the north of the Aiguille du Pissoir. Traverse the top of the Glacier des Grands and cross the snowy headland above the Croix de Bron. Now descend the Bron Glacier and continue down the large north-east combe (cross the small valleys and moraine lines, and ski on the right bank of the mountain stream). Once in the Trient valley, cross the mountain stream and continue on the right bank until you get to the bridge before the wood. Now join the track (left bank) that leads to the village of Trient.

On the Col du Pissoir

56.a   Pétoudes Glacier (PD).
After crossing the col near the Aiguille du Pissoir, go straight ahead and go to the left of the convexity in the glacier and take the north-east

branch of the Pétoudes Glacier. Take the north/north-east combe and now continue down the north combe of Les Autannes and stay well right of the mountain stream. After the moraine step you join the Trient valley and route 56.

56.b   North face of the Col du Pissoir (AD). From the Aiguille du Tour go to the right of Le Pissoir and the Col du Pissoir. Cross a headland (2974m) at the obvious small col, then continue down the steep north valley that leads to the top of the Trient Glacier. You can also access this steep glaciated valley to the left of the rocky promontory marked 3177m on the map (35-40°/250m, underlying layers of ice). Stay on the left bank of the valley and join the classic route (56).

57   POINTE D'ORNY   3269m
Arpette couloirs   AD+

⌐	1500m	⌧	February-May	⌐	sections of 45°
↗	D1+D2: 1700m + 120m	⌧	120	⚠	1
↘	D1+D2: 0m + 1820m	⏱	D1 + D2: 6 + $2^{1/2}$hrs	⊕	SP
⊕	North-east	⚒	4.1		

Perched just above the Trient Hut, this peak and its north face don't seem very impressive. However, the great snow conditions that you get on these routes are much appreciated by the local skiers and justify the long walk up the day before (unless of course you get dropped off at the Col des Plines by helicopter!).

D1   From Champex go to the Col des Écandies and the Trient Hut (ref.18).

D2   From the hut there is an easy climb to the summit of the Pointe d'Orny (20 mins). Descend a few metres on to the north face and traverse right crossing the small rock ridges and steep couloirs (sections of 45°). This leads you to the Arpette Glacier (35-40°/500m). At the bottom of the glacier head right to possibly more powder skiing and then follow the Val d'Arpette to Champex.

57.a   North-east couloir of the Petite Pointe d'Orny (3187m, D). From the hut follow the route you took up. A little way before the Petite Pointe d'Orny (at around 3000m) climb up around 80m to get to the start of the couloir (40-45°/350m). The cornice at the top often steepens the slope at the start.

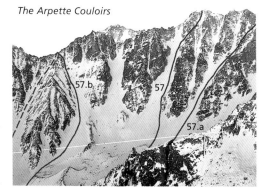

The Arpette Couloirs

57.b   Col d'Arpette (AD). From the hut pass the Col d'Orny and descend the left bank of the glacier to the small basin before the Orny Hut at around 2800m. Climb to the Col d'Arpette (2942m) and cross the crest a little higher up on the left. The couloir is not very steep, but faces the setting sun (snow sometimes crusty at the top).

57.c   Creux Magnin (PD). From the top of the La Breya chairlift follow the woodland track that takes you to the Val d'Arpette and leave it again at about 2000m. Traverse up to get to the bottom of a very large combe. Now climb to the top of the combe (2751m). The snow here is always excellent.

58   COL DE LA LYS   2703m
East face   PD

⬆	900m	🏔	January-April	⤴	sections of 35°
↗	1800m	📷	121	⚠	1
↘	1800m	☺	6hrs	🏥	SP
✦	East-north	🎿	2.3		

Col de la Lys and the Fenêtre d'Arpette

There are numerous possible combinations of routes in this area, but they each require several cars. In fact, the best strategy is to start from the Breya chairlift. Alternatively, you can park at La Poya (before Champex on the road from Les Valettes) and climb to the La Jure alpages (pastures). There is a long climb from Bovine that could serve as a good training route, bad weather trip or route for the start of the season. You could also combine this route with the Col de la Forclaz and route 59.

From Martigny, via the village of Le Bourgeaud, continue along the road to Bovine (steep and narrow woodland track). Climb on skis to the village of Les Assets and continue through the pastures (alpages) to the Bovinettes Chalets.

Taking the large cone above the larches, you get to an easy ridge route that leads to the small summit marked 2259m on the map. From here you can see the north face of La Giète (access from the Col de la Forclaz, route 59) and the rest of the route on the south-facing slopes. Leave the combe that leads to the Pointe Ronde quite early on and traverse at this level to the Chaux de Bovine to the foot of the spur that comes down from Pointe de Prosom. Climb up the combe to the highest skiable point and the Col de la Lys is just on the right. You could also carry on to the Someceon du Dru (2829m). The descent of the Chaux de Bovine is very aesthetic, but you must traverse left before the forest at around 2000m to get back to Bovinette. It is almost impossible to ski on the left bank of the mountain stream through the forest and undergrowth.

58.a   Fenêtre de Grône circuit (2686m, PD). From Champex climb up the Val d'Arpette to above the Rocher de la Barme at around 2250m. Take the right fork up the combe (Combe de Six Carro) and climb up the whole of the small steep valley. Now head towards the notch on the left (2686m, south-east facing couloir). The descent of the north face follows a couloir and then the north combe to the La Jure pastures (alpages) at 1666m. Now follow the summer path that leads to the Champex road (La Poya, 1285m), 5hrs (sections of 40°). The wild north face of the Liapey de Grône has several steep and narrow couloirs (cold snow and great atmosphere).

58.b   Fenêtre d'Arpette (2665m, PD). This is a variation of the Tour of Mont Blanc walking route and the snow is not often great in this area. From Champex climb up the Val d'Arpette to the Fenêtre d'Arpette.

59   POINTE RONDE   2700m
North face   PD

⚑	1526m	🏔	Decembeer-April	⛷	sect. of 35-40°
↗	1170m	◔	5hrs	⚠	1
↘	1170m	⚒	2.3	⊕	SP
✦	North				

A good trip for the beginning of the season or for training that can be combined with the Champex face (coordination of cars). There are great views from the summit of the Trient plateau and five or six different descent routes.

At the Col de la Forclaz follow the Bovinette-Champex path (to the east) and traverse the whole of the north face through the woodland (a few short descents and avalanche couloirs to cross that can often be icy, rope and crampons useful). At the Giète pastures (alpages) at 1884m (large stable) head up the combe to the south-east to the small headland (2259m) from where you can see the Chaux de Bovine. Climb south-west and follow the line of the ridge that goes to the summit. The descent of the same route is nice to do via the pretty Combe des Faces and you can finish on the road to the hamlet of Mintset (1300m, 3km down the valley from the Col de la Forclaz). For good skiers, I can recommend the descent of the north face (35°/200m). The top section is steep and sometimes has rocks showing through the snow at the beginning of the season. The Combe de la

Veudale has a 1400m descent on sustained slopes. Watch out for possible slab at the top of this face that is prone to avalanche (in the spring they almost reach the road).

59.a ▪ North-east couloir (AD). From the summit descend the steep ridge on foot for 150m to ski in to a lovely couloir on the north-east (35-40°/150m). The rest of the route is identical to route number 59.

59.b ▪ Prélayes face (PD). There is an easy climb up from the Col de la Forclaz via the Pro du Sex chalets and through the larches to the shoulder and the Prélayes pastures (alpages) at 2017m. Continue on the wide headland that steepens up above the Trient side (if there is not much snow you will have to climb on foot) and follow the ridge with rocky outcrops to the Croix des Prélayes (2365m). The route to the summit of the Pointe Ronde starts on the west flank near

Near the summit of the Pointe Ronde.

the ridge and includes some steep sections over grass and rock (III). Ski the pretty slopes on the north face then the Creux des Dérottes to the track at 1600m. The way back to the Col de la Forclaz includes two short climbs up. It is also possible to continue from the Croix des Prélayes to the Pointe Ronde and then follow route 59 on the descent, but the route is quite steep and exposed (1hrs).

60	**LES GRANDES AUTANNES** Tour		**2679m** **PD**
⚑ 1326m	🗻 January-April	⤬ 35°/50m	
↗ 1350m	📷 133	⚠ 1	
↘ 1350m	⏱ 5hrs	⊕ SP	
✦ All			

This is an excellent objective for a winter's day. However, take care as the banks of snow built up by the wind (fœhn and west wind) can cause unfortunate accidents.

From Trient go the hamlet of Le Peuty, at the end of the valley road, and follow route 56 in reverse to 2200m. Head right in the large south-east combe of La Chaux and climb directly to the summit. The slope steepens up at the top and there can be the risk of slab avalanches in the winter (caused by the wind from the west). On the descent you can follow the route you took up or you can follow route 60.a.

60.a   North face of the Grandes Autannes, Les Herbagères (PD). In comparison with the classic descent, this route offers a whole selection of steep slopes that are often covered in powder snow and it would be a shame not to mention it here. From the summit descend a little way down the east ridge (few rocks) and join the first combe to the north. A rocky constriction lower down forms a boundary for the second steep combe where there are always good snow conditions. Head right via the even slopes and you will presently reach the larch trees. The woodland is quite steep and you should stay on the slope that faces due north until you reach Trient. At the bottom of the second combe (at around 2000m), below the rock spur on the left, you can also traverse to the Col de Balme by 20mins of climbing (also see route number 65.a).

61   POINTE DU VAN   2278m
East face   PD

⚐ 1326m	🏔 jJanuary-April	⤵ 35°/100m
↗ 950m	📷 132	⚠ 1
↘ 950m	⏱ 4hrs	⊕ DP
✦ East	🎿 3.1	

You can quickly get to the top of this modest summit from the French ski lift station at Le Tour. In addition, I recommend that you ski this route in winter before the big spring avalanches start.

From the village of Trient, go to the hamlet of Praillon and follow the woodland path through the forest (Tour of Mont Blanc variant route). At the first bend, follow the steep path that goes to Les Tseppes. From the Tseppes Chalets (1932m) continue to Le Carraye (2132m) and go round it on the left (the track on the north face is often exposed to slab avalanches). Now follow the headland to the summit. On the descent you can follow the same track at first and then ski the whole of the east face between the Pointe de Van and the forest. Head towards the chalets at first and then in to the spring avalanche couloirs (Les Tournays).

LE TOUR

PRACTICAL INFORMATION

Chamonix Tourist Office: 04 50 53 00 24 / www.chamonix.com
Compagnie des Guides: 04 50 53 00 88 / www.cieguides-chamonix.com
Ass. Int. Guides du Mont Blanc: 04 50 53 27 05 / www.guides-du-mont-blanc.com
Office de Haute Montagne: 04 50 23 22 08 / www.ohm-chamonix.com
PGHM: 04 50 53 16 89
Weather forecast: 08 92 68 02 74 / www.meteo.fr
Snow report: 08 92 68 10 20
Taxis Michellod (Le Châtelard): (027) 768 11 58

SKI LIFTS

Charamillon: 04 50 54 00 58
SNCF station: 04 50 53 00 44 / train timetables: 08 36 35 35 35

ROAD ACCESS

■ Le Tour
From Annecy, Geneva or Sallanches take the A40 (or the N205) to Chamonix, then the N206 to Argentière. About 500m after leaving Argentière, at the Bovereau bridge, take the right turn to Montroc – Le Tour. Continue to the end of the road and leave your car in car-park for the Charamillon – Balme cable-car.

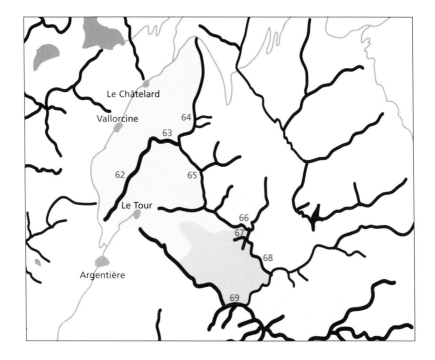

Previous page: On the Le Tour Glacier

The Le Tour ski station is served by the Charamillon-col de Balme lift systems. The skiing here is accessible, 'user-friendly' and good for all the family. For the more committed off-piste skier, there is also the descent to Les Jeurs in Switzerland on the north face, above Vallorcine.

However, as with any area at the head of a valley, Le Tour is subject to frequent changes in the air currents and you should be aware of what they are doing if you are planning to ski the routes here. In fact, although Le Tour has an image as an area for relatively easy 'moyenne montagne' skiing, you should not underestimate the ever-present risks. The accumulation of snow that occurs as a direct result of these specific conditions is responsible, each year, for a number of accidents and avalanches. The high mountains that overlook this mixture of forests and pastures form the eastern extremity of the Mont Blanc Massif and it has been quite calm here since the snout of the glacier avalanched.

Thanks to the neighbouring lifts at the Grands Montets (Argentière), it is relatively easy to access this high altitude area. Using these lifts, you can ski a number of these routes in a day. Moreover, if you stay at the Albert 1er Hut (unguardianed in winter) you can ski longer tours, notably in to neighbouring Switzerland.

Le Tour Glacier

MOUNTAIN HUTS

Ref.20 ▪ Albert 1er Hut (2700m, PD), access from Argentière

CAF, winter room unguardianed (30 places), guardianed at the weekend in May on request (153 places), tel: 04 50 54 06 20

From Argentière take the Lognan and Grands Montets cable-cars to the top of the Grands Montets and follow route 70 (Argentière section) to the Col du Passon. From the Col (3028m), descend the combe to the north and go round the base of the Aiguille Supérieure du Passon. There is now a traverse down the large glaciated combe to the right, without losing too much height. After a large flat section at around 2730m join the right bank of the glacier and beyond the small section of moraine is the hut.

	3233m		$2^{1/2}$ - 3hrs
	550m		680m + 330m

Ref.20.a ▪ Access via the left bank of the Tour Glacier (PD)

This route follows the classic descent of the Col du Passon (route 70, Argentière section). Although the climb up is quite long and steep, this is quite a safe route and can be used when the Argentière lifts are closed.

	1450m		3 to 4hrs
	1300m		

On the Col Supérieur du Tour

Ref.20.b ▪ Access via Le Tour (Charamillon lifts and Bec de Picheu, AD)

I am not giving a description of this route for safety reasons. Rarely in condition, this route is exposed to avalanches and some of the steep sections are very dangerous when the snow is hard and you cannot afford to slip or fall at all... unless there is no snow.

Ref.20.c ▪ Access from Switzerland

Follow the Three Cols route (68) or one of the variants, or go from the Trient Hut (see route 56).

62   AIGUILLETTE DES POSETTES   2201m
North-east ridge   F

2170m (ski lift)	Decembre-April	35°/250m
30m	129, 130	1
900m	2hrs	Dp
North-west	2.1	

Aiguillette des Posettes

62

If the ski lifts are not working or you would like an early morning start, you will have to climb 700m with skins to get to the summit (2hrs). However, thanks to the lift system in Le Tour we can dispense with this climb and concentrate on the ski down and getting the first tracks on this pleasant and regular north-west slope. You can complete this 'moyenne montagne' (middle mountain) round-trip by taking the train from the station at Le Buet back to the Chamonix valley. There is often powder snow on this face at the beginning of winter and even when there isn't much snow the grassy slopes underneath you won't ruin your skis. Avoid the direct descent of the north face because avalanches are frequently set off by skiers, snowboarders and freeriders above you. In fact, when there are lots of people on the mountain, the slope here that exceed 30° with their bushes, rhododendrons and dry grass can't hold the snow. In addition, the whole of the south-east face of Les Grosailles could be skied if it wasn't for the very serious risk of avalanche.

From Le Tour, via the Charamillon gondolas, go to the Col de Balme. Follow the piste to the Posettes draglift and join the north-east ridge on the right, from where you can reach the summit in a few minutes. On the descent, move along the south-west ridge for about 150m (generally on foot) then descend a large shoulder before heading down the north-west face (cornices). At the start of the first small valley head slightly left on to a headland (at the same height as the first bushes) to avoid the dangerous build-up of snow at the top of the couloir. Lower down (at around 1700m) return to the large central couloir and, a little way before the cone at the

Le Tour and the Posettes

end of the slope (at around 1400m), traverse left between the larch trees to get to the station and the Le Buet car-park. You can take the train to Montroc and then you can either walk or take the bus back to Le Tour.

62.a   Tête de la Jorette (F). From the top of the Posettes draglift, head south towards Le Tour (summer path). This is an excellent descent to do in the spring when the snow has been transformed. You can finish this tour via the track when there isn't much snow in the forest and you finish in the car-park at Le Tour.

63   TÊTE DE BALME   2321m
North face   PD

⌐	2190m (ski lift)	◰	December-April	↳	35°/150m
↗	130m	◔	3hrs	⚠	1
↘	1220m	⤼	2.1	⊕	DP
✛	North				

When the conditions are not great elsewhere there are some very pleasant descents to be done on the gentle 'moyenne montagne' slopes of this north face with its small valleys. However, watch out for the local winds that are very strong in this area and are constantly shifting huge quantities of snow from one section to another. Every year numerous accidents are caused by skiers and snow-boarders setting off slab avalanches here. It is for this reason that you are strong-ly advised not to access the north face directly from the summit of the Tête de Balme as windslab avalanches very frequently occur here and the entire sector is particularly unstable. It was in one of these small valleys, that didn't have much snow in it, that a friend of mine, the guide Jean-Pierre Devouassoux, was swept away by a small accumulation of snow in December 1998. He was most probably crushed to death by the weight of the snow and was reunited with our other sadly missed companions on the morning of 27th December. The night before, we had celebrated the arrival of the New Year early with a whisky as I would be on Aconcagua with a group of our clients by the 31st. That was to be a final farewell to this great guide and skier. Jean-Pierre was well respected for his wisdom and kindness and for his astute, and sometimes harsh, observations. He was a true mountain professional and was proud and respectful of the values handed down to him from his ancestors. His job as a guide, however, had also adapted to the evolving tourism in the valley and he was always pleased to pass on what he had learned with great generosity. Like many of the other great men from this valley his memory lives on in his large family and in our hearts. Rather than skiing all the way to the bottom of the Swiss side, you can join the Belle Place chairlift (150m before the reservoir) that takes you right back to the Le Tour ski area. You might, however, like to continue your trip in to Switzerland and sample some of the area's famous 'croûtes au fromage' (cheese dish) or some Fendant (local wine) - treasures of the canton of Valais!

From Le Tour take the ski lifts up to the Col de Balme (2191m) and traverse across horizontally to the restaurant. Descend a little towards the col and an easy climb now takes you, via a large 'hump', to the summit.
On the descent, ski to the north-east and go round the rock bands (marked 2333m on the map) passing below the Croix de Fer. Traverse across the west face and ski down the middle of the valley. You can follow the left or the right bank of the Nant de Catogne (stream) to reach the reservoir. Follow the path and, after having crossed the mountain stream, you come to the first of the Cretton chalets. Bear hard left and join the steep path in the wood that leads to the valley (metal barriers, dangerous icy patches under the trees). A 15-minute walk beside the road takes you to the Le Châtelard station where you can get the train back to Montroc.

63.a   Small Catogne plateau (PD). Follow route 63 and after the rock bands (marked 2333m on the map) and a small col, turn left on to a shoulder and continue into a steep couloir. Ski the north-west face and join route 63 on the right bank of the Nant du Catogne (stream).

63.b   North-west face (PD). From the Tête de Balme take a wide turn quite low under the west ridge (avoids dangerous top section of north face) and ski the whole north-west face from Belle Place to the Grand'Jeur chalets. Now go to the reservoir and follow route 63 out.

64   POINTE DU VAN   2278m
East face   PD

⌐ 2190m (ski lift)		◱ December-April		⌐ Sections of 35°	
↗ 130m		⌐◌⌐ 132		⚠ 1	
↘ 1000m		◔ 3¹ᐟ²hrs		⊕ DP	
⊕ All		⚒ 2.3			

For those who want more, a great combination of routes would be the descent of the east couloir of the Pointe du Van, then a climb up to the Tête de Carraye (route 61, previous section) and the descent of the north-west face to the Esserts reservoir. From here you can get the Belle Place chairlift to Le Tour. Do bear in the mind the ever-present avalanche dangers in this area as explained earlier (route 63).

From the Col de Balme (via ski lifts, see route 63), go to the Tête de Balme. Descend north/north-east and go to the first col, now traverse to the top of the large west slope (avalanche risk) below the Croix de Fer. From the next col you can get to the summit in 15mins or you can head north via the crest. You can descend just before the Tête de Caraye in the east combe (steeper with rock bands on the left, route 61). I would

East couloir of the Pointe du Van

recommend, however, that you continue traversing and join the Tseppes chalets. Now head right and join the bottom of the large couloir that takes you to Le

East face of the Pointe du Van

Peuty (village of Trient, route 61). You can ski quite close to the left bank (not too densely wooded).

You will have to plan transport for the end of the route rather than relying on the local taxi service (Taxis Michellod at Le Châtelard).

64.a   East couloir of the Pointe du Van (AD). After the Croix de Fer, on the south col of the Pointe du Van, this wide combe is steep in the middle (sections of 40°). Stay on the right bank to avoid the large avalanche at the bottom of the couloir.

64.b   Couloir to the north of the Pointe du Van (AD). Rarely in condition, this couloir can be very dangerous if there are avalanches, as there is a narrow funnel (rocks) in the middle section (40°/250m).

65   LES GRANDES AUTANNES   2680m
West face   AD

2190m (ski lift)		December-April		35-40°/200 m	
490m		133		2	
1230m		3hrs		SP	
West		3.1			

Although very windy the Autannes sector can be skied on all sides. A good knowledge of the terrain and conditions (weather and, more specifically, wind) will help you choose the best routes and ski some magnificent descents. The north-west slopes towards the Bec du Picheu below the Pointe de Bron are also

Les Herbagères and the Col de Balme

very pleasant to ski. Moreover, the walks up to the starts of the routes are definitely alpine in nature even if they don't look like much from below. If you follow the Autannes crest to the south, there are some great descents on the northwest face, but do be careful not to venture lower than 2300m on the west facing slopes of Les Esserins as they are difficult to ski and are prone to avalanche.

Aiguille Verte from the Autannes ridge

From Le Tour take the Le Tour-Charamillon gondola and then the chairlift, and climb straight up to the large combe above. The combe quickly steepens up and you will have to walk the last section. Join the headland on the left. There is some interesting, and sometimes technical, mixed climbing on the rocks and snowy steps here. You will need a rope and crampons if the snow is hard or windblown, and you can slip on the frozen ground. You reach the top of the ridge, and the border, near a collection of small peaks.

On the descent, the west couloirs near the summit can only be skied if there is good snow cover. It is better to continue along the ridge to the small col that lies between the point marked 2697m on the map and the Col des Autannes. From here you can take the easier of the two couloirs that lead to the large Lac de

Great skiing on the Bron Glacier

Charamillon combe and then follow the Combe de la Vormaine, on the left, back to Le Tour.

65.a   Les Herbagères, Swiss side (PD). The descent is identical to route 60.a (previous section), but the access is different. From the Col de Balme follow the north-west ridge of the Grandes Autannes to the summit (mixed PD, a little long). Then descent of the north face starts in an easy combe. A narrow gully leads to a magnificent second combe (route 60.a). If you have left a car in Trient you can continue right to Trient via the steep slopes in the larch forest (right of the Nant Noir). Alternatively, at around 2100m you can head left above Les Herbagères and climb (20 mins) to the Col de Balme.

65.b   East face (PD). From the summit ridge join the east face (route 60, windslab possible) and at around the same height as La Goye (local word meaning 'little lake'), head right to join the large combe below the Bron Glacier (route 56) and ski down to Trient by the left bank of the stream.

66   AIGUILLE DU TOUR   3542m
Normal route   AD

⚑ 3233 m (ski lift)	🏔 February-May	⌐ sect. of 35-40°
↗ D1 + D2: 530m + 840m	📷 127, 135	⚠ 1
↘ D1 + D2: 1060m + 2100m	🕐 3hrs + 7hrs	Sp
✣ All	⛷ 3.1	

The Aiguille du Tour rises up out of a huge glaciated area that is great for skiing. Access on the French side from the Albert 1er Hut is quite long, while access from the Swiss side and the Trient Hut is just as long and indirect, although it is a more varied and pretty route. I don't recommend that you ski the moraine under the Albert 1er Hut. Although the first section is superb to ski, the lower section is steep and exposed even if you follow the steep summer track under the EDF water supply points (cables at the start of the descent).

D1 ▪ Go to the Albert 1er Hut from Argentière or Le Tour (ref.20 and ref.20.a).

D2 ▪ From the hut, head due east above the moraine. Where the moraine starts to point north (cairns) leave it and join the glacier. Go to the left of the rock marked Signal Reuilly (also spelt Reilly) at around 2950m. Now climb diagonally up and south-east towards a large headland (crevasses) and join a second combe to the right that leads to the Col Supérieur du Tour. Barely higher than its neighbour, the Col du Tour, the Col Supérieur is

Below the Col Supérieur du Tour

easier to cross even if it is steeper at the end (take off your skis for 20m). Descend a few metres so that you can now climb diagonally northwards up the Trient side. A short steep slope followed by a long sloping plateau (crevasses) leads to the foot of the Aiguille du Tour. Ski towards the bergschrund and then continue on foot to the summit (1hr there and back, steep rocks at the top). The return journey follows the same route or directly in the middle of the Tour Glacier (go to the right of the

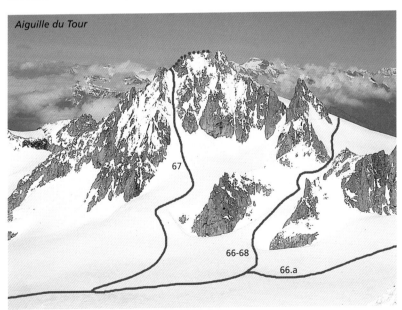

Aiguille du Tour

67

66-68

66.a

area with the large crevasses). Above the plateau, on which the huts sits (at about 2750m), traverse towards the left bank and continue to Le Tour.

66.a   Col du Tour (3282m, PD). Follow route 66 and pass the combe that leads to the Col Supérieur du Tour. Go round the base (west) of the Aiguille du Col du Tour. Climb up the next combe to the Col du Tour (short climb, 30-50m, grade II). Descend on to the other side and go left to avoid the steep slope (bergschrund). Cross the combe that comes down from the Col Supérieur du Tour and join route 66. Return via the Col Supérieur du Tour.

66.b   Tour of the Aiguille du Tour (PD). After having climbed to the summit (route 66), descend to your skis and head north. Cross the passage to the north of the Aiguille du Pissoir. Now join and cross the Col du Midi des Grands (3235m), which takes you to the south-west combe (40°/100m). Rejoin route 66 on the left bank (crevasses), and either ski back to the hut or direct to the Le Tour ski area via the left bank of the Tour Glacier.

67   AIGUILLE DU TOUR   3542m
Table Couloir   D

⚑	3233 m (ski lift)	🏔	February-June	⌐	40-50°/150m
↗	D1 + D2: 530m + 840m	📷	135	⚠	2
↘	D1 + D2: 1060m + 2100m	☻	3hrs + 5hrs	🏠	SP
✳	South	🎿	4.3		

On the summit ridge of the Aiguille du Tour

This couloir is skied quite often and is a good 'warm up' and training route for other more serious descents. The route was first descended by Garcia, the monoskier, who 'schussed' the whole way. His technique was quite spectacular and he appeared to be sitting right back on his monoski. Dominique Potard and Jean-Paul Lassale repeated this exploit in May 1979, reaching 150 kph! However, the list of candidates for this kind of feat requiring excellent technique and a masterful control of balance is not a long one... Although, there was the Japanese skier, Miura, whose direct descents of extreme slopes strapped to a parachute to reduce his speed were equally breathtaking. Using this technique he was able to descend from the South Col of Everest, among other things...Given the success of the these spectacular descents, why not stage freeride finals on the north face of the Aiguille du Midi, 'schussing' all the way?!...

D1   Go to the Albert 1er Hut from Argentière or Le Tour (ref.20 or ref.20.a).

D2 From the hut follow route 66. At around 3100m climb up the first combe that is bounded by the Aiguille du Tour and the Aiguille Purtscheller. The 'table' is an enormous block of granite that rests on a spike of rock. The couloir is to the right of the 'table' and is very visible from here. The bergschrund is usually easy to cross. The slope is 40° to start with and then slowly steepens up to 45°. The final few metres, near the steep rocky outcrop to the right are nearly 50°. The access route to the summit of the Aiguille is given PD, but in winter the start of the climb can be quite delicate as it is north-facing and it is often icy. Descend a little way to the south and climb up the final blocks that lead to the summit (1 1/2 hrs there and back). On the descent, the first gully often does not have much snow in it. Take the left bank at first and then move to the centre and then join the right bank for the final section. Now you rejoin your ascent route.

On the Table Couloir

68	**THREE COLS** Chardonnet, Saleina, Col Sup. du Tour		**3323m** **AD**

⚑ 3233m (ski lift)	🗻 February-May	⚗ 40-50°/80 m
↗ 1060m	📷 113, 127, 135, 138, 139	⚠ 1
↘ 2880m	🕐 7hrs	🧭 SP
✤ tAll	🎿 3.1	

In the winter (up to about mid-March) you can ski the Three Cols in a day. In the spring and when it is warmer, however, it is better to stay the night at the Argentière Hut and get an early start the next morning.

From Argentière and the Grands Montets (cable-cars), follow route 72 to the Col du Chardonnet. At the bottom of the couloir, traverse beneath the south face of the Grande Fourche and now climb up the combe to the Fenêtre de Saleina. Cross the Fenêtre de Saleina at 3276m (slope gets steep at the end). Ski below the north faces of the Tête Blanche and the Aiguille du Col du Tour to get to the Col Supérieur du Tour (3289m). There is a great descent down the west face of the Col Supérieur (route 66) and you now join the left bank of the Tour Glacier and the Le Tour ski system (route 70). You are strongly recommended to cross the Col Supérieur du Tour rather than the Col du Tour, which has become very steep and difficult to negotiate in the last few years.

Sunrise over the Saleina Glacier

68.a ▪ Fenêtre du Tour (3414m, PD). If you are late or you just need to get back to Le Tour quickly, it is also possible to join the Tour Glacier by crossing the Fenêtre du Tour just after the Col du Chardonnet. The climb up is steep (40°/80m). The direct descent passes by the north spur of the Aiguille du Passon and then follows the left bank of the Tour Glacier (route 70). Watch out for the crevasses and the serac fall beneath the north face of the Chardonnet.

68.b ▪ Tour of the Aiguille du Tour via the Col du Midi des Grands (PD). Follow route 68 to beneath the Col du Tour then follow route 66.b.

68.c ▪ Tête Blanche (3429m,F). This easy belvedere route gets slightly monotonous towards the end and its final plateau can be accessed from the Fenêtre du Tour, Col du Passon or the Argentière Hut.

69	**AIGUILLE DU CHARDONNET**	**3824m**
	Forbes Arête	**D**

⚐ 3233m (ski lift)		⛰ February-June		⤴ 45°/80m	
↗ D1 + D2 : 530m + 1120m		📷 139		⚠ 2	
↘ D1 + D2 : 1060m + 2100m		☉ 3hrs + 7hrs		⊕ HP	
✦ North/North-west		🎿 4.3			

Although it is very popular in the summer, the Forbes Arête does not get very many visitors in the winter even though there is great skiing from the ridge. You can ski the east couloir (45-50°/150m) of the Fenêtre Supérieure du Tour (3458m), but there is a large cornice that can make the start difficult. You can access the Saleina Glacier and go back again via the Fenêtre, although it can be dangerous and difficult (cornice, bergschrund, 45°/50m).

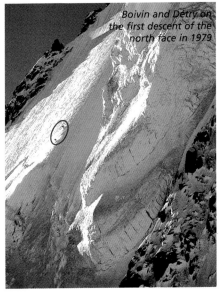

Boivin and Détry on the first descent of the north face in 1979

D1 ▪ Go to the Albert 1er Hut from Le Tour or Argentière (ref.20 and 20.a).

D2 ▪ From the hut follow route number 66 to around 3100m (beneath the spur of the Col Supérieur du Tour) and traverse due south to the foot of the Aiguille Forbes (3230m). The slope on the ridge is steep from the start. On the steep right-hand headland there are lots of seracs and there is a risk of windslab avalanche. Pass the ledge on the Fenêtre Supérieure du Tour (3458m) and head up and right via the 'La Bosse' (hump) to the rocks where you leave your skis. It takes about 3hrs to go to the summit from the ridge and back and it is an interesting traverse (airy climb with sections on the south face). You have to cross several steps and gendarmes (III) with exposed cornices. The descent follows the route you took up and you put your skis on a few metres below the ridge. From the foot of the Aiguille du Chardonnet follow route 68 back to Le Tour.

69.a ▪ **North face (TD).** This route deserves to be classified as much more than just a mere variant route. It is, however, very rarely in condition. The upper slope

Aiguille du Chardonnet and the Le Tour Glacier

is very steep (over 50°/100m). After the traverse above the suspended glacier the face is often icy and just as steep (50°/400m) and you almost always have to rappel for several dozen metres at the level of the seracs. The first descent was by Jean-Marc Boivin and Yves Détry in 1979.

69.b   Alternative access route (PD). From the Albert 1er Hut get on to the Tour Glacier and traverse due south, following the depression that avoids the crevassed area in the centre of the glacier. Climb below the Aiguille du Passon and then move alongside the north face of the Aiguille du Chardonnet going left to avoid the serac falls. Now go to the foot of the glaciated combe before the Aiguille Forbes (3230m).

69.c   Traverse (TD). From the summit of the Aiguille du Chardonnet join the western (subsidiary) summit and start the descent via the left-hand couloir whose slope gets progressively steeper. Continue down this narrow, very exposed couloir (55°/80m) and join the Col Supérieur Adams Reilly on the right (difficult, cornice). Continue via a steep glaciated 'hump' to the Épaule Glacier (crevasses) and then down to the Tour Glacier (50-55°/250m). You can also rappel the first 150m on the normal route to descend from the summit and avoid the left-hand couloir that is very exposed. As for many glaciers around the world, the Le Tour glacier is shrinking. It is therefore possible nowadays to ski down the left side of the glacier, starting at 2400m. These steep but regular slopes are less exposed than a few years ago, the glacier's retreat limiting the risk of serac falls. It is also possible on the right to turn around the lower end of the glacier and cross to the left around 2300m and join the latter descent.

ARGENTIÈRE

PRACTICAL INFORMATION

Chamonix Tourist Office: 04 50 53 00 24 / www.chamonix.com
Compagnie des Guides: 04 50 53 00 88 / www.cieguides-chamonix.com
Ass. Int. Guides du Mont Blanc: 04 50 53 27 05 / www.guides-du-mont-blanc.com
Summits: 04 50 53 50 14 / www.summits.fr
Office de Haute Montagne: 04 50 23 22 08 / www.ohm-chamonix.com
PGHM: 04 50 53 16 89
Weather forecast: 08 92 68 02 74 / www.meteo.fr
Snow report: 08 92 68 10 20

SKI LIFTS

Les Grands Montets: 04 50 54 00 71

ROAD ACCESS

From Annecy, Geneva or Sallanches follow the A40 (or N205) to Chamonix
and then take the N206 to Argentière.

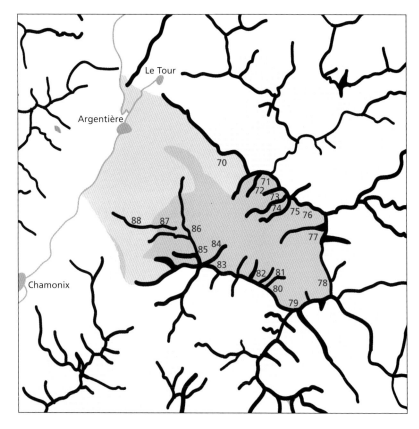

Previous page: The Aiguille Verte above the magnificent Argentière cirque.

The Argentière Basin is quite unique in the French Alps. From piste skiing to off-piste descents and ski-mountaineering tours, there is a fantastic selection of routes for all levels of skier on offer in this area. Freeriders and ski-tourers can take their pick of superb off-piste routes (Pas de Chèvre, Argentière Glacier...), the great couloirs (Chapeau, Poubelles...) and classic tours (Col du Chardonnet, Col du Passon...) and the big 'extreme' slopes (Courtes, Verte...). The Grands Montets is the starting point for the classic Chamonix-Zermatt Haute Route and it also allows access to Switzerland, via the Col du Chardonnet. This means that some of the tours can be done in a day or you can do them in two stages by staying at the Argentière Hut. Unfortunately, the popularity of the Grands Montets ski station sometimes distracts a little from the splendour of the surrounding landscape as the crowds of visitors to the slopes sometimes show a certain lack of respect for the environment that welcomes them. Nevertheless, with a little bit of effort you can still find peace and quiet and, more importantly, slopes of untracked snow here.

MOUNTAIN HUTS

Ref.21 ■ Argentière Hut (2771m, F)
CAF, guardianed from February to May (140 places), winter room not guardianed, tel: 04 50 53 16 92 / refugeargentiere@wanadoo.fr

From Argentière take the cable-cars to the top of the Grands Montets. From the top station follow the piste that descends the north-east face. Leave the piste quite quickly and go right of the rocky outcrop (3000m, crevasses). You pass quite close to the moraine on the left as you descend to the Argentière Glacier. Cross the glacier heading towards the Arête du Jardin on the Aiguille d'Argentière. Avoid the heavily crevassed right bank of the glacier by going right of it. The hut is clearly visible on a line of moraine.

    3233m   1¹ᐟ²-2hrs

    220m

    680m

Ref.21.a ■ Argentière Hut, alternative access route (PD)

This is a quicker and prettier route but it is hardly ever done before April when the crevasses have had a chance to be filled in a bit better. From the Col des Grands Montets head right and traverse downwards below the couloirs on the Aiguille Verte (watch out for the crevasses and serac falls). Pass above the Rognon Inférieur on the north ridge of the Grande Rocheuse (2886m) and join the Argentière Glacier.

Ref.21.b ■ Argentière Hut via Lognan (F)

Out of season, when the lifts are closed, follow the Pierre à Ric piste up to Lognan and traverse to the left bank of the glacier. Climb to 2550m and now follow directions given in ref. 21.

    1240m   4-5hrs

    1530m

70   COL DU PASSON   3028m
Traverse to Le Tour   AD

3233m (ski lift)		December-May		35°	
480m		127, 139, 144, 147		1	
2260m		4hrs		SP	
North/North-west		3.1			

This is a very popular route with has a very pretty descent into Le Tour. You can also use it to access the Albert 1er Hut or as an alternative to the Three Cols. You can ski the descent of the Bec de la Cluy when the conditions are at their best – in the morning in spring snow. Nevertheless, there is still quite often serious risk of snow slides and avalanches. Some of the variant routes (Bec de la Cluy, Peclerey) can be in condition from the beginning of the winter. The south-west couloir of the Col Supérieur Adams Reilly (50°/200m) is often skied but there is not always good snow cover in it and its narrow lower section as well as the dangerous bergschrund limit the time that it is in condition. The Col Adams Reilly is easier (40°/150m).

From the Argentière Glacier go to the steep slopes on the opposite face. An awkward ascending traverse (often hard snow, ski crampons) takes you round the base of the west shoulder (Épaule Ouest) of the Aiguille du Chardonnet. Climb up the large combe below the Aiguille du Passon. You reach the col by a climb on foot up a steep couloir (80m of 40-45°, rope useful). On the descent head northwards and then north-/westwards. Below the Bec Rouge Inférieur (2800m) head right to go round the rocky promontory marked 2722m on the map. Keep to the most direct line as you follow the edge of the snout of the glacier. If it looks like

The classic Col du Passon route

*Col du Chardonnet and the
Aiguille d'Argentière*

there is a risk of avalanche in this area ski on the snowy headlands even if the snow on them is not as good as elsewhere. At around 1650m traverse below the Tête des Cascades (steep at the level of the first trees). This route is safe but there is often crusty snow in the middle section near the glacier. Keep heading a little to the right below the glacier to join the Le Tour lift system (see also comment on p.140).

70.a Bec Rouge (PD). At the level of the Bec Rouge Inférieur descend right into a combe that is quite steep and often has powder snow in it. If there has been a big build up of snow this combe (slabs can be formed by the south and easterly winds) can also be avalanche prone. Rejoin route 70 at the bottom.

70.b Bec de la Cluy (Bec de Lachat) (AD). Go to the right of the Bec Rouge Inférieur. There is now quite a steep traverse to the left at the top of the combe. Climb up a little (20 to 40m) to get to the west ridge and follow it down. A few narrow and exposed sections take you to the Bec de Lachat cairn (2447m). Descend the large south-west combe (Rocheray Couloir). This is a direct line but the slope is steep. At around 2200m, traverse right to join the Grand Chantet Couloir or the slopes to the left of it. You arrive at Le Planet. The average gradient of the slopes is between 35 and 40°/300m. This route is exposed and can have hard snow and you should not attempt it if the snow layer is unstable or in the afternoons when it is hot.

70.c   **South-west couloir of the Aiguille du Passon (3383m, D).** 350m between 40 and 45°. First descent by Marc Ravanel on 7th April 1984.

70.d   **South-west couloir of the Col Adams Reilly (3365m, D).** I don't recommend you ski this couloir at the beginning of the season (40°/150m, crevasses, high bergschrund). The north face of the col can also be skied but is crevassed.

70.e   **North-east couloir of the Aiguille du Passon (3383m, D).** Sections at 50°. The lower section is often icy at the level of the bergschrund. First descent by Mansard, Gallan and Garde on 22nd April 1979.

71   AIGUILLE DU CHARDONNET   3824m
South face   TD

⌐ 3233m (ski lift)	📷 February-June	⌐ 45°/600m, sections of 55°
↗ D1 + D2 : 220m + 1130m	📷 144, 146, 147	⚠ 3
↘ D1 + D2 : 680m + 2800m	🕐 2hrs + 7hrs	⊕ HP
⊕ South-east	📐 5.1	

Owing to its south-easterly aspect, this face is not often in condition and the snow conditions can be tricky: the snow at the top can be too hard while the snow at the bottom turns 'bad' too quickly. Jean-Franck Charlet, Georges Bettembourg and a few other skiers from Argentière skied various sections of couloirs on this face and it was Daniel Chauchefoin who did the first official descent on 22nd April 1982.

In my opinion, the climb up the south face and the normal route followed by the descent of the west face is one of the best outings in the Chamonix Valley. The route up follows a technical line to a great summit and the descent is long and difficult without being extreme. This is real, top quality ski-mountaineering in a spectacular setting. Looking down on the 'ants' on the Lognan pistes, gives you such a sense of peace that you wish that time would stop and let you properly take in the place and its majestic surroundings.

South face of the Chardonnet

71.a

71

On the other hand, one Sunday in May quite recently, on the last day of the Grands Montets, I managed on my own to get to the summit at 12:15 from a lift at 9am and be back at Lognan for 2pm!

D1   From the Grands Montets follow ref 21 to the Argentière Hut.

D2   From the hut climb up the south-west face of the Col du Chardonnet. At around 3300m you get a good view of the south-east couloir and the cone at the foot of it. Climb up this cone for about 250m and cross a notch that gives access to a second couloir (traverse sometimes exposed). The last 100m are narrow and take you to the Forbes Arête (15m of climbing). A further 150m of mixed climbing along the ridge takes you to the summit. From the second couloir you can also take a third couloir (snow cover not so good at the top) to the left that leads directly to the summit. On the descent, you should be able to ski from the summit but the top section is very exposed. The passages to the middle couloir and from the second to the third couloirs are also exposed. There is also the risk of snow slides and rock fall etc in the gullies lower down. The final couloir after the gendarme, on the other hand, is very skiable.

71.a   West couloir (TD). This is a variant on the normal descent route. From the summit (opposite Lognan) descent the left side of the west couloir. The couloir steepens up and gets more narrow (between 45 and 50°/250m), and there is a delicate traverse (cornice at the end) to leave it that takes you to the top of the Col Supérieur d'Adams Reilly. The easiest route out from here is to descend the north face of the col and ski to Le Tour. However, there is a much more aesthetically pleasing line on the west face that joins up with the Adams Reilly Glacier (for this use the narrow couloir on the left, 45°/150m). Descend the right bank of Adams Reilly Glacier. Now join the Argentière Glacier from which you can get back to Lognan (see route 72). As this route follows the rotation of the sun around the mountain, you can try this tour in a day from Argentière!

Aiguille du Chardonnet at sunset

72 COL DU CHARDONNET — South-west face 3323m PD

3233m (ski lift)	January-May	35°/200m
770m	113, 145	1
2760m	$4^{1/2}$hrs	SP
South-west	2.3	

The Col du Chardonnet is the first stage in the celebrated Chamonix-Zermatt 'High Level Route', and despite being very accessible the climb up in the sun can be monotonous and draining when you are carrying a heavy rucksack. Nevertheless, as you climb up the odd glance gives you glimpses of the magnificent landscape of red and gold granite peaks that surround you. At the top of the col the hard slog is more than amply rewarded by the stunning panorama, and it is time to change your t-shirt! There is a great choice of routes on offer from the top of the Col du Chardonnet including: the Fenêtre du Tour, Fenêtre de Saleina, Cabane des Dorées (Dorées Bivouac Hut), Col des Plines, Saleina Glacier, Saleina Hut and the Three Swiss Cols, the Planereuses Glacier via Tita Neire, Grande Lui and even the north face of the Aiguille d'Argentière!

From Argentière via the Grands Montets join the Argentière Glacier (see ref.21). Cross the Argentière Glacier and climb up the Chardonnet Glacier. Cross the line of rocky moraine on the left bank after about 100m and now head towards the centre of the glacier. After two big hairpin bends (the first 300m are steep and the snow is often hard) you should arrive at a large relatively flat slope (watch out for crevasses). An easy walk leads to the back of the glaciated cirque, beneath the obvious Col du Chardonnet.
The descent follows the same route or the right bank of the glacier at the bottom (crevasses in the middle section). From the Argentière Glacier traverse at 2550m on the left bank to about 2340m and rejoin the pistes via a traverse to the left. You can ski to Lognan and then to Argentière via the Pierre à Ric piste or via the Refuge de Lognan. Although I have described the descent on the south-west face, the traverse into Switzerland is much more popular (following the Three Swiss Cols route or the beginning of the Chamonix-Zermatt High Level Route). The start is steep and narrow for 150m and you often need to put in a handrail.

Climbing up to the Col du Chardonnet

72.a Access via Lognan (PD). You can also access the Argentière Glacier from Lognan. Cross and climb up the left bank of the glacier to 2550m (this is also an alternative access route to the Argentière Hut).

72.b   Col Supérieur du Chardonnet (AD). Before you get to the col, climb up and left along a short steep slope that takes you to the upper col (3660m). The north-east slope is steep (50°/60m) but a technically interesting descent and can be a good test for steep skiing (in some cases it might be helpful to be belayed with a rope).

73   AIGUILLE D'ARGENTIÈRE   3900m
North-west face, X Couloir   D+

3233m (ski lift)	march-June	45°-50°/300m
D1 + D2: 220m + 1130m	114, 145	2
D1 + D2: 680m + 2650m	2hrs + 7¹/²hrs	HP
North-west	4.3	

There was a lot of snow in the winter and spring of 1980 and, with a couple of skiing and mountaineering afficionados, I managed to ski some really great descents during the summer that followed. I have great memories of skiing the west face of the Aiguille d'Argentière on 3rd August. Crossing the Argentière Glacier, on the other hand, was a little bit 'wet'! This was probably the first descent of the Aiguille d'Argentière by the original normal route, known as the Whymper Route, that used to be popular with mountaineers before the current Argentière Hut and the cable-cars were built.

D1   From Argentière, via the Grands Montets, go to the Argentière Hut (see ref.21).

D2   Follow route 71 to a first plateau at around 3000m and head towards the central rock spur. Climb up to 3600m via the large glaciated combe on the right (watch out for the crevasses between 3100m and 3400m). Take the cone furthest to the right to climb the X Couloir that is visible from the Grands Montets. There is a comfortable section along the ridge to the foot of the final steep section, below the summit. These last 120m are sometimes covered in powder snow, but are also often icy (wind and north-facing). In this case, you will have to go to the summit and back on foot. Don't forget to take gear for one or two rappels (abalakov kit). The descent via the same route varies in difficulty from being quite exposed at the top to very pleasant at the bottom. Return via routes 72 or 74.

74   AIGUILLE D'ARGENTIÈRE   3900m
Milieu Glacier   D

3233 m (ski lift)	February-June	45°/250m
D1 + D2: 220m + 1130m	113, 150	2
D1 + D2: 680m + 2650m	2hrs + 6hrs	SP
South	4.2	

This magnificent summit has a classic ski descent on it, and at the end of the winter when this route is really popular you even find moguls starting to form here. Skied in the 1940s by the guide André Tournier and Émile Allais, and then by James

Aiguille d'Argentière, Milieu Glacier

Couttet (Chamonix's World Ski Champion) the Milieu Glacier offers an irresistible invitation to great high mountain skiing. However, I was taking a couple of clients up the mountain one spring day when I watched three people fall and go over the bergschrund. They were each evacuated from the mountain by helicopter with serious injuries. These accidents could have been avoided by taking simple and prudent precautions. The sky was overcast that day and the sun had not sufficiently softened the snow and as a result you simply couldn't afford to make a single error. One should never overestimate one's abilities when it comes to skiing in a high mountain environment like this, despite the fact that a little bit of self-confidence is sometimes necessary to progress to the next level of difficulty. You should also be aware of the fact that weather conditions can change the grading of a descent, and a steep slope can be skied quite comfortably in soft snow but it becomes altogether a different proposition if the snow is hard. This area has a selection of complete ski-mountaineering routes. They require a very good, solid technique and a certain independence of spirit that allows you to take your own decisions irrespective of what the rest of the group thinks…

D1   From Argentière via the Grands Montets join the Argentière Glacier (see ref.21). If the weather is good and you are fit, you can do this route in a day. If this is the case, rather than going to the hut, climb up the left bank of the large combe below the Milieu Glacier.

D2   From the hut go to the combe mentioned above and join the glacier on the left. Climb up the glacier below the fawn-coloured granite slabs of the Arête Charlet-Straton. Watch out for the crevasses that are visible in the middle. Traverse right to 3200m or continue up the slopes that steepen up and then slacken off again as you reach a kind of plateau on your right. You can now easily join the system of bergschrunds on the left. The couloir is very large at first and then narrows and steepens up at the top (45°). The slopes beneath the summit (to the right of the col) slacken off a little (35-40°). Watch out for the enormous cornices that stand guard over the Swiss side of the mountain and the Couloir Barbey. The descent via the same route is quite easy if there is soft snow but can be very dangerous if the snow is hard and you fall. Follow route 72 to Argentière.

74.a   Couloir Barbey (D). Access the central summit of the Aiguille d'Argentière via the Milieu Glacier. There is a large cornice that sits above the couloir. You can be belayed as you look over the top of the cornice to see where the best point is to cross it (usually better on the right). The descent (see route 51) follows the final shoulder on the north face at first then heads right via a series of small secondary couloirs. Your route of descent (45°/400m, sections of 50°, 5.1) will be dictated by the terrain left after the numerous snow slides on this face. As a result, the deep central gully can be avoided by skiing the small face on the right. Watch out for the rocks that can be exposed at the bottom of the couloir. Go round the rock spur at the end of the descent and join the Saleina Glacier. At around 3050m put your skins back on your skis. If you are skiing back to France, head north-west to get to the Fenêtre du Tour (3414m) which, after 1 1/2 hrs of climbing up, gives access to the Tour Glacier and the Le Tour ski area. You can also climb up to the Col du Chardonnet (steeper) to join its west face, Lognan and Argentière.

75   AIGUILLE D'ARGENTIÈRE   3900m
Y Couloir   TD

⚐	3233m (ski lift)	🗻	March-May	⌐	45°/250m, sect. of 50°
↗	D1 + D2: 220m + 1130m	📷	151	⚠	2
↘	D1 + D2: 680m + 2650m	⏲	2½hrs + 8hrs	⊕	HP
⊕	South-east	🎿	5.2		

The Y Couloir on the Aiguille d'Argentière is a technically and physically demanding route that is also very rewarding and it brings with it quite a sense of achievement. Some years in the spring, when the snow conditions are good, this can be one of the ultimate extreme skis. The first descent was by Marie-José and Patrick Vallençant on the 7th July 1972. The conditions for skiing this route currently, however, are not as good as they were in the 1970s.

D1 ▪ From Argentière via the Grands Montets join the Argentière Glacier (see ref.21).

South face of the Aiguille d'Argentière

D2   Climb up the right bank of the Améthystes Glacier to around 3300m and where you can see the couloir after the pillars of the south point (Pointe Sud, large cone). You can follow the bergschrund from a funnel (mixed climbing), above which you climb on the right bank. The couloir is narrow at the start but gets wider at around 3500m where it forks and forms the Y shape. Take the left branch of the Y and a series of steep couloirs. A rock shoulder and a final cornice lead to the southerly summit ridge, 100m below the summit. If you take the branch that leads straight up, the couloir is easy to negotiate at first and then becomes increasingly steep and narrow. The exit from the couloir heads left and leads to the summit and goes round the end of the Flèche Rousse ridge.

On the descent, the choice of which branch of the Y to take is quite difficult given the often dicey snow conditions (at the top). The common couloir beneath the point where the two branches meet up, on the other hand, is less steep and is easier to ski even if the central gully can present further difficulties. Depending on the year and the conditions, you may have to rappel past the final gully and bergschrund. Follow routes 76 and 72 to rejoin the Grands Montets pistes.

75.a   Brèche Nord du Plateau (3300m, D–). From the Argentière Hut, climb up the right bank of the Améthystes Glacier and you will soon see two couloirs near the Brèche Nord du Plateau. The first one (40-45°/250m) is not very interesting. The second (45-50°/200m), in a beautiful rugged setting, is more attractive. These two couloirs can be backup objectives if the conditions are bad on the Y Couloir. Both of them were first descended by Daniel Chauchefoin in 1977.

76   COL DU TOUR NOIR   3535m
Améthystes Glacier   PD

⚐ 3233m (ski lift)	🏔 March-May	⌐ sections of 35°
↗ 1000m	📷 113, 150, 151, 153	⚠ 1
↘ 680m + 2300m	🕐 2¹/²hrs + 4hrs	✚ SP
✦ South-east	🎿 2.3	

The Col du Tour Noir is a highly prized and relatively easy ski tour. Having said that, the final plateau can seem endless as the heat, tiredness and blisters on your ankles start to get the better of beginners or those who are not in shape...

There are a few crevasses at the level of the last rise in the glacier at around 3250m below the Y Couloir. From the Col du Tour Noir you are rewarded with magnificent views into Switzerland and a stunning panorama of some of the great north faces. Moreover, the quality of the descent makes this route very special.

On the Améthystes Glacier

Argentière face of the Tour Noir

From Argentière via the Grands Montets join the Argentière Glacier. Now traverse to and climb up the Améthystes Glacier. Stick to the right bank to avoid the crevasses in the middle of the glacier. After a long section under the ridges of the Flèche Rousse you reach the col via a short steep slope. On the descent follow the tracks you made on the way up. If there is lots of snow you can join the left bank of the glacier and then move to the centre at around 3100m (line of moraine visible on the right). Lower down, on the Argentière Glacier, traverse to the left bank and rejoin the bottom of the Grands Montets pistes (see route 72).

Touching the clouds!

76.a   North-east face of the Col du Tour Noir (tour via Swiss side, D). From the col join the north-east face (45°/250m). Traverse right and pass the lower section of a nice little couloir that comes down from the west ridge of the Aiguille de l'A Neuve. Cross the final band of seracs via a small and narrow couloir. If there is lots of snow you can follow a gully on the right that takes you to the bottom of the slope, but the rock band is high and this is not the best route down. Take equipment for rappelling in case it is needed and join routes 68 or 72.

76.b   East shoulder of the Pointe Supérieure des Améthystes (3565m, AD–). Either on the climb up to or on the way down from the col, head towards the Tour Noir at around 3150m. Before you get to the middle of the combe head towards the east shoulder of the Pointe Supérieure des Améthystes. The slope steepens up considerably for about 50m (probable bergschrund). As this small slope faces north there is often good snow here and makes a good complement for the return from the Tour Noir with a more technical variant (45°/50m).

76.c ▪ Col Supérieur du Tour Noir (3690m, D). Climb up the right bank of the Améthystes Glacier and traverse across the top at the foot of the Aiguille de l'A Neuve. A distinct couloir on the right (40-45°/150m) leads to the Col Supérieur. If you decide to descend down the Swiss side, a first slope (cornice at the top) takes you down and left on to a snowy ridge. Cross this and join the large regular slope that faces north-east (50° at the top for 150m). Traverse below the Col de l'A Neuve (3406m). Now go round the west ridge of the Grande Lui and climb up a steep slope for 80m to join the normal route (47.b). Alternatively, if there is lots of snow and the A Neuve Glacier is well filled in, ski down the left bank, then the middle before moving back to the left bank of the glacier to La Fouly (route 47). For crossing into Switzerland this traverse is prettier than crossing the Col d'Argentière and more direct than the route over the Col du Tour Noir. If the conditions on the north-east face are not good enough, you can return via the west couloir that you took on the way up.

77 ▪ COL D'ARGENTIÈRE   3620m
Tour Noir Glacier   PD

⚑ 3233m (ski lift)	▥ December-May	↳ 35°/50m
↗ 1070m	▣ 151, 153	⚠ 1
↘ 680m + 2390m	◷ 7hrs	⊕ SP
✧ South-west	✗ 3.1	

Steeper than its neighbour, the Col d'Argentière is also much prettier. You can cross the Col d'Argentière into Switzerland but it is longer and more difficult with at the bottom with steep gullies to cross on the right, D+, 45°/600m, route 46.b). Watch out for the numerous crevasses at the bottom of the A Neuve Glacier. Join route 46.a to get to La Fouly.

From Argentière via the Grands Montets, join and climb up the Argentière Glacier. Pass the Améthystes Glacier on your left and climb up the Tour Noir Glacier. Stay on the right bank at first and then move to the centre and back to the right bank at around 3350m to avoid the system of crevasses. After a sustained section below the Tour Noir (crevasse on the right and bergschrund), come back right and head straight towards the col that is in fact called the 'Passage d'Argentière', the actual Col d'Argentière being lower down and unskiable.
The descent is by the same route and you are free to choose the best line from the various combes and slopes on the face depending on the quality of the snow.

77.a ▪ Rouges du Dolent Glacier (PD). You can access the Rouges du Dolent Glacier from the col and via a snowy saddle (3570m) on the right, below the Pointe Morin. When there is good snow cover crossing this saddle is relatively straightforward but these days, as the glacier is lower, you need a rope to get on to it. You find yourself in an isolated glaciated combe with a beautiful descent that is sustained at first. This combe and its descent complement the passage at the foot of the stunning granite formations of the Pointe Kurz. On the way up from the hut you can also stay right of the central rock spur and climb up the Rouges du Dolent Glacier itself. Now you either climb to the snowy saddle mentioned above or you can cross the steep slope to the snow saddle beneath it on the left, at around 3360m, and ski the north-west face (40-45°/100m).

78 COL DE L'AMÔNE   3550m
South-west couloir   D

3233m (ski lift)		February-June		45°-50°/300m
1000m		155		2
680m + 2320m		7hrs		HP
South/south-west		5.1		

Owing to its southerly aspect and the rock face that dominates the Col de l'Amône to the east there are frequent rock falls on this face and the couloir's funnel shape make it a bit of a bowling alley. And you should be aware of this. On the other hand, the final section towards the summit crest is very aesthetic and the view from the top over the north face and the chaotic A Neuve Glacier is quite breathtaking. For this reason and its sense of isolation, this route is a superb vantage point from which to check out all the other descents in the Argentière Basin, especially those at the back of the basin that are rarely in condition. For a long time now numerous skiers have dreamt of descending the steep and highly aesthetic couloirs such as the one on Mont Dolent (first skied by Daniel Chauchefoin and Yves Détry in April 1977; start 50m below the col, 2 rappels, 55°/350m) and the north face of the Aiguille du Triolet that was first descended by Jérôme Ruby and Dédé Rhem on snowboards on 16 June 1995. The two boarders were dropped off by helicopter and set off from the Col des Aiguilles du Triolet. They crossed the serac bands in three rappels and managed to descend 650m of terrain of between 50 and 55°. In the summer of 1973, Patrick Vallençant and I had a go at the very steep slopes to the left of

Col de l'Amône

the serac bands. The steepest slope at that time was right of the two rock rognons in addition to which the ice covering the face was much thicker making more of a skiable the slope below the seracs. Daniel Chauchefoin successfully skied the north/north-west face of the Aiguilles Rouges du Triolet (ABO, ice, sections of 60° with ice axe). Owing to the extremely hit and miss nature of their condition and 'skiability' I haven't described those descents here that are rarely in condition. That does not, however, detract from the extreme level of technical ability and commitment that they require and the exploits that they have witnessed…

From Argentière, via the Grands Montets, follow ref 21 and climb up the Glacier d'Argentière. Pass the ridge that comes down from the Pointe Kurz and continue up the right bank to the couloir (visible at the last moment) set in among the rock spurs. Cross the bergschrund on the right and climb up the couloir that gets steadily steeper. The last section is very narrow and exceeds 50° at the top. The start from the ridge is exposed and the first 60m are difficult to ski. The first descent was by Yves Détry in 1977.

78.a   Col du Dolent (TD). (55°/350m, start 50m below the col, rappels at the top). Also known as Col Nord du Dolent. First descent by Daniel Chauchefoin and Yves Détry on 17th April 1977.

78.b   North face of the Aiguille du Triolet (ED+). Maximum exposure and rarely in condition, descended only once, by snowboarders (50-55°/650m, minimum of 3 rappels).

79   COL DES COURTES   3569m
North-east couloir   D

3233m (ski lift)	March-May	45°-50°/500m
1020m	156, 160	2
680m + 2340m	7¹/²hrs	HP
North-east	5.1	

It is only quite recently that the Col des Courtes was added to the list of routes in the Argentière Basin. Separated from the summit of the Courtes by a long ridge broken by steep and jagged rock spires, the Col des Courtes is the lowest

From the Triolet to the Courtes

point before the summit of the Aiguille de Triolet that overlooks Italy to the south. The sheer variety of rock and ice routes and ski descents that can be done on the chain that separates the Argentière and Talèfre Glaciers is unique in the Alps. The majority of the routes here are pretty difficult, especially when it comes to the north faces. At the end of the winter and the beginning of spring, many of these routes can be done in a day, if it is cold, thanks to the Grands Montets cable-cars. Later on in the season it is better to start from the Argentière Hut. The first descent of the north-east slope of the Col des Courtes was done by Daniel Chauchefoin and a friend in May 1976.

From Argentière, via the Grands Montets, follow ref.21 and then climb up the right bank of the Argentière Glacier. Pass the base of the north/north-east face of the Courtes and go round its immense cone of debris. If you face the barrier of the Triolet, you will see the snowy slope that leads up to the Col des Courtes. The double bergschrund can be impossible to cross some years. The couloir running alongside it on the right can be less pleasant (gully and risk of rock fall). Further up, however, the huge slope is regular with a very steep section (55°) at the top and on the right bank. You arrive quite quickly at a shoulder uphill of the col (to the east and at 3612m) as the col itself is a deep and steep notch. On the descent, a nicer and more obvious line follows the right bank even if it is steeper here. Now the descent is more to the left and takes you to the bottom of the couloir, where the bergschrund is filled in above the cone of debris. Don't forget to check out the best line of descent on the way up as the conditions and the gradient of the slopes change from year to year.

79.a   Pointe Tournier, east couloir (D). This very irregular and steeper couloir was skied for the first time by Eric Ballot and Emmanuel Cottignies (45-50°/500m, sections of 55°).

80	**COL DES CRISTAUX**	**3601m**
	North-east couloir	D

⚑	3233m (ski lift)	📷	March-June	⌐	40°-50°/500m
↗	1050m	📷	156, 160	⚠	2
↘	680m + 2370m	⏱	7hrs	⊕	HP
✦	North-east	🎿	5.1		

The Col des Cristaux has for some time now been a classic route. It is often skied in winter as its left bank gets a good covering of snow and the ground itself is mixed without having icy sections. The final section below the col is steep and does not always have good snow cover whereas the rest of the slope is quite regular. On one trip, with a group of trainee guides from ENSA, I set off from the Aiguille du Midi to traverse the Aiguille du Tacul via the Couloir du Capucin, stayed the night at the Couvercle Hut, crossed the Col des Cristaux and the Col du Tour Noir (descending the north/north-east face) then climbed up via the Grande Lui and finished up in La Fouly. This is a great route whose descents are all on slopes with the same aspect. We did it in April and we had planned to do the complete traverse of the Massif starting with the Miage peaks and including Mont Blanc. The weather decided otherwise and we were reduced to more modest aims. It was nevertheless a truly stunning traverse!

From Argentière, via the Grands Montets, follow ref.21 and join the Argentière Glacier. Follow route 79 and go past the base of the spur that runs alongside the north/north-east face of the Courtes. It is quite easy going up to below the bergschrund which you can cross either in the middle, directly beneath the col, or to the right via the cone at the base of the secondary couloir. Above the bergschrund, depending on how hard the snow is, either head straight up or to the right of the couloir to join a secondary crest higher up (less monotonous!). Two-thirds of the way up the route heads left slightly, underneath the col. There is often some mixed climbing to cross the final 100m and it can reach 50° in places. Some years you often need to rappel past this poorly covered section on the descent. Lower down the snow is colder on the right (also slightly steeper) or you can go left to the transformed snow in the couloir that has the slight escarpment running alongside it. There can be a deep gully down the centre of slope.

80.a   North-east couloir of the Aiguille Qui Remue (3700m, TD). The middle section can be icy. The average slope is 45-50°/550m. First skied by Rémy Lécluse.

81   LES COURTES   3856m
North/north-east couloir   D

3233m (ski lift)	March-June	48°/400m
1300m	156, 159, 160	2
680m + 2620m	8hrs	HP
North/north-east	5.2	

The first descent of the north/north-east face was done by Serge Cachat-Rosset in April 1971. This route has become a classic descent and is a great introduction to true extreme skiing. On the other hand, it also represents the ultimate goal for some ski-tourers with limited technical abilities and the same is also true for talented skiers with limited mountaineering skills. I was to see this for myself the day after catastrophe had hit Chernobyl when I was skiing on this face with four ski-mountaineering clients, one of which was a very good skier who I didn't know very well. We all climbed up without difficulty until we got to 150m from the summit and a band of ice. I belayed each of my companions for the first 50m of the descent. The best skier of the group went last and wanted to stay on the rope for a little bit longer. Although the snow had quickly become softer and easier to ski, my client was reluctant to sever the 'umbilical cord' (providing mostly moral support) while his companions were enjoying the freedom of skiing independently while under the close supervision of their guide! In the end, the two of us skied the face's 600m roped together. This provided me with an excellent opportunity to refine my rope technique when skiing with clients that allows them the freedom to make their turns unimpeded by the rope. The technique I used involved belaying my client by passing the rope around my waist while myself being secured to an ice-axe placed uphill with the ends of one or two skis placed in the snow. Hold two or three loops of rope in your downhill hand to help the skier as he or she makes their turns; ask them to stop just after the turn to give you time to give them a bit of rope and then give a signal to make the next turn.

This kind of belaying is not good enough for steep slopes. However, if the skier makes gentle turns the system should hold given the elasticity of the rope, and the dynamic breaking system around the waist should hold the skier losing his or her balance. Belaying directly off an ice-axe or another direct anchorage point to the mountain, on the other hand, is dicey as you can't give enough slack before a turn and there is not enough give in the system if the skier falls as opposed to the dynamic system of belaying around the waist.

Aiguille Chenavier and the summit of the Courtes

From Argentière, via the Grands Montets and ref.21, climb up the Argentière Glacier to the cone below the north/north-east face of the Courtes (crevasses). Cross the bergschrund, which can often be quite high and easier to cross towards the right. The line up heads a little to the left at first, towards a snowy saddle. This first section is quite steep. Now use the snowy ridge and return to the face, heading towards the right. Once again the slope steepens up and the top section is about 50°. Follow the narrow ridge to the summit.

The start of the descent is very impressive and wide and you can pick a line that uses the areas where there is good snow. Lower down the slope slackens off and you can find colder snow on the slopes facing north, under the middle saddle.

81.a   Aiguille Chenavier, north-east couloir (TD). Descended for the first time by Pierre Tardivel on 17 June 1999 (45-50°/700m). Start at the top of the north/north-east face and then traverse beneath the small gendarme on the ridge and change faces. A system of diagonal ledgeson the right takes you to the couloir. There are a few narrow sections and gullies and then the slope widens out.

82   LES COURTES   3856m
Austrian Route   ED+

⌐	3233m (ski lift)	▨	Spring	⌐	50°-55°/850m
↗	D1 + D2: 220m + 1300m	⬚	160	⚠	3
↘	D1 + D2: 680m + 2600m	◔	8-10hrs	⊕	HP
⊕	North	✗	5.5		

The first descent of the north face of the Courtes by Daniel Chauchefoin (in soft snow!) was astonishing, even if he is one of the great extreme skiing specialists. After this success it became possible to think about skiing extreme lines elsewhere in the Massif. We started to think about skiing anywhere where the snow would stick and, if for some reason we couldn't ski the whole way down, we could always use a rope... This was how the north face of the Aiguille du Midi first entered the arena of possible of extreme skis. In the winter of 1977, favourable conditions and the numerous first descents that were being done created a congenial spirit of competition between the ski-mountaineers of the time. This led to a massive development of the discipline, which at that time was considered merely another kind of mountaineering. Nowadays, on the other hand, it is the ski-mountaineers and freeriders who come in large numbers to assault the extreme slopes and their soft powder snow in the winter. It is not easy to find out what the conditions are like on the faces here from May to June as the Grands Montets cable-cars are closed and the walk up from Argentière – at more than 3hrs - is a not a great pleasure...

From the Argentière Hut (see ref.21) go to the foot of the north face of the Courtes (see route 81). Traverse, heading left, to cross the bergschrunds at around 2900m. A first band of steep snow allows you to climb up to the right and below the steep buttresses of the central spur (north/north-east). Join the top of a snowy

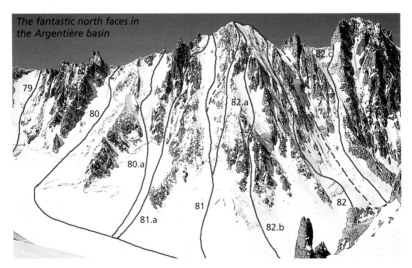

The fantastic north faces in the Argentière basin

79
80
80.a
81
81.a
82.a
82.b
82.c
82

promontory and climb straight up a section that includes, at first, some mixed ground. Now go up the steep slope underneath the Tour des Courtes. Keep heading right to climb over the step downhill of the face (a little less steep) to the level of the Tour Rouge. From here there is a system of steps that leads you to a final steep and exposed slope on the north face to the summit. The descent has all the ingredients for a great extreme ski. Each winter is different and the snow cover on these slopes can be quite hit and miss. This route should only be attempted by very experienced ski-mountaineering experts. On the first descent, Daniel Chauchefoin used the top of the Swiss Route.

82.a   North-east spur (TD). First descent by Pierre Tardivel on 11th June 1989 (45-50°/900m).

82.b   North-east couloir, near the Cordier Route (TD). First descent by Pierre Tardivel on 1st July 1987 (40-50°/750m).

82.c   Col des Droites (TD). First descent by Eric Monnier (July 1980). With the new millennium, this route has stared to become very popular and it looks like it will become another of the Argentière Basin's classic extreme ski routes (45-50°/600m). In the spring of 2001, Pierre Tardivel and Tim Dobbins on skis together with Bertrand Delapierre on a snowboard did the first descent of the north face of the Col de la Tour des Courtes (45-50°, 5.5, 2 rappels over seracs) which is just next to the Col des Droites.

83   COL DE L'AIGUILLE VERTE   3796m
North face   TD

3233m (ski lift)		march-June		50°-55°/850m
D1 + D2 : 220m + 1100m		162		3
D1 + D2 : 680m + 2560m		8-10hrs		HP
North		5.5		

Although a little shorter and less impressive than the Couturier Couloir, this route has virtually the same characteristics. By taking the variant start route from the west depression you avoid the upper ice convexity. In July 1975, accompanied to the bergschrund by the celebrated ski champion James Couttet, I quickly climbed to the top of the couloir. I was able to ski the first 150m of the descent as there was a thin layer of snow covering the ice below. However, once past the convexity in the ice my efforts to side-slip or to get any purchase on the slope with my skis was in vain as the thin layer of spring snow slid away to reveal the black ice below. Not wanting to cheat and set up rappels, I secured myself to the ice with an ice-screw and swapped my skis for crampons and climbed back up to the col. From the col I descended the narrow couloir on the Talèfre face (a first descent). Do I regret having turned back? Although it was a little painful, there's no doubt that I much prefer being here and able to write about it all these years later… The first 'official' descent of this slope, without skiing the upper section, was by Dominique Potard and François Williot on 10th April 1977. A variant route, via the west depression and avoiding the ice section, was skied by Pierre Tardivel in 1999.

Aiguille Verte

D1   From Argentière, via the Grands Montets, go to the Argentière Hut (see ref.21).

D2   From the hut join the bottom of the north face of the Col de l'Aiguille Verte via the glaciated combe. Cross the bergschrund that is surmounted by a rock step on the right (delicate and steep). Via the left bank (small snowy ridge runs along-side it higher up) climb to the ice convexity at around 3700m (55° or more for 30 to 50m). You end up at the east col (convenient place to put skis on) below the Signal Vallot. The couloir at the start of the descent very quickly becomes steeper and more narrow. The fold-like formations in the ice also make for difficult skiing. Lower down, the slope widens out and it is often better to keep to the right bank.

A system of mini-couloirs separated by snowy ridges means that you don't have to stay too long in the central gully (likelihood of rock fall and snow slides). The final 'hurdle' is the crossing of the bergschrund where the couloir is funnel-shaped and potentially dangerous. It can be more convenient to stay on the right bank to start off with, but the bergschrund is often too high to cross on this side. By following ref.21 and passing under the north face of the Aiguille Verte this route can be done in a day, but only if it is cold and by technically and physically strong ski-mountaineers. Note: The top section of the Lagarde Couloir on the north-east face of the Droites was skied by Emmanuel Ballot (several rappels at the bottom).

Using both poles for balance !

84   AIGUILLE VERTE   4122m
Couturier Couloir   TD

⚑ 3233m (ski lift)   🏔 March-June   ⌐ 55°/300m

↗ D1 + D2: 220m + 1470m   📷 162, 165   ⚠ 3

↘ D1 + D2: 680m + 2890m   ☉ 2hrs + 8hrs   ⊕ HP

✦ North   ⚔ 5.4

This is a real gem of a route for any extreme skier. The start on a prestigious summit, a regular and highly aesthetic line, essentially technical dangers and risks that can be overcome by mastering control (both mental and physical) of your body – these are all essential elements in an extreme ski descent. On Sunday 29 July 1973, two days after a big fall of snow, Patrick Vallençant and I climbed up through the deep snow to the junction with the Washburn variant. Rather than tempting fate and disturbing the fragile equilibrium of the top layer of snow, we stopped at around 3500m. As we skied the 55° slopes in powder snow we were sure that we would 'do' the Couturier the next day or the day after that. Drunk with fatigue and the effect of the sun, we stayed the night at the Grands Montets Hut (the Argentière Hut was being renovated). At 3 o'clock the following morning white clouds of snow enveloped the mountains and flashes of lightening and rumbles of thunder put an end to our second attempt. Three days later, seeing that the route was in condition (our tracks were the proof!), Serge Cachet-Rosset was dropped at the top by helicopter put at his disposal by his sponsor. It took him several tense and difficult hours to complete his descent of the route before being picked up by the helicopter below the bergschrund. The following Sunday we had another go. This time the hard snow meant we got to 4000m in 2hrs. We started down the descent before the sun made the condi-

tions too dangerous and we had an hour of absolute bliss on this remarkable route. We even took the time to film each other on the descent. The following week the weather forecast wasn't kind to us and we missed our chance to do the first descent of the Cordier Couloir. Note: The north-east face below the Col Armand Charlet was skied by Emannuel Ballot. The lower 350m were passed with the aid of rappels while the upper 600m vary between 50 and 55°.

D1 From Argentière, via the Grands Montets, go to the Argentière Hut (see ref.21).

D2 Cross diagonally back across the glacier the above the rock spur

Patrick Vallençant on the Couturier

marked 2886m that comes down from the north-east ridge of the Grande Rocheuse. Via a combe to the right of the ridge, you arrive at a glaciated cirque at 3000m below the north face of the Aiguille Verte. The bergschrund can be negotiated to the right. Head up the couloir for the first 200m (51°). After the first junction stay close to the central gully to avoid making a classic mistake higher up: that is to head straight up (you can climb up at night) and then have to traverse right for several pitches. As there is a serac at the top, it is better to stay a little on the left of the couloir and to climb to the summit on this side (55°/100m). The serac to the east of the small snow dome has been threatening to collapse since the end of the 1990s, and so it is not a good idea to spend too long beneath it…You can either climb straight up to the summit or to the right via the less steep snow dome (45° maximum). Start your descent on the snow dome but watch out for the windslabs here that can be extremely dangerous. You can descent quite quickly into the couloir via the left bank, which faces north-east at its start. Traverse to the large regular slope on the right (55°) to get away from the central gullies. Now move back to the centre until you get to the bergschrund depending on the state of the gullies. Join the Argentière Glacier and the Grands Montets pistes to get back to Argentière (route 70).

84.a   (D+) Direct access from the Grands Montets in a day. Traverse below the bergschrunds on the Grands Montets ridge and just past the bottom of the Cordier Couloir, to get to the foot of the couloir. You reach the bergschrund by the left of the cone that is already quite steep.

85   AIGUILLE VERTE   4122m
Cordier Couloir   ED

⚑	3233m (ski lift)	📱	March-May	⏷	55°-57°/300m
↗	D1 + D2 : 220m + 1470m	📷	162, 165	⚠	3
↘	D1 + D2 : 680m + 2890m	☺	2hrs + 8hrs	⊕	HP
⊕	North	⚔	5.5		

Skiing the Cordier Couloir is at the limit of what is reasonable as it is very steep and the snow cover here is not great. More important, however, are the objective dangers in the couloir (seracs, rocks, snow slides). After our descents of the Couturier in the summer of 1973, Patrick Vallençant and I made an attempt on the Cordier at the beginning of August. As we approached the 3600m mark the snow started falling away under the beams of our head torches. I still have vivid memories of our miserable and hair-raising retreat back down the slope, down-climbing over icy snow in rigid ski boots with our skis on our backs. That was out last attempt that year. In March 1977, two days after Yves Détry's successful first descent (6 March with two short rappels), I tried again and, as the conditions were exceptionally good, I was able to do the whole thing in four hours. I didn't have to set up any rappels as the wind had blown enough snow onto the ice.

D1   From Argentière, via the Grands Montets, go to the Argentière Hut (see ref.21).

D2   Via route 84, climb to the glaciated basin below the Couturier and descend a little below the rocky triangle of the Verte. Climb the couloir and at around 3400m head towards the rock ridge. Now head left to go round 250m of sustained slope broken by seracs. Get on to the snow dome and continue up a slope that gets less steep (risk of slabs) up to the summit. Your line of descent will depend on the conditions you have encountered on the way up. The 'serac field' changes from year to year and has steep and exposed sections, it can be quite straightforward if the snow is good (50°). The couloir below the Col du Nant Blanc becomes very steep (more than 55°). At the level of the central gully, there is often an icy section (snow slides) for several dozen metres and then the slope widens out but remains sustained (around 55° in the middle) until the bergschrund.

85.a   Col du Nant Blanc (3776m, ED+). The first descent was by Daniel Chauchefoin on 3rd June 1978. This is the direct descent of the Cordier Couloir. Below the point where the two branches of the glacier are split by a rocky ridge, at around 3500m, there is about 250m of ground at between 55 and 58°. This section is narrower and rarely has as much snow as the route described above.

85.b   North couloir of the Aiguille Carrée (3600m, TD) and the Gigord Couloir (3500m, TD). These two steep couloirs that come down from the Arête des Grands Montets are rather in the shadow of their famous neighbours, the Cordier and the Couturier. However, the first one is narrow and difficult to ski with slopes that face the other way and is rarely skied owing to the frequent lack of snow. It is unlikely that you would be able to ski it from the top. The Gigord Couloir, on the other hand, is shorter and more skiable and resembles the Chevalier Couloir. Both couloirs are on more or less the same gradient and vary from between 50°/500m to 600m. Moreover, as they both face due north, you can avoid some of the rock fall in this very rocky area. Both very skied for the first time by Dominique Neuenschwander, in 1985.

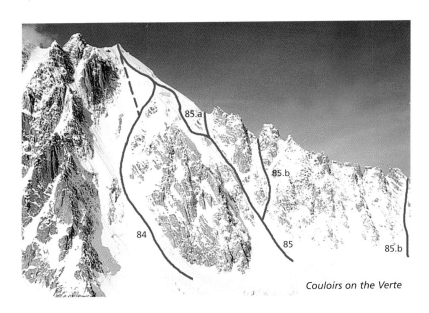

Couloirs on the Verte

86   PETITE AIGUILLE VERTE   3512m
Chevalier Couloir   D

⌐	3233m (ski lift)	⬜	February-May	⌐	45°-50°/350m
↗	360m	📷	141	⚠	2
↘	2280m	◔	5hrs	⊕	HP
✦	East/north-east	✗	5.2		

Descending a couloir that you have checked out in the way up is always the safest option. With the Chevalier Couloir, however, the fact that it is very easy to access it from the north face makes it a special case. In fact, a walk up with skins on your skis to the bergschrund at 3400m followed by a short climb (52°/70m) of the curving snow crest or 'demi-lune' gives you access to the top of the couloir. In addition, there is a cornice that overlooks the route and can give you an idea of

On the Chevalier Couloir

the conditions in the couloir. Moreover, a general awareness of the conditions in the mountains is always helpful before setting off on this kind of a route. Of course, you can also observe the route from the bottom of the couloir. I have skied the Chevalier Couloir with my students quite regularly since the 1970s. Although I have rarely climbed it from the bottom, I am so often in the area that I can quite easily pick the best time for the descent. The role of a guide is, after all, to know when to wait and when to go for it. Only the mountain's 'occasional visitors' and journalists on the look-out for a juicy story call it 'lethal'…

From Argentière and the Grands Montets, descend the start of the Rognons Glacier (to the east of the Col des Grands Montets) and follow the beginning of the piste and the base of the east face of the Petite Aiguille Verte until you see the couloir above the distinct bergschrund. Cross the bergschrund well to the left and climb up the couloir, which narrows 100m from the summit. The final 40m are very steep and there is often not good snow cover here. Once you have arrived at the 'demi-lune' you can finish up on the north ridge and put your skis on below the final set of rocks, although normally the classic descent starts at the 'demi-lune'. If the cornice is very large, the first few skiable metres can be more than 55° (you can belay people with a rope at the start). After this the couloir widens out but remains sustained.

86.a   North face of the Petite Aiguille Verte (D). The fact that this route is so near the lift system means that some years it gets skied from the beginning of the winter if the autumn snow was able to stick to the ice on this small north face. You can also ski the short very steep slope below the shoulder on the right. Depending on the conditions, you can train in this area right up to the summer. From Argentière and the Grands Montets go to the Col des Grands Montets via the metal staircase and climb straight up to the first 'balcony' towards the Petite Aiguille Verte. Go right to avoid the two crevasses. Join the bergschrund, which can sometimes be quite high, and cross it on the left. Via the 'demi-lune' or straight ahead below the rocks, you reach the top of the skiable slope (25m below the summit). If the bergschrund is impossible to cross (which is often the case, especially on the way up), it is easier to take the normal route up the right shoulder. A short ridge leads to the rocky summit (50-55°/80m).

87   AIGUILLE DES GRANDS MONTETS   3295m
Pas de Chèvre   AD

⚑ 3233m (ski lift)		🏔 December-April		⌐ 35°/300m	
↗ 50m		📷 168		⚠ 1	
↘ 2180m		🕐 2¹⁄₂hrs		🏕 DP	
✦ West		🎿 3.1			

This route can sometimes look like a piste with moguls, and unfortunately it does not always get skied in good conditions. In fact, the development of wider skis and of snowboards has encouraged skiers and boarders to try this in the afternoon sun. As a result, when these tracks refreeze it is sometimes almost impossible to ski this route in the morning when the snows is colder and firmer.

There is also a variant route to the left of the Rectiligne Couloir that is less aesthetic, more dangerous and has a delicate section across rocks. From this part of the Pas de Chèvre you get an impressive view of the west face of the Aiguille Verte that really gives you an idea of terrain on the Nant Blanc Glacier. The Nant Blanc face was skied for the first time by the ski-mountaineer Jean-Marc Boivin on 12 June 1989 and snowboarded for the first time by Marco Siffredi on 17 June 1999. Obviously, setting off down this route involves risks: the quality of the snow varies, you have a choice of routes and you have to choose carefully where you set up rappels. You need a really solid technique and an

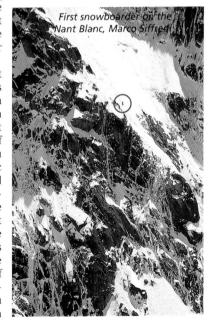

First snowboarder on the Nant Blanc, Marco Siffredi

The Verte and the Drus under their snowy mantle

88.a

88

87.a

87

equally solid confidence in your ability if you're going to try the Nant Blanc face as you simply cannot afford to fall here. Do remember that the first descent (by J.M. Boivin) took five hours (to allow time for the really hard snow to soften!) while the climb up only took an hour and a half…

From Argentière, via the Grands Montets, go down the metal staircase and head west on to the Grands Montets Glacier as its gets less and less steep.

At around 3100m, go straight on and into a large combe that is steep at the top (risk of windslab with northerly or easterly winds). Lower down, the combe narrows and becomes a steep gully. If you continue left, a rock spur divides the Pas de Chèvre into two parts. The real Pas de Chèvre crosses a small col that leads to a very

steep section (20m rappel) and the right-hand combe. However, if there is enough snow both the combes can be skied even though the quality of the snow in them will be very different. In the right-hand combe (steep at the top) the snow stays quite cold, whereas the snow in the left combe becomes crusty quite quickly and can be unstable as the layers of snow sit on smooth slabs of rock and grass. At the bottom of the

Perfect powder on the Pas de Chèvre!

face (at around 2100m), it is imperative that you head left. Look out for a large larch tree standing on its own and, still heading left, descend a steep section full of 'varosses' (green alders). After the moraine, you join a rocky couloir (often doesn't have good snow cover, risk of rock fall). Often, if there is poor snow cover, you will have to stay on the moraine (for about 200m leftwards) to get to a second couloir known as the 'Couloir des Chaussettes' ('Sock Couloir'). It gets its name from the woollen socks that the first tourists to cross the glacier would wear over their leather boots to stop them slipping on the ice… At the bottom of the couloirs you reach the Mer de Glace, which you follow. You leave the glacier lower down, on the left bank, and there is a short walk up to the Buvette des Mottets (small cabin that sells refreshments) from where you join the track down to Chamonix.

87.a   Rectiligne Couloir (AD). Follow the same start as for the Pas de Chèvre and at around 3500m stay left opposite the Drus. You should see the start of a rock spur on your right as you join the couloir that is quite steep and narrow at its start (45°/40m then 35-40°/300m). This takes you to the Nant Blanc Glacier. Go to the left bank of the glacier (crevasses). From here, in good conditions, you have the choice of several superb routes beneath the north face of the Drus and the Flammes de Pierre. Watch out, the direct descent in the centre leads to rocks bands. Head right as for the Pas de Chèvre or head sharp left and look for a steep couloir after the larches.

88   AIGUILLE À BOCHARD   2766m
Poubelles Couloir   AD

⚑	3233 m (ski lift)	🗻	January-March	⛷	40°-45°/250m
↗	50m	📷	168	⚠	2
↘	1720m	⏱	2hrs	⊕	DP
🧭	South/west	🎿	4.1		

To conclude our tour of the numerous extreme and 'expert' descents in the Argentière Basin, I have to mention Bruno Gouvy's descent of the Niche des Drus. While many people dream of the perfect route with the ideal approach and descent, Bruno managed to pull it off: he jumped out of a helicopter with his paraglider and landed virtually on the summit of the Petit Dru, he then rappelled down to the Niche des Drus, snowboarded the slope and with his paraglider flew back down to Chamonix. This truly was a fantastic achievement worthy of this visionary mountaineer, skier and parachutist, to name but a few of his many talents. His thirst for new challenges led him to his final descent of the Aiguille Verte. He was dropped off by helicopter. He had overestimated the thickness of the snow on

Poubelles Couloir

the ice on the north face, and his snowboard took him on one final descent of the Couturier Couloir …

From Argentière, take the Lognan cable-car and the Bochard gondola to reach the top of the couloir that is right opposite the upper Bochard lift station (80m west, barriers). The descent starts in this very narrow couloir. You usually rappel past the first 20m and then put on your skis. After having descended to couloir, pick up the bottom of the Pas de Chèvre on the left. The ease of access to the Poubelles Couloir means that it is quite often skied. However, the narrowness of the top section of the couloir and the banks on either side make it rather delicate if the snow is hard. If you fall, you will go into the steep rock sides of the couloir…

88.a   Chapeau Couloir (AD). From Argentière take the Lognan cable-car and the Bochard gondola and follow the Pendant pistes. Now there is a long diagonal traverse beneath the west ridge of the Aiguille à Bochard to join the large combe. Stay left so as to traverse as high as possible towards a shoulder, and now climb up for a few metres. This impressive looking couloir is quite steep at the beginning (35-40°/450m). Try to stay on the left bank and pick a route that uses the best snow conditions. The final section is crossed by a rock band (ice-fall). Traverse left just above to join the Chalet du Chapeau. Follow the track that goes to Le Lavancher and the road to Argentière (bus) or the cross-country ski tracks to Chamonix (sign on left, at the beginning of the Le Lavancher track, via the Arveyron climbing area). This couloir is orientated to the west and therefore receives lots of sun in the afternoon. Its snow is transformed very early in the season. Beware of avalanches above the bottom ice-fall.

TALÈFRE-LESCHAUX

PRACTICAL INFORMATION

Chamonix Tourist Office: 04 50 53 00 24 / www.chamonix.com
Compagnie des Guides: 04 50 53 00 88 / www.cieguides-chamonix.com
Ass. Int. Guides du Mont Blanc: 04 50 53 27 05 / www.guides-du-mont-blanc.com
Summits: 04 50 53 50 14 / www.summits.fr
Office de Haute Montagne: 04 50 23 22 08 / www.ohm-chamonix.com
PGHM: 04 50 53 16 89
Weather forecast: 08 92 68 02 74 / www.meteo.fr
Snow report: 08 92 68 10 20

SKI LIFTS

Aiguille du Midi: 04 50 53 30 80 / reservations: 08.36.68.00.67 /
www.aiguilledumidi.fr
Montenvers: 04 50 53 12 54

ROAD ACCESS

From Annecy, Geneva or Sallanches follow the A40 (or N205)
to Chamonix.

We are now on the south side of the huge and austere rocky walls that make up the north faces of the Aiguille Verte, the Droites and the Courtes. We leave behind us the vertiginous ice slopes that fall straight down to the Argentière Glacier. But don't for a minute think that things are going to be easier on this side, because that certainly isn't the case! Whichever side you are on, the slopes here are just steep. Neverthless, the history of extreme skiing has made light work of these south and west faces. Whether it's the Charpoua

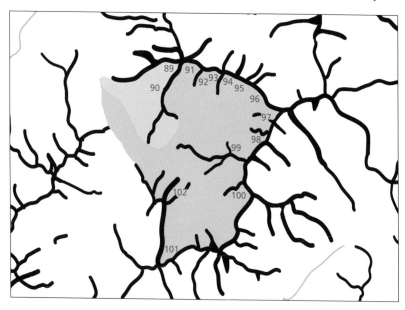

Previous page: Climbing up to the Périades Bivouac.

cirque, where Jean-Marc Boivin and others pioneered routes, or the south faces of the Droites and the Courtes, nothing is as it seems. These routes are consistently exposed, and so to the risks of the routes themselves you should add those that their orientation brings (rock fall, avalanches…). Although accessing these routes was made a little bit easier by the construction of the Aiguille du Midi cable-car and the Montenvers railway, few of them can be done in a day. Moreover, some of these areas, such as the Courtes Glacier, are very broken up and crevassed which makes accessing them quite a hit and miss affair… The Talèfre Glacier has receded so far since 2000 that you can now avoid the dangerous and tiresome trudge up the Leschaux Glacier moraine. This convenient gap in the glacier means that, on the climb up, you can easily get to the foot of the Pierre à Béranger via the west face of the old line of moraine. The descent, down the right bank, is even easier still. Don't let this picture of ease and comfort fool you, the skiing is hard here and these are 'real' mountains! To ski here you have to be an experienced mountaineer as well as skier. All that said, this area has great routes to ski, to dream about and to remember for a long time to come… One of the main reasons I like coming to this area so much is the fact that it has been the scene of so many legendary first ascents. You cannot fail to admire the pioneering first ascents of the British adventurers such as Mummery, Hudson and Whymper, who were led by such accomplished guides as Almer, Biner, Burgener and Croz. That's not forgetting, of course, Armand Charlet who, later on, was to become so fascinated by the Aiguille Verte and its surrounding peaks. Just for the record, Armand Charlet had 100 ascents of the Aiguille Verte to his name, 16 of which were first ascents with clients.

MOUNTAIN HUTS

Ref.22 ▪ Charpoua Hut (2841m, AD)
Private hut (reservations in the summer season through Compagnie des Guides de Chamonix), open in winter, 12 places

From Chamonix take the Aiguille du Midi cable-car and descend the Vallée Blanche (route 120) to around 2000m. At the level of the Charpoua moraine follow the old access route to the hut via the left bank of the couloir or, still following the old access route, join the line of moraine of the Rognon de la Charpoua (ladders below the hut). If the conditions on the Vallée Blanche are not good (beginning of winter, open crevasses…), you can join the access route described above from the Montenvers station.

⚑ 3790m   ⏱ 3¹ᐟ²hrs

↗ 840m

↘ 1790m

Ref.23 ▪ Couvercle Hut (2684m, AD-) via the Aiguille du Midi
CAF, 151 places, often guardianed in the spring (May weekends), winter room (30 places), tel: 04 50 53 16 94 (04 50 47 23 99 when not guardianed)

From Chamonix take the Aiguille du Midi cable-car and descend the Vallée Blanche (route 120). Pass the Salle à Manger beneath the Requin Hut and join the

Couvercle Hut

Leschaux Glacier (2130m). Climb up and left on the glacier and traverse towards the high moraine line on the right bank. Head up and left of the moraine via the depression whose sides get more pronounced and leave the depression via a steep section to the right. Go left and round the Pierre à Béranger (2466m) and follow the slope that gets steeper and which overlooks the small valley where the Talèfre Glacier used to finish in the 1980s. Join the Talèfre Glacier a little before 2600m. For the Couvercle Hut join the right bank, climbing slightly up the middle of the glacier, and climb up the line of moraine opposite in a steep traverse leftwards. You will get to the winter room in 15 minutes. Once there is sufficient snow cover, on the descent you can go right of the snout of the Talèfre Glacier (sections of 35°). However, watch out for snow slides and lumps of ice coming down the right flank. Otherwise descend via the same route you took up.

⛳ 3790m   ⊙ 3h

↗ 540m   ↘ 1660m

Ref.23 ▪ Couvercle Hut via Montenvers (AD–)

This access route, via Montenvers (open in winter), is generally used in spring when the Vallée Blanche is no longer in condition or in winter when the weather is not great or there are too many people at the Midi. At the upper Montenvers station descend to the Mer de Glace (gondola, ice cave) and after a long climb cross the rocky junction with the Leschaux Glacier. You can also walk up from Chamonix via the Mottets track (2hrs).

⛳ 1909 m   ⊙ 3h

↗ 1030 m

Ref.24 ▪ Leschaux Hut (2431m, PD)
CAF, 16 places, not guardianed in winter or spring but open (to be enlarged in 2005)

From Chamonix via the Aiguille du Midi and the Vallée Blanche (route 120), join the Leschaux Glacier and climb up it. Towards the right bank after 2km of vir-

Leschaux Hut

tually flat ground you should spot the hut below a rock band, 80m above the glacier and between two deep avalanche couloirs. You can access the hut via either
the left-hand couloir (steep traverse) or the right-hand one (one move of III, rope
in place).

  3790m   2¹/²hrs

  290m   1660m

Ref.25 ■ Requin Hut (2516m, PD)
Cie des Guides & CAF, 50 places, guardianed in winter and spring, tel: 04 50
53 16 96 (04 50 47 21 89 when not guardianed)

From Chamonix, via the Aiguille du Midi, descend the Vallée Blanche (route 120)
or the Envers du Plan. After the Géant ice-fall, at around 2550m, head left. Climb
up from Montenvers in 2hrs.

  3790m   1¹/²hrs

  1280m

Ref.26 ■ Périades Bivouac (3450m, AD)
2 to 3 places, blankets

This looks like a Canadian tent made out of wood! It is uphill and west of the
Brèche Puiseux (route 105) on a steep rocky ridge.

  3790m   4-5hrs

  1000m

  1350m

89   AIGUILLE VERTE   4122m
Y Couloir   TD+

  3790m   March-April   50-55°/300m

  D1 + D2: 640m + 1280m   176   3

  D1 + D2: 1790m + 2370m   D1 + D2: 4 + 6hrs   HP

  South-west   5.4

In July 1973, after having finished our guide's course, Patrick Vallençant and I
had to turn back during our first attempt on the Y Couloir before bad weather
set in. A further attempt the following spring, after having come down the Vallée
Blanche, had to be abandoned by the time we got to the bergschrund again
because of the weather. Finally, on 3rd July 1977, I had soloed past the lower wall
but decided to turn back at the Y itself as the snow had not refrozen sufficiently
the night before. That same day, however, Daniel Chauchefoin managed to descend the south face of the Courtes in summer conditions. He was successful
despite a few hairy moments caused by soft snow avalanches (even though he
was attached to a rope on rappel!). The first descent of the left-hand branch was

done by Jean-Marc Boivin on 27th February 1985. Eric Bellin snowboarded the right-hand branch a few years later.

The majestic Aiguille Verte

D1   From Chamonix, via the Aiguille du Midi and the Vallée Blanche (route 120), climb to the Charpoua Hut via ref.22 (open, blankets).

D2   From the Charpoua Hut and via the headland that quickly joins the glacier, climb up the west-facing section of the glacier to the steep couloir below the bergschrund (3380m) at the back of the combe. In 1977, the rock wall above the bergschrund could be crossed from left to right, or at its centre (60°/60m), or more easily via a small couloir to the right follo-wed by a long horizontal traverse left. Above this, the slope becomes less steep and splits at around 3700m. Continue straight forward. The couloir gets very steep between rocks (chimney beneath a large block jammed between the rocks). A final easy snowy headland takes you to the Moine ridge near the summit. The left-hand branch is slightly less steep (50° below the Sans Nom Ridge) but exposed.

On the descent, the gradient exceeds 55°/300m at the top of the slope and, if the gully is very deep, you will need a rope. Lower down the slope is never more than 45°/300m. The lower wall can, on the rare occasion, have enough snow cover to allow you to side-slip down it. If not, you will need to set up one or two rappels to get past it and the bergschrund. The rest of the route is 'easy' and you follow the route you took up from La Charpoua hut.

The Charpoua face of the 'ecclesiastical' chain

89.a   Brèche du Cardinal, west couloir (3497m, D). Climb up the Charpoua Glacier and head under the Cardinal then right, into the couloir. Climb up the left bank to the notch at 3497m. The central gully (50°/400m, 5.1) can make the descent quite delicate. You could choose to wait for the sun to soften the snow (beginning of the afternoon) but by that time the slopes beneath the Charpoua will be more dangerous. The first descent of the Brèche was by Daniel Chauchefoin and Pierre Tardivel on 19th April 1981.

89.b   Petit Dru, south-west couloir of the brèche (ED+). 450m with sections of more than 50°, very exposed and with a long obligatory rappel. First done by Jean-Marc Boivin (17 April 1987, with a heli-drop). This is a very 'alpine' route and is not very interesting in terms of the skiing in it.

90   BRÈCHE NONNE-ÉVÊQUE   3306m
South-west Couloir   D+

3790m		February-May		50°-55°/500m
1300m		176, 177		2
4050m		8 to 9hrs		HP
South-west		5.1		

Because of the way it faces this route can be done in a day. Having said that, you have to be quite quick and choose the best time to do it (in winter you have to have a good forecast). After having skied this route, you can spend the night at the Charpoua Hut and try one of the descents described in routes 89.a, 90 and 90.a (Cardinal, Brèche Moine-Nonne).

From Chamonix, via the Aiguille du Midi and the Vallée Blanche (route 120), follow the start of the route that climbs to the Charpoua Hut (see ref.22). Above the moraine head towards the Éperon du Géographe (2512m) and carry on, keeping a little to the right. The cone of snow at the foot of the couloir is easy to spot, whereas the route itself is steep-sided and is less easy to pick out. The lower section can be icy. The Brèche Nonne-Évêque is the only route that can be accessed easily from the Talèfre Glacier (see route 91.a). The descent is serious if the snow is hard. Take a snow anchor (snow stake, plastic bag…) for a possible rappel in the gully at the bottom because there are no spikes among the rocks here. Of the three couloirs here, this is the narrowest and steepest one. First descended by Boivin and Pellegrin on 21st April 1984.

Couloir on the Brèche Nonne-Évêque

90

90.a ▪ Brèche Moine-Nonne (3198m, D). Although this couloir is a little less steep (42°/500m) than the last one, it faces the same way and you follow the same access route from the Charpoua Glacier, up to 2500m, as the previous route. It is also much more skiable (4.3). It was first done by Jean-Marc Boivin on 21st February 1985. This is quite an accessible route for those starting out in extreme skiing and you can put your technique to the test here without running too many risks. Having said that, do take care if the snow is hard as any fall could have serious consequences… As this route faces west you can do it in a day, but only if you access it from this side.

91 AIGUILLE VERTE   4122m
Whymper Couloir   TD+

⌐ 3790m	⬘ May-June	⌐ 45°-55°/550m
⟋ D1 + D2 : 500m + 1430m	📷 176, 182	⚠ 3
⟍ D1 + D2 : 1650m + 3070m	⏱ D1 + D2 : 4 + 9hrs	⊕ HP
⊕ South/south-east	🎿 5.3	

The Swiss skier Sylvain Saudan, helped by the guide Dominique Mollaret and the aspirant guide Pierre Meunier, successfully made the first descent of the Whymper Couloir on 11th June 1968. Having decided to wait until the middle of the day and for the snow to soften, Saudan avoided the afternoon avalanches and descended to below the bergschrund before the climbers. The latter, however, were caught up in a snow slide and after being catapulted into the air they were swept over the couloir's rocky section. Although badly bashed about, they were alive and Pierre Meunier managed to alert the mountain rescue team who took them off the mountain. This proved to be an important date in the history of extreme skiing as it marked the arrival of 'skiing the impossible' for Sylvain, and gave some of the discipline's future adventurers something to dream

Anselme and Edouard Baud, father and son, on the summit of the Aiguille Verte

about... Thus, one weekend in July 1973, during our guide's training scheme, Patrick and Marie-Jo Vallençant and I managed to do the first repeat descent of the Whymper in soft snow and good conditions between 8 and 9 o'clock in the morning. The Whymper can be skied right up to the beginning of summer, but in the spring when there is lots of snow the heat of the sun can set off enormous and deadly avalanches. I repeated this serious descent 28 years later with my son Edouard in July 2001. After having climbed up the Couturier and having skied the first section (first third was icy and the snow in the rest of the couloir was dangerous), we climbed back

Anselme Baud on the start of the Whymper, 1973

up to the summit and set off down the Whymper at the not very favourable time of 11 o'clock in the morning. The skiing at the top of the face was good, but lower down the ground quickly became dangerous as the gullies funnelled the snow slides down the east face. It was certainly quite a 'full' day!

D1 From Chamonix, via the Aiguille du Midi, follow ref.23 to the Couvercle Hut. You can also access the hut from Montenvers (see ref.23.a).

D2 Climb up the moraine and join the right bank of the Talèfre Glacier. Follow the base of the 'ecclesiastical' chain of mountains and go past the foot of the Moine ridge that comes down from the Aiguille Verte (3350m, crevasses). Take care not to set off up a similar looking couloir just after the Cardinal (turn off your head torches to get a better look!). Higher up, from a sloping plateau, you should be able to identify the base of the Whymper Couloir and the bergschrund that you cross on the right. Join a secondary couloir (comes down from the Grande Rocheuse) that has rocks above it. Move back left on to a small headland that you follow for a few metres before continuing up the left bank of the couloir. There are now two or three gullies to cross and then you climb directly up to the Col de la Grande Rocheuse (4050m). The access to and the descent of this peak are not very interesting on skis. You spend most of your time side-slipping diagonally with an ice-axe... But is still quite a special moment to stand on the summit of the Aiguille Verte! The upper section of the start of the couloir becomes steep very quickly (55°/100m). It is funnel-shaped and when the snow is hard it is exposed. Lower down, the right bank is less awkward but the gullies are quite deep. Turn left. You may need to set up a rappel to pass the final section and the bergschrund.

91.a Brèche Nonne-Évêque, east couloir (3306m, AD). From the hut, climb up the moraine on the left bank of the Talèfre Glacier. Pass the Moine and the Nonne and join the second couloir on your left that is snowy (couloirs starts at around 3200m). The top section is steep (almost 50°/30m) and the rest of the couloir has about 150m of great skiing at around 45°. This is the only easy route that takes you from the 'ecclesiastical' ridge to the Charpoua side of the mountain. In addition, this is an excellent place to test your steep skiing technique without objective dangers (4.3, danger level 1).

92   COL ARMAND CHARLET   3998m
South couloir   TD

⌐ 3790m	📖 April-June	53°/200m
D1 + D2: 500m + 1310m	📷 176, 182	⚠ 3
D1 + D2: 1650m + 2950m	D1 + D2: 4 + 8hrs	HP
⊕ South	5.2	

Although the middle section of the south couloir of the Col Armand Charlet is less impressive than the Whymper Couloir, this descent is similar to the latter and there is less risk of rockfall here. In July 1975, after several long months of enforced inactivity (eight days in a coma, three operations and four months in hospital thanks to a single blow to the head from a rock), I wanted to prove to myself that I could go back to extreme skiing. This descent, accompanied by a new approach to risk (before the accident I had a feeling of invincibility even when it came to falling rocks…), was a test that I simply had to take. Thus, I went up to the hut

Start of solo descent of Col Armand Charlet

with some friends and skied this first descent on my own on 6th July 1975, almost a year after my accident on the north face of the Courtes. This descent proved to me that the idea of going back to guiding wasn't just a dream after all, despite the pessimism of the surgeons. The confidence that my family and close friends had in me had not been in vain…

There was also a positive side to the accident. Among other things, I started to be a little more circumspect in my approach to projects and with regards to generally accepted ideas. Was I still not all there after my days in a coma? Well, it's certainly a good 'excuse'!

D1 From Chamonix, via the Aiguille du Midi, follow ref.23 to the Couvercle Hut. You can also access the hut from Montenvers (see ref.23.a).

D2 Follow route 91 to the bottom of the Whymper Couloir. Go past the snow cone and, after a depression, climb to the bergschrund below the Col Armand Charlet. Cross it on the left and climb up the central gully or via the steep slopes to the side of the right bank. Below the summit, it is better to take the steeper couloir that comes down from the east ridge of the Grande Rocheuse as the exit from the direct route leads to a very narrow col. On the descent and depending on how high the cornice is, the slope can reach 54° for several metres. Lower down the slope slackens off in the centre of the couloir, but only the steep slopes on the side can be skied. Take gear to rappel past the high bergschrund (take an ice-axe that you can pull out afterwards or leave a snow anchor). The rest of the descent follows the route you took up or a route directly below the Jardin de Talèfre.

92.a   Col de l'Aiguille Verte, south-west couloir (3796m, D). During an attempt to ski the north face of the col in summer 1974, poor conditions meant that I had to climb back up the 150m of the Argentière face I had skied. Back at the col, and although I didn't really know what the conditions were like on the Talèfre side of the col, my only choice was to ski down that side. There are rock spurs and crumbly bits of rock on either edge of the couloir, which can lead to rockfall. The descent was quick and I rappelled past the high bergschrund. Lower down I rejoined the Jardin de Talèfre via the left bank of the glacier. In fact, even if the bergschrund blocks access to the couloir, it is well worth skiing the slope back down to the glacier below.
Get to the base of the Whymper Couloir (route 91) and continue to the glaciated combe beyond the Aiguille du Jardin. Try to cross the bergschrund on the right, below the depression to the east of the Col de l'Aiguille Verte. Climb up the narrow couloir until you reach the top. You can only ski this route when it has excellent snow cover in the spring. First descent probably by Anselme Baud in July 1974 (45°/300m, sections of 50°, 5.1).

93   LES DROITES   3984m
West summit   TD

3790m		February-May		45°-55°/500m	
D1 + D2: 540m + 1310m		182, 184		3	
D1 + D2: 1650m + 2230m		D1 + D2: 4 + 8hrs		HP	
South-west		5.2			

The south face of the Droites was the scene of a superb descent by two famous names in extreme skiing. One fine Sunday in May 1982, Daniel Chauchefoin and Pierre Tardivel skied the south-west face beneath the west summit of the Droites (variant route). They managed to ski this very committing and technical route, which is not obvious from below, thanks to very rare favourable snow conditions. To be successful on these kinds of routes you quite often have to wait, sometimes even years. So, in a discipline that some consider the privilege of the reckless or the mad, they are in fact quite reasonable and patient...

D1   From Chamonix, via the Aiguille du Midi, follow ref.23 to the Couvercle Hut. You can also access the hut from Montenvers (see ref.23.a).

D2   From the Couvercle Hut pass the steep moraine and join the Talèfre Glacier by traversing above the Jardin de Talèfre. Now head towards the central spur of

the Droites and go round it on the left (crevasses and bergschrund). You can cross the rock barrier on the right via a snow bar and join the lower section of the west summit. If there is enough snow, you can stay right of the lower rock spur and, 100m higher up, cross it on the left. Climb up left and pass two ribs of rock to continue in the upper section that almost faces due west. The final couloir finishes among the rocks on the summit ridge.

On the descent, if the northerly wind has filled the south-west face with snow, the face can be very skiable. Nevertheless, initial observation of the route from the right bank of the glacier (below the Évêque) is

Talèfre face of the Droites

essential, as the couloir can have deep gullies in it. Moreover, it is also essential to check out your descent route as you climb up. This is an ambitious route to ski given the objective dangers and the highly committing technical level, but it

From the Verte to the Courtes

is the only logical route of descent from the western summit of the Droites on skis.

93.a ▪ East summit of the Droites (4000m, D+). The most direct route follows route 93 in the beginning to get to the couloir south-west of the eastern spur. From the top of the couloir you cross several gullies and ramps on the right to get to the bottom of the east face. There is an easier and longer access route: follow route 94 to the Col des Droites and at around 3600m, head to your left to get to the bottom of the east face (35 to 40°, small rock spurs and snowy gullies). Continue a little to your left to join quite quickly a rocky area towards the ridge that you climb up (III for 80m). Climb a final snowy face and then follow a ridge that leads to the rocks on the summit. The ski descent starts a few metres below the rocks. You will need to set up one or two rappels to get past the rocky constriction at around 3800m. Lower down, depending on what you saw on the way up, descend either the south-west couloir (45°/150m) or the huge slope below the Col des Droites. The first descent was by Rémy Lécluse in winter 1987.

94	**COL DES DROITES** **South face**				**3733m** **AD**

⌐	3790m	🏔	February-May	⤵	40°/400m
↗	D1 + D2: 540m + 1040m	📷	182	⚠	2
↘	D1 + D2: 1650m + 2680m	☺	D1 + D2: 4 + 8hrs	⊕	SP
✦	South-west	🎿	4.1		

This route can be done in a day, preferably during a cold spell at the end of winter. If you do it then, you have to be quick and travel light to climb the 1500m before midday to avoid the rapid warming of this south face that can make it very dangerous. Another solution is to sleep at the Requin Hut (open in winter), which means you can access the south-facing slopes of the Droites early in the morning. In both cases, you gain some altitude and save more than an hour of hard work by avoiding the detour to and from the Couvercle Hut.

D1 ▪ From Chamonix, via the Aiguille du Midi, follow ref.23 to the Couvercle Hut.

D2 ▪ Join the glacier and go round the Jardin de Talèfre in the direction of the Glacier des Courtes. Gradually move back left (towards the main cone at the bottom of the col), avoiding the heavily crevassed section between 3000m and 3100m. You quite easily cross the bergschrund at around 3300m and zigzag up to the col, if the snow is good enough, or else climb straight up the slope using crampons. The top part of the slope is a bit steeper. On the way down, you choose from various lines of descent and your choice of route will depend on the different snow conditions. Watch out for the gullies that can often be deep in spring. Stay quite high on the Talèfre Glacier and, via the left bank, rejoin ref.23.a (access to the Couvercle Hut via right bank). The first descent was by Louis Lachenal and Maurice Lenoir on 21st April 1946.

95   LES COURTES   3856m
South-west face   AD

⚑ 3790m	▨ May-June	⌐ 40°-45°/550m
⬈ D1 + D2 : 540m + 1150m	🖸 182	⚠ 2
⬂ D1 + D2 : 1650m + 2790m	◐ D1 + D2 : 4 + 9hrs	⊕ SP
✦ West	✗ 4.3	

The summit of the Courtes has an 'airy' feel to it and the slopes of this magnificent mountain act as a magnet to ski-mountaineers. Thus, Daniel Chauchefoin has skied several first descents here. The principles that guide this unassuming and efficient skier from Annecy, are that steep skiing should be fun and in some way in harmony with nature. He is another of the great names from 1977, the year of all the magnificent first descents. Among others, he skied first descents on the west face of the Buet, the Diable Couloir on Mont Blanc du Tacul, the Mallory on the Aiguille du Midi, the Austrian Route on the Courtes and the south-west face of the central spur on the Droites (with Pierre Tardivel). Also a guide, in his day he was a brilliant climber on the limestone crags in the Annecy region and put up numerous high quality and astonishingly difficult routes in the 1970s and 80s.

D1   From Chamonix, via the Aiguille du Midi and the Vallée Blanche (route 120), follow ref.23 to the Couvercle Hut.

D2   The next day, follow route 94 and cross the bergschrund below the south face of the Col des Droites at around 3300m. Head right to get to a first slight ridge on the face. Now head straight up and then right again and traverse beneath the Tour des Courtes to reach the summit ridge. The start of the ridge is

Les Courtes and Le Triolet

exposed and above the north face. Descend from the ridge onto the south/south-west face (45° for a few metres) and continue, keeping close to the route you took up. The top section is difficult and committing and there is a traverse across steep and quite broken ground (possible rocky ribs).

95.a Col de la Tour des Courtes, south face (3720m, D+). The couloir here is narrow and the gully that runs down the centre of it will probably pose the greatest problems (sections of 50°). It is often only a matter of chance or patience that conditions are good… So, all that it then takes is to be in the right place at the right time, not to lose your nerve and to make sensible decisions. The first descent was by Daniel Chauchefoin on 20th June 1977 (40-45°/550m).

96	**LES COURTES** South face			**3856m** TD

꒐	3790m	꒐	May-June	꒐	40°-45°/700m
꒐	D1 + D2: 540m + 1170m	꒐	182, 184		sections of 55°
꒐	D1 + D2: 1650m + 2810m	꒐	D1 + D2: 4 + 9hrs	⚠	3
꒐	South	꒐	5.2	꒐	HP

In the world of extreme skiing, the Courtes are inextricably associated with not only Daniel Chauchefoin but also Pierre Tardivel. Pierre, also from Annecy, has recently skied two superb new routes here, dedicated to his wife and daughter. This, of course, was not Pierre's first trip to the Courtes and he already has first descents on the north-east couloir of the Aiguille Chenavier, the north-east spur and the north-east couloir of the Courtes, the Col de la Tour des Courtes to his name… As to the rest of the Massif and among his other notable firsts, his superb descents of the Col de la Brenva and the Grand Pilier d'Angle once again pushed back the limits of what was thought possible in extreme skiing.

D1 From Chamonix, via the Aiguille du Midi, follow ref.23 to the Couvercle Hut. You can also access the hut from Montenvers (see ref.23.a).

D2 Even though, seen from the hut, it looks quite skiable, it is still a huge route that should not be undertaken without great caution. Accordingly, you are not obliged to climb up the route that the descent follows, bearing in mind the fact that the lower rock bar, above the sometimes high bergschrund, can be difficult to cross. Therefore, I prefer to follow the normal route up (see route 95).
Starting at the summit, the descent route starts in a couloir that faces slightly south-west. Follow this couloir to get to the large face and keep heading right until you reach an obvious headland right at the bottom. There are a few more metres to cross diagonally and then there is a long rappel (50m) past some small rock bands and the bergschrund. The first descent was by Daniel Chauchefoin and Pierre Tardivel on 4th March 1979, the second by Edouard Baud and Benoît Fanara in April 2003.

96.a South/south-west couloir (D+). This is very direct, and deep and steep-sided high (especially at the bottom). It was christened 'Couloir Angélique' by Pierre Tardivel who did the first descent on 25th May 1999 (45-50°/600m).

96.b   South couloir of the Aiguille Croulante (D). More skiable that its neigh-bour, this couloir, especially the upper section, is difficult. If the snow is hard enough I recommend climbing up on foot. On the other hand, it is less exposed to rock fall than the Couloir Angélique. It has an average gradient of 40-45°/500m and was des-cended for the first time by Pierre Tardivel and Fabien Meyer on 26th April 2000.

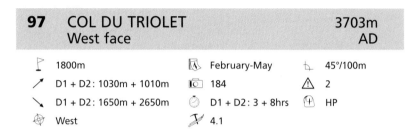

97   COL DU TRIOLET   3703m
West face   AD

⚐	1800m	🏔	February-May	⤵	45°/100m
↗	D1 + D2 : 1030m + 1010m	📷	184	⚠	2
↘	D1 + D2 : 1650m + 2650m	🕐	D1 + D2 : 3 + 8hrs	⊕	HP
✦	West	🎿	4.1		

Also known as Pointe Isabelle, this route has declined in popularity since acces-sing the final section became more difficult. Until 1981, helicopters were allowed to drop skiers at the col. However, the French President Valéry Giscard d'Estaing outlawed heli-drops in the Massif at this time and since then this magnificent 'belvedere', or panoramic viewpoint, is only visited by the most determined ski-mountaineers. The views on all sides here are superb: there are the sunny valleys of Italy at your feet and in the distance the Swiss 4000-metre giants of the Oberland and the Valais regions. A quick traverse to the northern extremity of the plateau (rocky point marked 3719m on the map), gives you an amazing view loo-king out over the whole of the Argentière Basin. With its stunning views of the tapering narrow crests of the surrounding north faces and the imposing Mont Blanc Massif, this is one of the best spots in the Alps. Add another hour (there and back) on to the timings for this route, if you want to climb to the summit of Pointe Isabelle itself (3753m). This entails a short bit of mixed climbing up the west face followed by a short rappel, or down climb, to get back to the Col du Triolet.

D1   From Chamonix, go to the Montenvers ref.23.a to the Couvercle Hut or via the Aiguille du Midi and the Vallée Blanche (route 120), follow ref.23.

D2   You can access the Talèfre Glacier by traversing across the moraine higher up (2650m), but if there is not enough snow you will have to retrace your steps sligh-tly back to your approach route. You reach the beginning of the Courtes Glacier (a few crevasses) via the middle of the glacier. Climb up to the plateau (3400m), staying quite close to the rock faces. There have been crevasses and seracs guarding the access to this area since the 1980s, so it is rare to be able to climb directly up the glacier. I prefer to climb up via the right-hand spur, which requires basic mountai-neering training (have to use mountaineering equipment in the first section). After a huge dome (crevasses), you join the final, easy section below the Col du Triolet. Your line of descent depends on the difficulties presented by the upper section, and can vary greatly from year to year. Don't underestimate this route: it is long and requires mountaineering skills. If you choose to descend via the glacier (a little bit less exposed than via the spur), you will quite probably have to rappel past the seracs (take snow anchor or plank of wood). At the end of the winter, it is possible to descend the right bank of the Talèfre Glacier down to the Leschaux Glacier.

After having rappelled past the Triolet seracs

97.a Petite Aiguille du Triolet, west/south-west face (3806m, AD). Short slope of 45°/80m, first descent by Louis Agnel in 1941.

98 COL DE TALÈFRE 3544m
West Couloir D

3790m	February-May	40-45°/350m
D1 + D2: 540m + 860m	188	2
D1 + D2: 1650m + 2500m	D1 + D2: 4 + 8hrs	HP
West	4.3	

The Col de Talèfre is not often skied, although it is quite often visited by mountaineers on crystal-hunting trips. Up here you never tire of the magnificent views towards Mont Blanc and the Chamonix Aiguilles. This is another good reason to plan to ski this descent in the morning sunlight, even if the route itself is not as rewarding as its neighbours. The fact that this route faces west means that it can also be done from the Requin Hut which is further away but guardianed in the winter.

D1 From Chamonix, via the Aiguille du Midi and the Vallée Blanche (route 120), follow ref.23 to the Couvercle Hut.

D2 Descend to the Talèfre Glacier and traverse east to climb up to the small glaciated cirque below the Col de Talèfre (crevasses in the steep section that you cross towards the left). The bergschrund is not very big in the spring and gives

Southern part of the Talèfre basin

access to a narrow couloir. Climb up this couloir to the col. From the col there are impressive views over the Triolet Glacier on the Italian side of the chain. It is safer to descend after the hard snow has started to melt a bit.

99   POINTE SUP. PIERRE À JOSEPH   3472m
North/north-east couloir   TD–

⌐	3790m	▣ May-June		↳	50°/350m
↗	1330m	▣ 188, 189, 190		⚠	2
↘	2420m	◔ 8-9hrs		⊕	HP
✦	North-east	✗ 5.1			

1977 marked a defining moment in the history of extreme skiing. Having been born more or less as a result of the exploits of the Swiss (from the Valais region) skier Sylvain Saudan, the discipline literally exploded on to the scene during the winter season of that year and the following summer. The majority of the glaciated slopes were in excellent condition, and what had hitherto been considered impossible all of a sudden seemed possible after all. Thus, the Cordier Couloir on the Aiguille Verte (Détry), the Mallory on the Aiguille du Midi (Détry, Chauchefoin, Baud), the ridge on the Aiguille Blanche de Peuterey (Baud, Vallençant), the north face of the Aiguille du Plan (Boivin, Giacomini), the Austrian Route on the Courtes (Chauchefoin) and the north face of the Chardonnet (Détry, Boivin) were all skied for the first time that year. The slopes at over 55° were also starting to be chalked up. Routes following obvious couloirs were becoming more and more tortuous, crossing rock bands and areas full of seracs. To skiing skills, you had to add those of the mountaineer (the use of arti-

Climbing up to the Couvercle Hut

103.a

ficial aids such as rappels were becoming more common). Since then the winters simply haven't been comparable, but extreme skiing continues to attract more and more practitioners thanks also to the impressive evolution of the equipment.

From Chamonix, via the Aiguille du Midi, follow ref.23 to the Talèfre Glacier. Head east via its left bank and pass a first north spur of the Aiguille Pierre à Joseph (2904m), leaving it on your right. Now go round a second, south/south-east, spur, again leaving it on your right, and join the large combe at the foot of the north face of the Aiguille de Talèfre. On your right, you should be able to just make out the cone at the bottom of the north/north-east couloir. Cross the bergschrund on the right and climb the slope to the summit. Follow the same route on the descent. The snow is often in good condition (cold, well protected from the sun). Watch out for the rocky outcrops at the top.

99.a   Col des Aiguilles de Talèfre (3580m, ED). This face (also know as the north face of the Aiguille de Talèfre) is rarely in condition. The first half of the route is steep (55°/300m) and the there is the top of a spur on the left that is less sustained (45°/50). The final section is over 50°/100m and is often icy. We don't know the details of the true first descent of this route as the skier fell to the bottom of the route. As luck would have it, he recovered from his injuries. Subsequent attempts have started somewhere down the slope and have avoided the top section! Therefore, if this north face is not in condition, it is recommended that you descend via the slope opposite (see route 99.c).

99.b   Descent via the Pierre à Joseph Glacier (D+). This is a nice-looking slope and it starts at 50°/80m and then becomes 45°/250m. After the couloir follow route 99.c.

99.c   Aiguille de Talèfre, west face (TD). From the Leschaux Hut, climb up

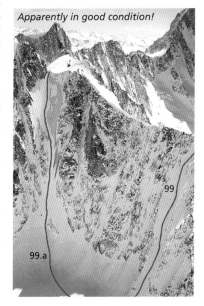

Apparently in good condition!

99

99.a

Aiguille de Talèfre and the Aiguille de l'Éboulement

the right bank of the Pierre à Joseph Glacier. Via the back of the glaciated cirque, leave the slopes below the Col des Aiguilles de Talèfre on the left and join the south-west couloir on the right. The start of the climb is not easy to identify. This is a very aesthetic route in a very wild setting, and you have to expect a few difficulties due to the irregular snow cover in the area. The best conditions are usually to be found towards the end of the winter (lots of cold snow!). First descent by Patrick Gabarrou (45-50°/450m).

100   AIGUILLE DE L'ÉBOULEMENT   3599m
South couloir   D

⚑ 3790m		🏔 February-May		⌐ 40°-45°/500m
↗ D1 + D2: 280m + 1170m		📷 190		⚠ 2
↘ D1 + D2: 1650m + 2250m		⏱ D1 + D2: 4 + 8hrs		✚ HP
✦ South		🎿 5.1		

This couloir is a little bit off the beaten track and is tucked away at the back of a small glaciated cirque where only a few mountaineers and skiers ever venture. On the other hand, you get a good view of the couloir from the Mont Mallet Glacier and its straight line is quite attractive to skiers, and seen face on it is impressive! The first descent of this route by a visually impaired skier was probably by Gérard Mang (roped to a guide) in the spring of 1997. That same spring Mang also skied the west couloir of the Brèche Puiseux, the Chevalier Couloir, the Amône, and Persévérance among others. He deserves at least the same honours as the most famous of the extreme skiers: you try turning on a 50°-slope with your eyes closed and you'll understand!…

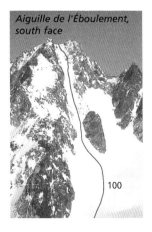

Aiguille de l'Éboulement, south face

*South couloir of the
Aiguille de l'Éboulement*

D1 From Chamonix, via the Aiguille du Midi and the Vallée Blanche, go to the Leschaux Hut (see ref.24).

D2 Descend back on to the glacier and head towards the Petites Jorasses to go round the crevassed area at around 2600m. Climb up the left branch of the glacier where you will find the couloir hiding between two rock spurs. There is generally enough snow here and the climb up does not usually pose too many problems. The steep upper section (52°/80m) slackens off as you arrive at the small col to the left of the summit. On the descent, owing to its orientation, it is better to wait for the sun to soften the snow that has refrozen in the night, even though the slope often has cold powder snow in it. If you are really fit and you catch the first lift up, you can ski this route in a day, and it can be done up to the end of April. The first descent was by Bertrand Delafosse, Daniel Lauzier and Jean-Pierre Mansard in July 1977.

101 COL DU MONT MALLET   3481m
East face   PD

⚑ 3790m		🏔 January-April		⤵ 30°-35°/200m	
⬈ D1 + D2: 0m + 1340m		📷 192		⚠ 1	
⬊ D1 + D2: 1270m + 2820m		🕐 D1 + D2: 1 + 9hrs		🏔 SP	
✦ East		🎿 3.1			

Place names are the collective memory of an area: they tell us about the local natural environment, how the land is used and what it represents in the popular imagination. Thus, some of the names of the peaks in the Mont Blanc Massif may sound a little strange: Mont Maudit ('Accursed Mountain'), Combe Maudite ('Accursed Combe'), Aiguilles du Diable ('Devil's Needles')... You have to remember that only a few generations ago this massif wasn't yet a tourist haven, rather a place of fear, a place that brought more bad luck than good (avalanches, landslides, floods...). They brought so much bad fortune, these accursed mountains were surely the playground of the Devil and his helpers?... Times have changed, yet some of these names still bear witness to the beliefs of the past.

Mont Mallet (left) and the Capucin Couloir (centre)

D1 From Chamonix, via the Aiguille du Midi and the Vallée Blanche, follow ref.25 to the Requin Hut.

D2 Continue descending on the right bank of the glacier until you get to the junction with the Leschaux Glacier (2140m). There is now a long climb up this glacier (3km to the bend to the right) and when you reach about 2500m the route heads south-west and you get to the Mont Mallet Glacier. Don't hesitate to traverse higher and to the left to avoid the crevassed area before heading towards the Capucin du Tacul. You soon come to a large steep slope after which you will see a headland further left, which you follow. Go past the Brèche des Périades and then the Brèche Puiseux (Périades Bivouac is at the top of the ridge on the right). The Col du Mont Mallet is on the right-hand edge of a small glacial plateau. You should be on the descent quite early, before the sun melts the snow too much. You can more of less follow the route you took up. First descent by Armand Charlet and Henri Fournier in 1927.

Col des Grandes Jorasses

101.a   Mont Mallet bergschrund (3800m, PD). Continue up the glaciated combe, which is steeper but the snow is colder, to one of the higher crevasses on the glacier. If you want to carry on up the Aiguille de Rochefort you will have to cross a very high, sometimes double, bergschrund (extra 2hrs if the section is passable). Lower down, the descent is the same as route 101.

Bergschrund on Mont Mallet

101.b Col des Grandes Jorasses (3825m, D). Spend the night at the Leschaux Hut (see ref.24). Follow the access route to the Col du Mont Mallet (route 101) until 3500m. Now head left and climb up a large slope. The final section (50°/100m) is exposed, often icy and is rarely skied. The gradient of the slope above the bergschrund is 45-50°/100m. The first skied descent was by the Italian mountaineer and journalist Guido Tonella and two friends, in 1931.

102 COL DU TACUL   3337m
North couloir on the Capucin   D+

⚑ 3790m	🏔 February-May	⌐ 45°-50°/300m
↗ 920m	📷 192	⚠ 2
↘ 3660m	🕐 8hrs	⊕ HP
✳ North/north-east	🎿 5.1	

The Capucin Couloir is one of the rare few descents that can be skied without necessarily seeing it first, on the way up. There are several reasons for this:
it faces north and this means that the snow will always be cold the entire length of this deep couloir that is also well shaded;
- owing to the often poor quality, crumbly and unstable snow here, the climb up this north face can be long and tiresome, which explains why it is not often used on the approach;
- sliding some snow down from the top of the slope is quite an effective way of clearing it before you set off and protecting yourself to a certain extent from avalanches;
- Accessing this route from the Aiguille du Midi is not only very convenient, but is also an athletic and alpine route in a remarkable area where your tech-

At the start of the Capucin Couloir

nical skills will be put to the test. For all these reasons, I ski this descent almost every year with my clients and trainee guides from ENSA.

From Chamonix, via the Aiguille du Midi and the Vallée Blanche (route 120), go to the Salle à Manger and climb up via route 104 to the bergschrund on the Col du Tacul. Climb straight up and head towards the notch on the right.

If there is good snow cover, you can ski the whole couloir from the top. If the conditions are not very good, especially if there are lots of tracks in it and exposed rocks, you will need a hand-rail (rappel) below the col. Just after the start of the descent, the slope is very steep (nearly 55°/50m) and the couloir is very narrow. The slope soon widens out on the right and there are rock ribs, which allow you to regain your balance and get your breath back. Lower down, the slope opens up and is less steep at the junction with the left couloir. The bottom of the couloir (possible gully) is about 40°. Cross the bergschrund towards the right. The slope remains sustained through a nice series of turns as it is sheltered from the sun by the Capucin du Tacul. Follow the right bank, then move to the centre at around 2600m and then go to the left bank at the end of this steep-sided Capucin Glacier. Now rejoin the Leschaux Glacier and the Vallée Blanche (route 120).

GÉANT

PRACTICAL INFORMATION

Chamonix Tourist Office: 04 50 53 00 24 / www.chamonix.com
Compagnie des Guides: 04 50 53 00 88 / www.cieguides-chamonix.com
Ass. Int. Guides du Mont Blanc: 04 50 53 27 05 / www.guides-du-mont-blanc.com
Summits: 04 50 53 50 14 / www.summits.fr
Office de Haute Montagne: 04 50 23 22 08 / www.ohm-chamonix.com
PGHM: 04 50 53 16 89
Weather forecast: 08 92 68 02 74 / www.meteo.fr
Snow report: 08 92 68 10 20

SKI LIFTS

Aiguille du Midi: 04 50 53 30 80 / reservations: 08.36.68.00.67 /
www.aiguilledumidi.fr
Montenvers: 04 50 53 12 54

ROAD ACCESS

From Annecy, Geneva or Sallanches follow the A40 (or N205) to
Chamonix.

The Vallée Blanche forms the backbone of this area and it can be accessed quickly from the Aiguille du Midi, the starting point for routes on the Géant Glacier, the Tacul and the Périades. Unlike the routes in the previous chapter, most of the tours here can be done in a day and the height gains are not excessive (maximum of 900m). Also, in this part of the Massif there is a

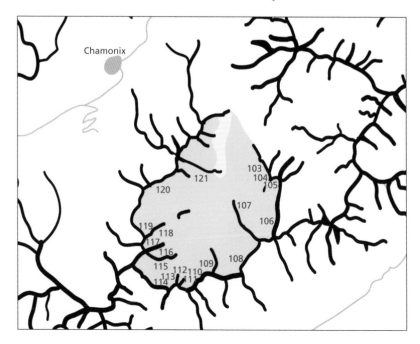

Previous page: Dent du Géant and Grandes Jorasses from the Blanche de Peuterey

broad range of routes, and you will find steep slopes and classic tours next door to each other. For all these reasons, this is a very popular area. There are lots of people on the easy routes by the Aiguilles Marbrées and the Col d'Entrèves, while the Brèche Puiseux area is less popular, but also more and more amateur extreme skiers are trying routes on the Tour Ronde and the big couloirs on the Tacul (Diable, Gervasutti, Jager). However, these figures pale into insignificance compared with the hordes of skiers and boarders who can be found on the world-famous Vallée Blanche from the beginning of the winter right through to the end of May. Indeed, you feel the contrast most strikingly once, with skins on your skis, you start climbing up towards the less accessible routes…

MOUNTAIN HUTS

Ref.27 ◼ Cosmiques Hut (3613m, F)
Private hut, 140 places, guardianed from February to October, tel: 04 50 54 40 16

From the top station of the Aiguille du Midi cable-car descend the exposed north-east ridge. Traverse beneath the south face of the Aiguille du Midi and climb up for 10mins to reach the hut that is easy to spot. In winter you can also stay in the Abri Simond (22 places).

⚐ 3790m	⏱ 30 mins to 1hr
↗ 70m	
↘ 230m	

Ref.10 ◼ Torino Hut (old hut 3371m, new hut 3322m, F)
CAI, new hut (180 places, guardianed in summer, tel: 0165.84.40.34), old hut (70 places, guardianed from December to June, tel: 0165.84.64.84)

From the top station of the Aiguille du Midi cable-car descend the north-east ridge and follow route 108 to the Col des Flambeaux (cross the Vallée Blanche). Go to the top station of the Pointe Helbronner cable-car via the small winter cable-car or ski and walk round the summer hut.

⚐ 3790m	⏱ 2$^{1/2}$hrs
↗ 200m	
↘ 600m	

Ref.25 ◼ Requin Hut (2516m, PD)
Cie des Guides & CAF, 50 places, guardianed in winter and spring, tel: 04 50 53 16 96 (04 50 47 21 89 when not guardianed)

From Chamonix, via the Aiguille du Midi, descend the Vallée Blanche (route 120) or the Envers du Plan. After the Géant ice-fall, at around 2550m, head left and traverse along to the hut.

⚐ 3790m	⏱ 1$^{1/2}$hrs
↘ 1280m	

Ref.26 ▪ **Périades Bivouac (3460m, AD),**
3 places, blankets

Follow route 105 to the Brèche Puiseux. The hut,
also know as the Chevallier Hut, is a little higher
up and to the left.

Périades Bivouac

⚐ 3790m   ⏰ 4-5hrs

↗ 1000m

↘ 1350m

103 AIGUILLE DU TACUL   3444m
North-west shoulder   D

⚐ 3790m	🏔 April-May	⌐ 45°/100m
↗ 920m	📷 189, 198, 202	⚠ 2
↘ 1330m + 2390m	⏰ 7hrs	⊕ SP
✦ West	🎿 4.3	

The Aiguille du Tacul is quick and relatively easy to get to. It is an aesthetic peak
and its massive north-west shoulder is very skiable. Leaving your audience of
admiring onlookers far below you on the Vallée Blanche, all you have to think
about is making great tracks!

From the Aiguille du Midi cable-car descend, via the Vallée Blanche (route 120),
to the Salle à Manger. At around 2420m, traverse right beneath the Séracs du
Géant (Géant Icefall) and climb up the right bank of the Périades Glacier. After
the crevassed area, cross the steep morai-
ne and climb up in the direction of the small
valley that goes to below the col. Pass the
Chandelle, Clocher and the fragile-looking Épée
on your left and continue leftwards. Climb
up the steep slope that leads to the west ridge
and head right above the bergschrund (35°
then 40°/250m). After the snowy saddle and
via the awkward chim-

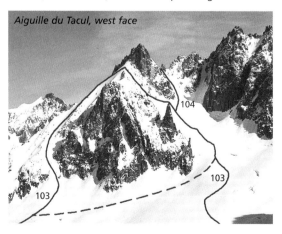

Aiguille du Tacul, west face

neys, you can (rock)climb to the summit of the Aiguille du Tacul (2hrs there and back, not very interesting). Descent: at the start, on the shoulder (3350m), the slope is quite exposed but not too steep. Ski on the slight headland that faces the Aiguille du Grépon the go to the left of the large blocks (3100m). Follow the slope down to the start of the third couloir that faces the Dent du Requin (don't go down the first, second or fourth couloirs as you need to rappel). At the bottom the couloir narrows to a steep gully (40-45°) that is often quite awkward to negotiate because of snow slides. After the bergschrund you can ski the superb slope on the right that leads to the lateral moraine of the Tacul Glacier (Vallée Blanche) or descend the slope immediately opposite the Requin Hut. You can also descend the route that you followed up the mountain or follow route 103.a.

103.a   North/north-east couloir of the point marked 2615m (AD). At the bottom of the west couloir descend right so as to go round the rocky face marked 2680m on the map. Climb up 50m (15mins) to a rock saddle. Via the narrow couloir on the right (40°/150m) or a passage that goes through the rocks on the left-hand saddle, descend on to the large north-east combe. Join the Leschaux Glacier to the right of the moraine. The snow stays cold here...

104 COL DU TACUL   3337m
West face   AD

⚑ 3790m	🗻 January-May	⌐ 40°-45°/200m
↗ 920m	📷 198, 202	⚠ 2
↘ 1330m + 2390m	◷ 6 to 7hrs	⊕ SP
✦ West	🎿 4.1	

This area gets quite a bit of traffic from the start of the winter as there are good views of it from the Vallée Blanche and it is often in good condition from quite early on in the season. You can do this route over two days and take the train up to the Montenvers (open throughout the winter) and go up to the Requin Hut in the late afternoon. An early start the next morning means you can climb the Épée du Tacul, for the photo opportunity, naturally...The climb includes a short pitch of V and you can pull on the loop of rope to do the last move (replaceded in summer 2002). You will need five carabiners and a 50m rope.

From the Aiguille du Midi, descend the Vallée Blanche (route 120) and follow route 103 to the top of the small valley below the Col du Tacul (3150m). Put on your crampons to cross the bergschrund. Now climb up a couloir (wide at first then narrows and steepens up at the top) to the left of the rock spur that separates the north and south cols. The north col, which is a little higher and to the left, gives access to the

Mont Mallet Glacier

ridge that leads to the summit (1 1/2 hr there and back of not very difficult but exposed rock climbing). The south col is also the start of the couloir on the north face, on the Capucin Glacier (route 102).

The descent follows the route you took up and you ski on the right bank to start with. The central gully is often deep in the spring. Go round the Chandelle on the left (crevasses near rocks) and lower down, traverse right as the north-west facing slopes often has good snow (see also route 103.a). Rejoin the Mer de Glace then the end of the Vallée Blanche and Chamonix via Les Mottets.

105 BRÈCHE PUISEUX   3432m
Traverse   AD

⚐ 3790m	⛺ February-May	↳ 45°/50m
↗ 970m	📷 192, 200, 202	⚠ 2
↘ 1330m + 2380m	◔ 7hrs	⊕ HP
✧ North-east	🎿 4.1	

To make the most of this magnificent descent below the Grandes Jorasses, you have to be quite disciplined about sticking to your timetable. It is recommended that you get an early start from the Requin Hut, although the best option is to

South-west couloir of the Brèche Puiseux

ref.26

105.a

Climbing up the south-west couloir

stay the night at the little wooden cabin that is the Périades Bivouac (maximum of 3 places, blankets). This will certainly be a memorable night, and the hut's unique situation allows you the luxury of choosing the best time in the morning to set off through the glistening crystals of the perfect snow on the Mont Mallet Glacier.

The only problem is if it turns out you're not the only group wanting to stay at the Périades Hut that night. One solution to this problem might be to attach a 'reservations card', with the date of your planned trip, to a stake posted at the start of the climb up to the hut. This should help avoid unfortunate surprises and much gnashing of teeth...

From the Aiguille du Midi follow route 120 to the Salle à Manger. At the start, follow route 103 up the right bank of the Périades Glacier, then head east up to 2900m. Go round to the right of the isolated central spur (crevasses and steep step) to reach the cone at the foot of the couloir and the bergschrund. In the centre of the couloir there is a gully that is often quite deep, which means you will have to use the steeper slopes on the right. The middle section is less steep, but the last few metres steepen up again. From the col there is a short steep descent (very narrow for 50m above the bergschrund) that joins the magnificent route on the Mont Mallet Glacier (see route 101).

105.a   South-west couloir (D+). The gradient given for this slope (45°/350m) is based on the average slope of the central gully. However, it is more often the case that you will use the slopes on either side of the gully and they exceed 50° at the top and above the bergschrund, which can be wide open in the winter. This couloir is not often used on the descent and the majority of the visitors here traverse the mountain via the Mont Mallet Glacier.

106 ÉPAULE DU MONT MALLET   3800m
West slope   D+

⚐	3790m	▨	April-May	⌐	45°-50°/450m
↗	1340m	📷	202	⚠	2
↘	1330m + 2000m	◔	8 to 9hrs	⌂	HP
✦	West	⚒	5.1		

The 'Pan de Rideau' (large slope on a face) on Mont Mallet was descended for the first time in June 1977, by Jean-Marc Boivin and Patrick Gabarrou. An enormous amount of snow had fallen that winter, a number of routes were skied for the first time and the west face was also in excellent condition. Will we be able to ski it for much longer? After a dozen hot and dry years (little snow in winter, except for February 1999), dare we believe that the snowy seasons of long ago will ever come back or are we the powerless witnesses of the effects of global

Mont Mallet and the Dent du Géant

warming? In any case, there was definitely a marked improvement in the air quality in the valley while the Mont Blanc Tunnel was closed. Can we seriously allow ourselves to continue polluting the Alps for much longer? From the tourist's pleasure at arriving in Chamonix to the local's pride in his alpine home, these are all reactions to the being in the mountain environment. Thus, we all have a responsibility to help to protect this precious heritage for future generations.

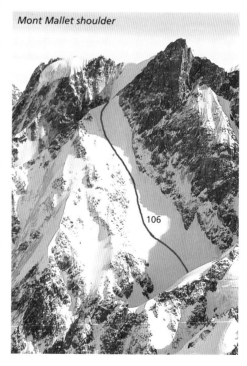

Mont Mallet shoulder

From the Aiguille du Midi follow route 120 to the Salle à Manger, then follow route 105 to 2900m. Now climb up the Périades Glacier towards the Dent du Géant. Some winter the crevasses can be quiet open, which makes accessing the upper combe at around 3300m quite tricky. Head due east on the large slope below Mont Mallet, towards the rocky outcrop marked 3769m. Uphill of this point you join a snowy ridge that leads to the shoulder. On the descent of the snowy saddle, join the first

Making every turn count...

steepest section or use the couloir on the right bordered with the rocks.
Although the bottom of the face looks more 'comfortable' on the left, but the bergschrund can be very high and difficult to cross. Follow the approach route up to route 104. The greatest danger is from the serac band between the Dent du Géant and the Pointe Yeld.

107 GLACIER DE LA NOIRE   3560m
Traverse   AD+

⚑ 3462m	◮ March-May	⚲ 45°/50m
↗ 280m	▣ 202	⚠ 2 (seracs)
↘ 2000m	◷ 6hrs	⊕ HP
✦ All	⚟ 4.3	

It is difficult to give a name to this superb ski-mountaineering traverse. It is near the Pointe Yeld and you ski the top section of the Glacier de la Noire and then you are mainly on the Périades Glacier. This in no way distracts from the high mountain atmosphere of this great descent. On foot, this is quite a risky route as it crosses steep and heavily crevassed glaciers. Nevertheless, even on skis, it is a good idea to be prepared in terms of equipment and training for crevasse rescue.

From the Pointe Helbronner, descent to the Col du Géant and head left at the foot of the north face of the Aiguilles Marbrées. There is a flat traverse across for 1500m to get to the foot of a wide couloir that faces south. Climb up this couloir keeping close to the ridge and then head right to reach a notch 100m to the south of two large blocks on the ridge.
Descend via the north combe heading for the slight notch on the right-hand edge of the sloping plateau of the Glacier de la Noire. Climb up for a few metres on foot (bergschrund) and join the crest that gives access to the second glaciated plateau, the Périades Glacier face. The conditions on the descent of this north-east face change according to the season and you start off on the left side and then move to the right. In any case, the relatively steep slope in the middle leads to the Glacier des Périades, below the impressive band of seracs. Traverse to the right bank of the glacier where you pick up the Brèche Puiseux route (number 105). You can also use this route to join the foot of the slope the west Pan de Rideau (large slope on the face) of Mont Mallet. Take care on the traverse as you are travelling parallel to the line of crevasses and you pass under the seracs.

108 AIGUILLES MARBRÉES   3483m
West couloir   AD−

⌐ 3790m	🏔 February-May	↳ 40°-45°/120m
↗ 350m	📷 204	⚠ 1
↘ 340m	◔ 6 to 7hrs	🏠 SP
✪ West	⚒ 3.1	

Dent du Géant and the Aiguilles Marbrées

The west face of the Aiguilles Marbrées is a short route that is good altitude training requiring a bit of technical skiing in a narrow and relatively uneven couloir. Not only does it give the chance to spend the day in a high mountain environment, this magnificent 'belvedere' gives you great views of the numerous climbing and skiing routes to be done in the area. From here you can also get a good look at the direct descent of the south-east face. There is a steep descent on the east face (you will need a rope) that joins up with the route number 40 on the Italian side of the Aiguilles Marbrées.

Note: for routes 108 to 115, the quickest access route is from the Torino Hut. You can get to the Torino Hut from Courmayeur (Mont Blanc Tunnel and cable-cars) or from the Aiguille du Midi and the gondola at the top of the Pointe Helbronner, which is not generally open before the beginning of May.

From the Aiguille du Midi, descend the start of the Vallée Blanche (route 120), then, at around 3200m, head south-east. Climb back up to around 3150m and pass the Col des Flambeaux, then cross the Col du Géant plateau eastwards. There is a Y-shaped couloir between the two summits of the Aiguilles Marbrées. The left branch of the Y is often the better bet as it has better snow in the top section. On the descent, rejoin the Vallée Blanche via the combe on the right of La Vierge (watch out, this is a heavily crevassed section, stay clear of La Vierge at the start).

108.a **Col de Rochefort (3389m, F).** A trip to the Col de Rochefort can be quite rewarding enough if you have modest expectations, or if, for instance, the conditions are bad. From the Col des Flambeaux, go to the foot of the Aiguilles Marbrées and go left of them to reach the col. This might equally serve as a reconnaissance trip if you were planning a descent of the impressive south-east face of the Aiguilles Marbrées (Italian face, route 40), which has become a classic winter route. You can also continue to the foot of the Arête de Rochefort (Dent du Géant) and descend the right bank of the Géant seracs. You would have to check the conditions of the route as this really are too many crevasses at the beginning of the winter...

108.b **Rochefort Ridges (4001m, D–).** In the spring, the traverse of the Rochefort Ridges, although long and difficult, gives access to the top of the Mont Mallet Glacier. It is one of the best ridge routes and ski-mountaineering routes in the area, and it is seriously committing.

109 AIGUILLE DE TOULE 3534m
North-west face AD

3790m		April-May		40°-45°/100m
700m		205		1
640m + 1700m		5hrs		SP
West		4.3		

As it is so near, the Aiguille de Toule is a great place to train. The route describes access from the French side of the Massif, but it is quicker to access it from the Helbronner cable-cars (Italy).

From Chamonix and the Aiguille du Midi, follow route 108 to the foot of the Pointe Adolphe Rey. Move up slightly diagonally below the crevasses in the direc-

Grand Flambeau, Aiguille de Toule and Aiguille d'Entrèves

tion of the Col d'Entrèves. After a large crevasse at around 3360m, head left and climb to the right of the face near the rocks. Follow the easy terrain on the north ridge to the summit. Except near the rocks, the snow on this face can often be hardened by the wind. The descent is via the same route, then follow route 120.

109.a   North face of the Aiguille de Toule (D+). The lower bergs-chrund is often very high and the face icy. The slope is given about 55°/120m. Between the summit ridge and the face, the headland can be rocky and icy and the snow can be hard.

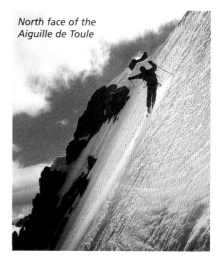

North face of the Aiguille de Toule

110   COL D'ENTRÈVES   3527m
North face   F

⌐	3790m	▨	February-May	⌐	sections of 30°
↗	380m	▣	205	⚠	1
↘	3120m	⊙	6hrs	⊕	SP
✳	North	⚊	2.1		

Italy has produced some very good extreme skiers who have chosen the Mont Blanc Massif as their playground. One of these talented skiers, Stefano de Benedetti, was to be very influential in the discipline of extreme skiing. For him the extreme was everyday and the Massif was the arena where the barrier between the possible and the impossible was to be rolled back. From his first amateur ventures to the great lines he opened in the Massif, he was always compelled by the same passion with a taste for primarily rocky routes. These routes demanded detailed preparation: you don't set off on extreme ski routes with your head down and eyes closed…! Among other routes, he did the first descents of the east face of the Aiguille Blanche de Peuterey, the Major Route, the central couloir on the Freney, the Gréloz-Roch on the Miage face of Mont Blanc, not forgetting of course, the south face of the Innominata Ridge! The Col d'Entrèves is a classic route that is skied from January, but watch out for the deep crevasses.

From Chamonix, via the Aiguille du Midi, follow route 108 to around 3300m and climb up the combe north of the Col d'Entrèves (a few large crevasses). In the winter you can ski all the way down to Chamonix via the Vallée Blanche or to Montenvers from around the end of March.

110.a   North face of the Aiguille d'Entrèves (3600m, AD). From the col descend the right bank of the small valley and climb up a little below the Aiguille.

Going round the summit, you come to a sort of snowy saddle. Below it the north-facing slope exceeds 40°/80m. You can either follow the direct descent (steeper) or head right above the rocks and the bergschrund. Lower down, at around 3350m, you rejoin the normale route you took up below the Aiguille de Toule (crevasses). You can also join the west face of the Aiguille de Toule (route 109).

111 TOUR RONDE   3792m
Normal route   D

⚑ 3790m	🏔 March-May	⤵ 40°-45°/200m
↗ 600m	📷 207	⚠ 2
↘ 600m + 2000m	⏱ 7hrs	⚕ SP
🧭 East	🎿 4.1	

To ski the normal route on the Tour Ronde, you need to be really motivated to do it and to have excellent control of your skis. This is real ski-mountaineering! In fact, the magnificent descent of the Brenva Glacier (route 35) is more than reward enough for the climb up the Tour Ronde.

From Chamonix, via the Aiguille du Midi, join the foot of the Aiguille de Toule (via route 109). Climb towards the Col d'Entrèves and the start of the large plateau (around 3500m). Head in the direction of the snow cone that has come down from the couloirs on the south-east ridge of the Tour Ronde. Avoid the left-hand couloir that doesn't lead straight to the normal route, even if it does look like the obvious way to go. Cross the bergschrund and follow the line on the left that quickly gets steep and narrow (large rocks). To the right, below the ridge, climb a steep section to just below the rocky outcrop that goes to the summit (35m, grade

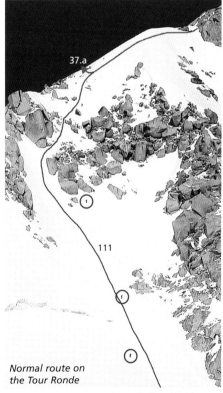

Normal route on the Tour Ronde

III climbing). The skied descent of the normal route is technical: the skiable sections are interspersed with quite exposed traverses and periods of side-slipping. Watch out for the rocks that lie just beneath the surface of the snow. At the bottom of the face, rejoin the Vallée Blanche via the route you took up.

112 TOUR RONDE
North face
3792m
TD

⚑	3790m	🏔	May-June	⚊	53°/250m, sect. of 55°
↗	590m	🕐	7hrs	⚠	3 (rock band)
↘	640m + 2000m	🎿	5.3	🅟	HP
✦	North				

In the past few years, the sense of exposure on this descent has increased as the snow cover on the middle section has decreased. On the first descent, 20th July 1971, Patrick Vallençant found the route very committing. But let's not forget that, in the early years, to ski 'extreme' things on stiff 2.07m skis you needed a very good sense of balance, a great deal of strength and a lot of bottle… During a guide's training course in June 1997, we encountered extreme conditions at the top where the ice was covered by a thin film of cold snow. This was in stark contrast with the slope lower down, where there was over a metre of powder snow in which we would have gladly rolled around! When I descended the route in spring 2002, however, I encountered soft snow right from the top and it was falling away as snow slides!

From Chamonix and the Aiguille du Midi follow the start of the Vallée Blanche to the Pointe Adolphe Rey. Climb up the left bank of the glacier and go south and round the Pointe Adolphe Rey. At around 3350m, cross the glaciated plateau (watch out, you will be skiing parallel to crevasses) and go to the foot of the north face of the Tour Ronde. Now cross the bergschrund on the right and climb up left of the rocks (snow more solid here) to the middle narrow section. Cross the steps (ice or mixed climbing, section of 55-60°) to reach the upper slope. This slope often has hard snow that has been 'worn away' by snow slides, but you can also sometimes find powder snow up here too. The final ridge abuts the rocky outcrop that is the summit. The round trip to the summit takes 1 1/2 hrs.

The descent proper starts on the ridge at around 3740m. You can do a few turns to warm-up at the top. Then for

Edouard Baud at the top of the north face

the next 150m the slope is even and exceeds 50°. The lack of snow in the midd-le section makes it more complex and you will sometimes have to set up a hand-rail (not obvious places for securing the rope) or put on crampons to cross the mixed ground. You can also cross straight over the central gully with a rope (will need slings). On the lower section, the snow is sometimes better on the right bank.

113 TOUR RONDE   3792m
Gervasutti Couloir   D+

⚑ 3790m	🗺 February-June	📐 45°-50°/200m
↗ 590m	📷 210	⚠ 2
↘ 590m + 2000m	🕐 7hrs	⊕ HP
✦ West	🎿 5.1	

Other than on the rare occasions when this slope has powder snow on it, I have, each time I have skied this couloir, found it to be technically and mentally com-mitting. I asked my friend and ski partner Patrick Vallençant, a little while befo-re his fatal climbing accident, to ski this route with me for a Japanese television programme. In August 1989, there weren't really any other couloirs with enough snow. This was to be our last adventure in the mountains together, and it was to be by no means the least exciting as the central gully was very icy and we had had to put in a 20m rope to enable us to ski it on the way down!

From Chamonix, follow route 112 and go round the base of the Tour Ronde to the steep-sided Gervasutti Couloir, nestling on the west face. The bergschrund can be quite high and difficult to cross. Climb up the left bank without straying too far from the central gully. There is often mixed ground to cross on the final 80m lea-ding to the heavily corniced summit ridge that overlook the north face. The start of the descent is not too steep and it allows you to get a feel for the snow beneath your skis. After the top section that you usually have to side-slip (under-lying rocks), you head left, then back right and finally back left again on to the side slopes. This takes you to the slopes to the side of the central gully that are steeper than the gully and in better condition.

Top of the Gervasutti Couloir

Bottom of the same couloir

A very snowy looking Gevasutti Couloir

113

113.a   East col of the Tour Ronde (3627m, D). The middle section of this col called East col but located on the west ridge of the Tour Ronde, is often icy, which usually makes it impossible to ski (55°/180m). It is used quite often as an approach route for the Italian side and the descent of the Brenva Glacier (route 37).

114 COL DU TRIDENT   3679m
North-east face   AD+

⚑ 3790m	🏔 March-June	⌐ 40°-45°/120m
↗ 480m	⏱ 5hrs	⚠ 1
↘ 600m + 1900m	🎿 4.1	⊕ SP
✦ North-east		

In a great situation, the Ghiglione Hut used to be guardianed for a period in the summer and for decades it was the starting point for big routes on the Envers du Mont Blanc or the 'other side of Mont Blanc'. The wearisome work of the guardians and Italian volunteers attempting to stop the snow from pushing the hut off the ridge was abandoned at the end of 1980, and the hut was dismantled. This was a great shame, even if it wasn't the warmest or most comfortable of huts. The Col du Trident gives access to the descent of the Brenva Glacier (route 37). All you have to do is descend a few metres on to the south-west face below the hut, and then traverse across the slope on the left (crests and gullies).

From Chamonix and the Aiguille du Midi, follow route 112, pass the Tour Ronde and join the right bank of the Combe Maudite. The glaciated dome on the right of the col should be visible. Climb up near the left-hand rock spur. The bergschrund can be difficult. The top section of the rope used to access the Ghiglione Hut can still be used. The descent follows the same route, then you rejoin the Vallée Blanche.

114.a   North face of the Trident or the west col of the Tour Ronde (3661m, TD). To get good continuity footage for our filmed descent of the Aiguille Blanche de Peuterey and the Peuterey Ridge, we skied this face twice in 1977. Although it is very steep, it was covered in snow and the conditions were good (about 55°/120m). It is on the left, virtually immediately above the start of the climb up to the Ghiglione Hut.

115 BRÈCHE DU CARABINIER   3792m
South face   PD

⚑	3790m	🗻	February-May	⌖	40°/50 m
↗	590m	📷	211, 212	⚠	1
↘	590m + 2740m	🕐	4 to 5hrs	⊕	SP
✦	South	🎿	4.1		

Despite its name, the Combe Maudite ('Accursed Combe') is a delightful corner of ice and light whose beauty is enhanced by the granite needles and peaks that surround it. Indeed, it is well worth ski-touring up just to see the combe itself. While you are there you can also pick out historic routes such as the Kuffner, skied for the first time by Jean-Marc Boivin, or the south face of Mont Blanc du Tacul, skied (with rappels) by Benoît Chamoux and Georges Gauthier in 1982. From the col you also get a good view of a route that is rarely skied, the north-east face of the Col du Diable (first descended by Daniel Chauchefoin and Pierre Tardivel on 12th April 1981). Although the slope barely exceeds 50°/350m, the access to and the exit from this route increase the difficulty of this descent. This very aesthetic area is attracting more and more people who want to try their hand at steep skiing.

57° slope opposite the Brèche du Carabinier

115.a

115

From the Aiguille du Midi, follow 112 towards the Combe Maudite until you get to the foot of the famous Grand Capucin (3400m). Climb up the right-hand couloir. Some years the lack of snow at the top makes it difficult to ski, but it does come in to condition quite early on in the spring. On the descent, follow the route you took up and rejoin the Vallée Blanche.

East face of the Tacul

115.a ▪ Couloir des Aiguillettes (TD). This narrow couloir between the Grand Capucin and the Trident has been skied since the 1980s, notably by Jean-Marc Boivin. Pierre Tardivel skied the whole route from the top in spring 2002.

116 MONT BLANC DU TACUL — 4248m
Diable Couloir — TD+

⚑	3790m	◹	March-June	⌐	50°-55°/800m
↗	950m	◻	212, 213	⚠	2
↘	490m + 2400m	◷	7hrs	⊕	HP
✦	South-east	✗	5.4		

As a whole, this route is less exposed than the Gervasutti Couloir (overlooked by a band of seracs and cornices), but the skiing here is more tricky and less even. The first complete descent was by Daniel Chauchefoin on 13 June 1976. A few years (and a few descents) later, a talented female Norwegian skier became the first person to ski it on telemarks.

From Chamonix via the Aiguille du Midi descend the Vallée Blanche (see routes 109 and 110) and stay near the base of the Pointe Lachenal. Traverse to around 3250m, below the south-east spur of the Mont Blanc du Tacul. Climb up the glaciated combe (one or two crevasses between 3350m and 3400m) to the bergschrund that you cross on the left. The key section on this route is a rough-

Anselme Baud on the Diable Couloir in 1975

ly 80m long narrow couloir that has an icy step. Higher up, climb up the centre of the couloir then on its left bank after the Y of the Isolée Couloir (more technical cramponning). The upper section is wider but strewn with rocks. Take the left branch and join the narrow ridge that takes you to the east summit. If this final section is too rocky, you can drop behind onto the south face and go round the final rock step and then climb up the slope between the east and west summits. Access from above is not obvious. The line of descent follows the route you took on the way up. Watch out for the rocks at the top and for the crusty snow that could collapse as it sits on a layer of hard snow left over from the winter. Lower down, the left bank will have transformed snow whereas the snow on the right bank stays col-

Isolée Couloir

der for longer although it is steeper (55°). The narrow lower gully can be crossed with a rope and you should take a snow anchor (technical difficulty and danger increased by the snow slides). Depending on the time of year, you can climb back up to the Aiguille du Midi or continue down the Vallée Blanche.

116.a   Isolée Couloir (TD+). This drops straight down from the sharp point at 4000m and is so named because of its isolated situation. This is the direct branch of the Y, which is also narrower, steeper and more difficult to ski (55°/150m) than its neighbour. Accessing the route from the north face of the Tacul is not recommended unless you have very precise information on the condition of the snow in the route. So the only way to be sure of a route is to climb up it – there are already too many other dangers to contend with.

117   MONT BLANC DU TACUL   4248m
Gervasutti Couloir   TD

3790m		March-June		45°-55°/700m
950m		212, 215		3 (seracs)
490m + 3200m		8hrs		HP
East		5.3		

This huge chute is one of the major reference points in steep skiing. In June 1976, the filmmaker René Vernadet asked if he could film me on my descent of the Gervasutti. Having spent the night at the Rognon, where he had set up his cameras, I set off for the first repeat of Gervasutti, after Sylvain Saudan's first descent in October 1968 helped by his guide friends. My solo ascent of the couloir took one hour and, after having crossed the high cornice, I started out on my descent of this magnificent slope at 7am and it took me just 20 minutes. The snow perfect: it was evenly hard with two to three centimetres of softened snow on top. Having filmed it a first time, I set off to film it again this time with Patrick Vallençant after our success on the Peuterey Ridge in May 1977. This time it was a bit more difficult as the north wind had hardened the snow to ice at the top and it took a great deal nerve to control our slalom skis (2.04m at that time!). Since then, I have skied this couloir several times and each descent has been in different conditions. Adaptability – that's the secret to successful extreme skiing!

From Chamonix via the Aiguille du Midi, go to the foot of the couloir at around 3350m (route 120). Climb up on the left of the bergschrund and then climb up the left bank of the couloir. After the first third of the way up, the central gully can be very deep for about 50 to 100m. Higher up, continue on the left bank near the rocks that are less exposed to the seracs. The cornice on the summit is generally lower on the right. If the snow is hard you can continue to the top and the time it takes for the sun to soften the snow a little. You may have to fix a rope to a wooden stake, which you can leave up there, in order to cross the cornice. The line of descent is to the right for the first half of the route (better snow, wider slope, more even and more protected). You must have complete trust in your equipment. In fact, your skis and their bindings are put under enormous pressure when you ski steep slopes, on hard snow and the bindings should be tightened to their maximum point.

117.a   Direct line from the summit (ED). Exposed, ice showing through (55°/100m).

Patrick Vallençant at the top...

... and in the couloir 60 minutes later!

118 MONT BLANC DU TACUL   4248m
Jager Couloir   TD+

⚐ 3790m	🏔 March-May	⌐ 45°-55°/700m
↗ 950m	📷 212, 215	⚠ 3
↘ 490m + 2400m	🕐 8hrs	⊕ HMP
✦ East	🎿 5.4	

The Jager Couloir was skied for the first time by the Saint-Gervais skier Jacky Bessat, on 7th March 1977. Eric Bellin, Philippe Besse, Christophe Crétin and Bruno Gouvy snowboarded it on 6th January 1990. The couloirs on this side of the mountain face east, have snow in them quite early on and some years they can be skied from January to the end of June. As the Cosmiques Hut opens earlier and earlier in the winter and the Montenvers train is open virtually all year, it is not difficult to plan to ski routes in this area. From the bottom of the gullies on the right of the Pointe Lachenal to the Jager Couloir, there are several other very steep descents, which don't start from the summit and can be done on this east face of Mont Blanc du Tacul. In particular, there is a couloir-gully to the left of the Quille Pillar (slopes approaching 60°) that rarely has enough snow.

Gervasutti and Jager Couloirs

From Chamonix via the Aiguille du Midi, follow route 120 to south of the Pointe Lachenal. The Jager Couloir runs parallel and to the right of the Gervasutti. The bergschrund on the climb up can be quite high and this makes the climb quite long but technically interesting. You can follow the ridge to get to the summit of Mont Blanc du Tacul on skis (1hr there and back).

On the descent, the start of the couloir is impressive (funnel that quickly narrows). The sections next to the central gully are difficult to ski.

The advantage of the Jager Couloir, even if it is less skiable that the Gervasutti, is the fact that there are fewer objective dangers as you are not below seracs for the whole way down!

119 TRIANGLE DU TACUL   3970m
North-west slope   TD

⊥ 3790m		🏔 May-July		⌐ 50-55°/200m
↗ 440m		📷 216, 237		⚠ 2
↘ 250m + 2200m		🕙 5hrs		⊕ HP
✦ North-west		🎿 5.1		

At first glance, Mont Blanc du Tacul would seem to be the ideal mountain for skiing: its slope is sustained, faces north and therefore has good snow. Moreover, the average gradient of the slope, which is neither too steep nor too shallow, means that snow fall brought by the west wind quickly evens itself out. However, the Tacul is also exposed to the north and north-east winds and, as it is a glacier, you will find numerous cracks in the snow here, caused by the underlying crevasses. These faults in the slopes lead to windslab avalanches. It is therefore a good idea to wait until spring before setting off down these slopes and proceed with caution. The two variant routes mentioned here would be the main routes on the mountain, if they were to be found in other massifs. Here, however, they are training routes…

From Chamonix via the Aiguille du Midi, follow route 120 to the Col du Midi and then traverse below the Cosmiques Hut (open for part of the winter) and go to the bottom of the north face. The first slopes to climb up on the right steepen up to 40° before the first crevasse and the large valley after this is less steep. Now head left to climb the main steep slope up to the col to the right of the rock (3970m).

North face of Mont Blanc du Tacul

Hard snow on the Triangle du Tacul

119.a   North-east slope of the Triangle (TD). The descent from the summit is exposed as a result of the risk of slab avalanche or ice in the upper section. It is better to stay on the lower slopes and use them as a 'training area' (between 45 and 55°/250m).

119.b   Contamine-Mazeaud Route (ED). This is certainly the more daring and impressive of the two variant routes as this descent is very exposed above the rock bands. There is rarely enough snow on this route and it is not often skied for this reason and because you have to rappel past the narrow section. Moreover, if the top section is not skiable the lower section can be used for training (55°/80m).

120 AIGUILLE DU MIDI   3842m
Vallée Blanche   PD

3790m	jJanuary-May		sections of 35°
40m	218, 219		1
2740m	3hrs		SP
All	2.3		

Thousands of skiers jostle their way across and follow each other down the Vallée Blanche every day in the season. There are a few variant routes that can be done here, if the snow cover is good enough. Although the skiing itself in this area is not necessarily great, the landscape is quite spectacular and, thanks to skis and Mother Nature, novices can discover for themselves the enchanting high mountain environment that this privileged trip in to the heart of the Massif affords. The summit ridge is equipped with a handrail and stakes, and skiers can walk down it without having to wear crampons, although do take the precaution of being roped together. The rest of the descent does require a certain amount of caution and don't let your sense of euphoria at being there overcome you! Also, don't forget your 'reserve of courage' as you stand at the top of the ridge with Chamonix 2600m below you. Bearing in mind the fear some people experience while going down the ridge, it might dissuade them from describing the famous Vallée Blanche as 'an easy piste' to future 'consumers'!

From Chamonix via the Aiguille du Midi, go to the exit of the left-hand tunnel (in the direction of the Pointe Helbronner gondola). Descend the north-east east ridge which is equipped with a handrail and stakes from the end of February to

Aiguille du Midi

the end of May. Don't put your skis on until you have got to the large platform at around 3700m. Competent ski-mountaineers sometimes put their skis on at the top of the combe next to the south-east rock spur. Traverse the large combe below the south face of the Aiguille and pass the Col du Gros Rognon (3415m). Ski towards the Pyramide du Tacul then take a long, wide turn to the left (crevasses). There is now a long diagonal traverse to the left to get to the top of the seracs. Pass through the seracs by staying on the left bank (can be steep, icy and narrow). You will end up at the same height as the Requin Hut and you will see the access route to the hut. Go down from this level and traverse to the right bank of the glacier via the Salle à Manger (2400m). Descend via the middle of the glacier to the same height as the junction with the Leschaux Glacier on the right. Now, via the centre of the glacier, pass the Montenvers station (or take the gondola on left up and catch the train down the Chamonix). Before the end of the glacier, exit left to pick up the track that leads up to the little Mottets buvette that sells

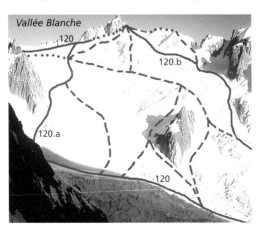

Vallée Blanche

refreshments and snacks (20mins). Follow the path back to Chamonix via the Les Planards pistes.

120.a 'Vraie' ('True') Vallée Blanche (PD). This route has become quite popular since the end of the 1990s. The shape of the glacier offers you a better route that starts with you going left of the small rock spur, crossing the centre of the valley, and skiing nearer the foot of the Gros Rognon. The slope is not excessively steep (30° maximum), but some of the sections near rocks can be very steep and there are a lot of crevasses (cause of Louis Lachenal's fatal fall in 1955).

120.b ▪ **Envers du Plan (PD).** Follow the start of the Midi-Plan ridge, then after a steep section of about 50m (35-40°), the descent now continues round several series of crevasses, staying on the left bank of the glacier. At around 3100m, cut right of the Petit Rognon and rejoin the classic Vallée Blanche (this is the 'Petit Envers' variant). Alternatively, you can carry on via the Envers du Plan Glacier, which is steeper and naturally known as the 'Grand Envers' variant: leave the glacier on the left, below the Dent du Requin, and then descend via the steep convexity in the centre of the glacier (35-40°/150m) or

Envers du Plan

more to the left (possibility of rock slabs and ice) to join the large steep combe (35°) down to the Mer de Glace. Owing to its popularity, this route can sometimes feel like a mogul field. Nevertheless, don't forget that the terrain is still heavily crevassed and the final section is steep and exposed…

121   AIGUILLE DU PLAN   3673m
South face   AD

⚑ 3790m		🏔 February-May		⬦ 40°/200m	
↗ 520m		📷 219, 220		⚠ 1	
↘ 640m + 2620m		⏱ 6hrs		⊕ SP	
⬦ South-east		⛷ 4.2			

This is a route that you can do from the Requin Hut (guardianed in winter) either by going to the hut from the Aiguille du Midi the day before, or by going up from Chamonix or Montenvers (2hrs). The Aiguille du Plan was one of the first alpine peaks to be skied and was first done in 1925 by Armand Charlet and André Roch. In skiing the mountain, this famous ice-climbing partnership (soon to be become world-famous), created a new form of winter mountaineering (or rather spring mountaineering, they did it in April!). It was very unusual to use skis for mountaineering at this time, especially on steep slopes. Bearing in mind the fact that their wooden skis didn't even have metal edges to them and

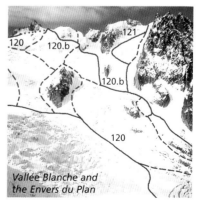

Vallée Blanche and the Envers du Plan

Pain de Sucre, north face

121.a

they were heavy and didn't slide well, it required a great deal of effort (both moral and physical) to make them turn especially as they were wearing soft leather boots whose only bindings were at the front and in the middle of the ski…Moreover, after the 'Great War' the techniques they were using were very limited: snow-plough, scissors and other stembogen techniques and telemarks… The 'flexion-extension' style of un-weighting was not really used at that time and their equipment was far from efficient.

André-Pierre Rhem – Dédé – young aspirant on the Guide's training scheme was, to me, a young man full of extraordinary inner energy. His ever present smile and the twinkle in his eyes were evidence of his abundant enthusiasm. In the Alps, the Himalaya, and in Russia, where he chose to end his winter season in 2004, his achievements, especially snowboarding, speak volumes. Back in his home mountain range, on that spring day, and excited at the prospect of a beautiful ride, maybe he underestimated the quality of the snowpack under the Helbronner cable car. The avalanche swept him off this exposed slope, here where the proximity to the cable car, more than anywhere, lends a false sense of security. It's a trap!

From Chamonix, via the Aiguille du Midi, follow route 120.b. Stay on the left of the glacier and go to the bottom of the Rognon du Plan at around 3150m. Climb up the right bank of the Envers du Plan Glacier via a steep slope with crevasses and seracs (some years the central section can be in condition). You reach the foot of the Col Supérieur du Plan via a large, less steep combe. Above the bergschrund the slope steepens up to 35° and then more than 40°. On the right of the col (3535m), follow the ridge that is steep to start with to get to the rocks before the summit (30m, III). On the descent, go back to the col and descend the glacier to rejoin the classic route (120.b). You can also do this route from the Requin Hut.

121.a   North face of the Pain de Sucre (TD+). First descent by Pierre Tardivel on 1st June 1990 with the first snowboarded descent, by Jérôme Ruby and Dédé Rhem, coming two days later on 3rd June (55°/350m).

CHAMONIX

PRACTICAL INFORMATION

Chamonix Tourist Office: 04 50 53 00 24 / www.chamonix.com
Compagnie des Guides: 04 50 53 00 88 / www.cieguides-chamonix.com
Ass. Int. Guides du Mont Blanc: 04 50 53 27 05 / www.guides-du-mont-blanc.com
Summits: 04 50 53 50 14 / www.summits.fr
Office de Haute Montagne: 04 50 23 22 08 / www.ohm-chamonix.com
PGHM: 04 50 53 16 89
Weather forecast: 08 92 68 02 74 / www.meteo.fr
Snow report: 08 92 68 10 20

SKI LIFTS

Aiguille du Midi: 04 50 53 30 80 / reservations: 08.36.68.00.67 /
www.aiguilledumidi.fr
Montenvers: 04 50 53 12 54

ROAD ACCESS

From Annecy, Geneva or Sallanches follow the A40 (or N205)
to Chamonix.

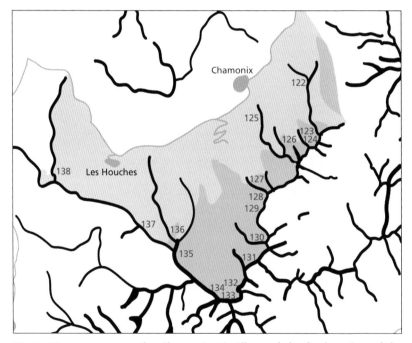

We now come to the Chamonix Aiguilles and the final section of the Mont Blanc Massif. You can't miss the Chamonix 'Needles' as you arrive in this, the capital of mountaineering. Above and behind them, forming the heart of the Massif, sit Mont Blanc and its surrounding peaks (the Tacul, Maudit and Goûter), which have made the valley famous.

Previous page: On the north face of Mont Blanc du Tacul

There are two different approaches to skiing in this area:
- classic ski-touring, with its 1 to 2-day climbs and long descents that require mountaineering skills and experience as this is a high mountain environment crossing glaciated terrain;
- the 'new wave' of freeriders. Using the cable-cars means you can shorten or completely avoid long climbs up to some of the routes in this area, and the approach to the valley's 'mythic' descents, such as the north face of the Aiguille du Midi, can be relatively quick and easy. In fact, from the start of winter a veritable festival of freerider descents is played out before our eyes. Just after a large fall of snow, the slopes on the Glacier Rond, the Cosmiques Couloir and many other routes become almost 'snow parks', which would have been inconceivable 30 years ago...

MOUNTAIN HUTS

Ref.27 ■ Cosmiques Hut (3613m, F)
Private hut, 140 places, guardianed from February to October, tel: 04 50 54 40 16

From the top station of the Aiguille du Midi cable-car descend the exposed north-east ridge. Traverse beneath the south face of the Aiguille du Midi and climb up for 10mins to reach the hut that is easy to spot.

⛳ 3790m   🕐 30 mins to 1hr

↗ 70m

↘ 200m

Ref.28 ■ Plan de l'Aiguille Hut (2205m, F)
Very basic winter room, 12 places

From Chamonix, take the first section of the Aiguille du Midi cable-car to the Plan de l'Aiguille. Follow the less steep slopes on the large north/north-west facing headland, and lose 100m in height to get to the hut, which is virtually below the cables.

⛳ 2310m   🕐 15 mins

↘ 100m

Ref.29 ■ Grands Mulets Hut (3051m, PD)
CAF, 68 places, guardianed from March to September, tel: 04 50 53 16 98

From Chamonix, take the first section of the Aiguille du Midi lift to the Plan de l'Aiguille and traverse beneath the north face of the Aiguille du Midi to a kind of balcony above the old Glaciers cable-car station (you are not allowed to ski downhill of this traverse line as controlled avalanches are set off here using Gasex explosions). From this promontory, the first difficult section is the descending traverse to the Bossons Glacier. You can either take your skins off here or leave them on, depending on the snow conditions and the track. This traverse can be dangerous (risk of sliding after a fall and, in the afternoon, risk of avalanches above). Cross the Bossons Glacier via Plan Glacier and traverse towards the left bank up to La Jonction (crevasses, seracs). Now zigzag your way up the section of glacier beneath the Grands Mulets Hut (steep at first, 45 mins). Leave your skis at the foot of the rock and follow the cables to the hut (5 mins).

P 2310m   ☺ 3hrs

↗ 800m

↘ 60m

122 AIGUILLE DE L'M   2785m
Traverse of the Col de la Bûche   AD

P	2310m	🗻	January-May	ꙮ	40°-45°/200m, 2 sect. of 50°
↗	470m	📷	224, 225, 228	⚠	1
↘	1750m	☺	4hrs	⊕	SP
⊕	West and east	🎿	4.1		

As it is quick to access, and if you have a good idea of the conditions when you decide to ski it, the Col de la Bûche is one of the classic descents in the valley. In the winter, and if you are fast, you can do this traverse in an afternoon especially if the track going up is already there. This is an example of a route that has been optimised by the use of the cable-car, although you should try to keep to a steady pace so as not to exhaust yourself before you get there. You should also respect the time it takes for the snow to stabilise – minimum of two to three days.

Bûche Couloir

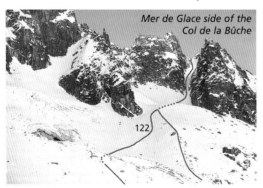

Mer de Glace side of the Col de la Bûche

122

From Chamonix, via the Plan de l'Aiguille cable-car (2310m), traverse eastwards to the foot of the first, pronounced line of moraine (below the Lac Bleu, 2299m). Cross this crest and pass below the Blaitière Glacier and go to the top of the second line of moraine at 2475m. Continue, on a flat traverse, to a third line of moraine and watch out for windslab formations. If you are unsure of the conditions on this traverse, just before it you can climb up another 50m to a kind of shelf. From here you can descend along the line of the rocks to the foot of a final rock spur, where you can shelter. From here, you can see the final accumulation zone to cross. You sometimes have to go all the way round the top of this section to the moraine. A short descent

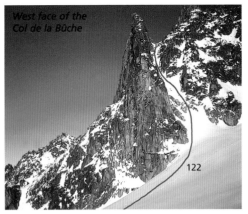

West face of the
Col de la Bûche

122

now takes you to the Nan-
tillons Glacier, which you
cross to its right bank (one or
two crevasses at the beginning of the season). The
climb to the bottom of the
couloir provides you with an
excellent opportunity to
practice your kick turns. Now
the slope steepens up to 40°.
The snow may be hard in the
morning and it is often easier
to walk up. The descent of
the east face, above the Mer
de Glace, is normally in powder snow because it protec-
ted by the Trélaporte ridge. There is a big cornice at the col and sometimes you will
need to be belayed past it. Cross the cornice on the right and move back to below
the Aiguille de l'M. At the bottom, the couloir narrows and early in the season it
can be rocky (30m rope useful). Head right, below the Petits Charmoz and join the
top of the moraine of the Thendia Glacier. If the snow cover is good, follow the
glacier on the right and at the narrow section, go left before the moraine. There
is now a descent on a very pleasant slope. Head left again and a final small couloir
takes you to the Mer de Glace. If the snow cover is not good, descend rightwards
below the Thendia Glacier and exit it through the rocky points before the path to
the Envers des Aiguilles Hut. Whatever happens, it is best to avoid the middle of
the combe. Join the Vallée Blanche (route 120) and return to Chamonix.
Note: Emmanuel Ballot skied a section of the north face of the Grands Charmoz
(several rappels).

122.a   North couloir of the Col Blanc (AD). Descend 100m via the east
couloir, then climb up for about 60m to the Col Blanc (2755m). The descent
is relatively straightforward, although it narrows at the bottom. You end
up above some large north-west slopes (Gasex). Now follow 125.a or b to
Chamonix.

123 COL DES NANTILLONS   3292m
North face   AD

⌐ 2310m		🏔 February-June		⌐ 35°-40°/200m	
↗ 980m		📷 226		⚠ 2 (seracs)	
↘ 2250m		🕐 5¹/²hrs		⊕ SP	
✦ North/north-west		🎿 4.1			

The Col des Nantillons is one of the most accessible and impressive cols in the
Chamonix Aiguilles. The delicate and narrow Pic de Roc heightens the feeling
one has of floating above the Mer de Glace. Opposite, the Aiguille de Tacul, the
crenellated Périades ridge and the long, steep barrier formed by the peaks on

Col des Nantillons and the
Aiguille de Blaitière

the Franco-Italian border put this little corner of the Alps into perspective. However, the uncertainties that one associates with high mountain terrain and steep glaciers, have earned the Col des Nantillons its place as a ski-mountaineering destination. You can see the Spencer Couloir from here and this can also be an alternative route to the Spencer Couloir. Why don't ski-mountaineers carry on up to the Grépon, a peak so emblematic of Chamonix? The short and varied climbing on this slender sliver of granite and the 20m of cragging in the sun on the Knubel Crack (section of V plus, rock shoes useful!) to get to it is glorious. Indeed, Gaston Rébuffat said that 'climbing this mountain [was] a delight'!

From Chamonix, via the Plan de l'Aiguille cable-car, follow route 122 to the Nantillons Glacier (1hr). To start with, climb up in the direction of the Doigt de l'Etala, then head towards the centre of the glacier. Now continue up the left bank of the glacier and stay out of the central section that is exposed to serac fall. If the climb up is icy or the upper seracs look too menacing, you can climb up the central spur (100m of II and III). Traverse quickly below the band of seracs towards the Grépon (crevassed area). Continue to the middle of the small steep glaciated valley above the seracs. At around 3250m, there is a traverse left from where you easily reach the Col des Nantillons. The main exposed section on the descent remains the zone below the seracs. If this feels too dangerous, you can descend via the rocky rognon (60m rappel). Continue your descent via the Plan de l'Aiguille or go back to Chamonix via 125 and one its variant routes.

124 BRÈCHE DE BLAITIÈRE   3449m
Spencer Couloir   D

2310m	March-June	45°-50°/250m
1140m	226	2
1140m + 1300m	7hrs	HP
North/north-east	4.3	

The first to dare to descend the Spencer Couloir was the Valais skier Sylvain Saudan, on 26th September 1967. Thanks to some spectacular photos of the descent, this was the start of his career, in the eyes of the public, as the 'skier of the impossible'. From 1968 onwards, with the help of his loyal friends (also guides), he started to add to his list of impressive descents, such as the Whymper, Gervasutti and Marinelli Couloirs. He became the steep-skiing specialist and was the subject of several films and talks, and he would refer to his unconventional technique as his 'windscreen wiper' turn. It was inevitable that he was going to have his rivals and his fans. That is how I came to accompany him on one of his descents in the USA, where I was working with a group of youngsters at the foot of Mount Hood in Oregon. I was convinced, following this adventure, that I could have a go at skiing everywhere, wherever I saw white, a dream I had had since my first experiences on skis!

Start of Spencer Couloir

From Chamonix, via the Plan de l'Aiguille cable-car, follow route 123 to the foot of the Spencer Couloir. The bergschrund is quite easy to cross, and you do this on the right. After a few pitches you get to a narrow section, which is the steepest section. After this, you get to the rocky crest between the two summits of the Blaitière. On the descent, if there are gullies in the first section, you can traverse right to the 'demi-lune' (curving snow crest) where the snow stays colder. On the other hand, there is ice just beneath the snow here and the slope does exceed 50°/100m. The Spencer Couloir gets the sun quite early from the spring onwards. Therefore, an early start is a good idea even if this means you have to wait for the snow to soften once you get to the start of the route. You can either go back to the Plan de l'Aiguille or follow route 123 to Chamonix.

Spencer Couloir in July 2001

124.a   Right couloir (AD). On the climb up, before you traverse towards the upper serac band, look out for the shortcut on the right that is sometimes possible to follow directly to the Spencer Couloir (see photo, steeper, less dangerous, 40°/100m).

124.b   Contamine Couloir (D). Follow route 122 and, after having crossed the final line of moraine on the left bank of the Nantillons Glacier, climb straight up towards a couloir that faces slightly left. After a steep diagonal climb you quickly reach the upper section of the Nantillons Glacier. After a final steep section, you pass under the Contamine Couloir from where you can join the Spencer Couloir. When there is lots of snow, this is the quickest access route and the least exposed to objective dangers. This is also the access route to the Contamine Couloir. The Contamine is narrower, the snow cover is not as good and its lower section is more sustained than the Spencer. It was skied for the first time by Serge Cachat-Rosset in July 1971 (50°/200m).

125   PLAN DE L'AIGUILLE   2310m
Pré du Rocher   F

⚐	2310m	🏔	Winter	⮎	sections of 35°
↘	1300m	📷	228, 230	⚠	1
✥	North	🕓	45 mins	⊕	DP
⚒	1.3				

The Glaciers cable-car was built between the wars, although its final section, up to the Col du Midi, was never finished, and it was replaced in 1954 by the current cable-car. Its two sections, instead of the three envisaged in the original project, join Chamonix with the Aiguille du Midi. The first Kandahar race was run on the piste that went from the top of the first station, in 1948. The race was won brilliantly by the young Chamoniard James Couttet, on 2.07m skis, and behind him came a band of Austrian skiers and the second Frenchman was a certain François Baud. Nowadays, the section above the Mont Blanc Tunnel is officially closed at certain times so that the slopes can be 'purged' by controlled avalanches using Gasex explosions, which are set off from the valley.

From the Plan de l'Aiguille mid-station, head north and descend a series of small valleys that get progressively steeper. At around 2100m, via a crest and the first

The Chamonix Aiguilles

Grand Chalet descent toward Les Planards

larches trees, come back a little right (summer path). This is the steepest part of the descent. Follow the series of north-facing clearings (sites of old chalets), which soon brings you to a well- marked path (1600m). The path takes you back to the Aiguille du Midi car-park.

125.a   Blaitière-dessus (PD). From the Plan de l'Aiguille traverse as high as possible towards the Blaitière Glacier moraine. The traverse of the lines of moraine and the steep combe above the Torrent de Blaitière can be dangerous (windslab). When you reach the same height as the first larches, ski in to the pretty north-west face where you will find the renovated Blaitière-dessus chalet (1926m). Ski through the wood on the right to get to the Blaitière-dessous chalet (1708m). Take the left-hand track to cross the Torrent de Blaitière and join the Pré du Rocher descent.

125.b   Grand Chalet (PD). Climb up via route 122 to get to the nice moraine slopes between 2400m and 2500m and descend either via Blaitière-dessus or via the Grand Chalet (or more rarely on the north face, via Les Fontanettes). Make sure you come back via the path on the left. Good snow at the start of winter.

125.c   Grands Bois (F). From the Plan de l'Aiguille head south in to the small valley that is before the Glacier des Pélerins. Immediately descend the north face or traverse further, depending on the quality of the snow (faces more or less north-west). At 1800m, where the small valley narrows, come back right (path). A large part of this woodland was destroyed by the storms of 1986-7. The Service des Eaux et Forêts has planted thousands of larches here. As a result, you should on your guard and try not to cut the tops off the trees. If the snow cover is bad, it's better to follow the path to pick up route 125.

125.d   Former Piste des Glaciers (PD). Climb to the top of the Pélerins Glacier moraine, at 2500m, and ski in to the valley or climb up higher and continue right, below the north face Aiguille du Midi to get to 2600m (1 1/2 hrs). Descend the steep slope near the old Piste des Glaciers and from there go to the tunnel entrance. If the pollution and heat created by the traffic haven't melted the snow, you can continue right, via the track, to Chamonix.

126 AIGUILLE DU PLAN
North face
3673m
TD+

⚑ 3790m		🏔 May-June		↳ 45°-50°/500m (sect. of 55°)
↗ 200m		📷 230, 231		⚠ 3
↘ 1350m		🕐 3-4hrs		⊕ HP
✦ North		🎿 5.3		

This face is too visible from Chamonix not to mention it here, even if most people will only ever ski it in their dreams… In December 1975, Patrick Gabarrou and a client climbed up a new route on the north-west face of the Aiguille du Plan. Emmanuel Ratouis was the first to ski it, in 1998. Ski-mountaineers on the look-out for good lines to ski are always interested in what the ski lifts have to offer, and that is why the Aiguille du Midi area is so popluar. Among the extreme routes done around here there's the descent of the route that Robert Chéré first climbed in 1976. The first person to ski it was none other than Jean-Marc Boivin. He descended this 1000m slope, with the help of a few rappels, which is for the most part between 50° and 55° and even has sections of 65° (he got past these sections with a rope!)…

North face of the Aiguille du Plan

From Chamonix go to the Aiguille to Midi. Follow the Midi-Plan ridge the Col du Plan (steep sections on the Vallée Blanche side). This traverse includes a section of down-climbing and a 25m rappel on the east face. Alternatively, you can climb up the south face of the Envers Glacier (see route 121). Join the shoulder (50m below the rocky summit of the Aiguille du Plan). The first descent of this impressive face was by Jean-Marc Boivin and Laurent Giacomini in June 1977. It was repeated by Eric Bellin and Jean-Franck Charlet (both guides) among others, but the snowboarder Alain Moroni's fatal accident seem to have put an end to subsequent attempts. It normally takes three rappels to cross the seracs at the top, then there is a longer one to cross the lower seracs. The conditions on this face vary considerably, and it seems it is impossible to ski the whole descent without rappelling past some of the sections.

126.a North face of the Col du Plan (TD). Several skiers claim to have done the first descent of this face, including Dominique Neuenschwander. However, Yves Détry appears to be the first person to ski it, in 1977, using three short rappels. In spring 1975, I climbed up the entire length of the left couloir hoping to exit from the upper gullies, but there wasn't enough snow. I ended up skiing the lower section, and later on, for a film, I skied the upper section. This face is rarely in condition and looks much more attractive from afar than it actually is up close. Make sure you are properly equipped (ropes, snow anchors etc) if you go there, so as to avoid having to be helicoptered off the face, as happened to a group of Americans in spring 2000…

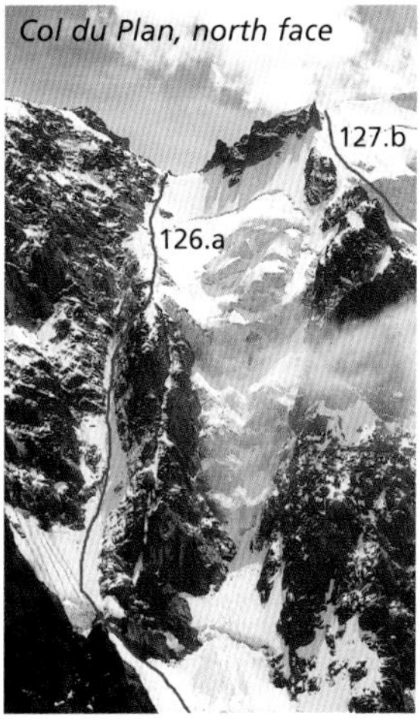

Col du Plan, north face

127 AIGUILLE DU MIDI 3842m
Mallory Route TD+

3790m	April-May	50°-55°/500m (sect. of 58°)
1500m	228, 231, 232	3
North	2hrs	HP
	5.3	

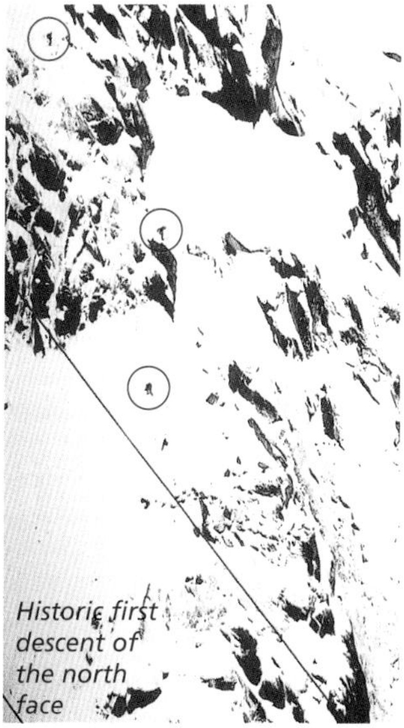
Historic first descent of the north face

I had wanted to ski a route on this north face for some time, as you get a very good view of it from the valley. On my first attempt I got as far as the hanging glacier, and I felt ready to try the descent proper. One Monday, after a descent of Mont Blanc had been cancelled, I found myself at the Aiguille du Midi in the hope of trying a first descent of the Mallory and I just had time to catch up with Yves Détry and Daniel Chauchefoin who had set off a little before me that morning. The top of the face was in good condition and it took me just five minutes and a few turns in powder to surprise my friends at the 'demi-lune' (curving snow crest). The difficulties started lower down and the risks increased significantly after the sharp rocky outcrops. After the soft snow on the crest that reminded me of a tightrope, came the Pan de Rideau, which was steep with hard snow and was shiny and smooth-looking following the snow slides of the day

Aiguille du Midi, north face

before. Although ideal for climbing up in crampons, this top layer offered little purchase for skis, despite their good, sharp edges. A few cautious turns and some judicious side-slipping and we finished this hard diagonal traverse and found ourselves above the rock bands. We had to put in a 25m handrail to get to the last section, which was relatively easy. Since then, this descent has been repeated several times. It is, nevertheless, rare for the snow to be soft from the top to the bottom of this route. You have to choose between relying on your technique in hard snow conditions, where you simply cannot afford to fall, or your nerve as you head down it in soft snow trying not to get swept off your feet as the snow falls away under your skis…

On 26 May 2001 I had just come back from a trip to Nepal and I was filled with doubt and some trepidation as I watched my son Edouard and one of his friends ski the same route. I was reassured by the fact that he had climbed the route the day before to check the conditions, but I was still a little worried by the fact that he was using light and soft ski-touring equipment, which I didn't think would help him on the hard snow in the lower section.

The Mallory is one of the few routes that can be seen in its entirety from the cable-car. You start from the platform of the east tunnel (exit for the Vallée Blanche). Descend the first slope for about 100m until you get to the hanging glacier. The slope is slightly less steep and you have to traverse left towards headland that sometimes consists merely of seracs. Lower down, on the first descent, the rocks barely showed through the snow, whereas now you have to go round them and go to the 'demi-lune' that is above the extremely steep north/north-east couloir (3350m). After 80m of this couloir that is squashed in between the glacier and a wall of rock, you arrive at the top of the north/north-west Pan de Rideau (large slope). This descent of this is exposed and it is above a band of rocks. The snow here can be 'glass-like', as it was when we first skied it, at around 11 o'clock in the morning. The diagonal slope steepens up before joining a very small passage, above the north gullies. Descend this passage and side-slip towards the edge of the left-hand side where you set up a 25m rappel (need gear). This gives you access to a distinctive diamond-shaped névé on the north/north-west face. Come back right to get in to a narrow couloir/ledge that faces north/north-east for 150m. You now join a final, wider couloir that comes down from a notch under the cables of the cable-car. After a small bergschrund the couloir widens out into a large cone at the bottom of the couloir, which you exit on the right to get back to Plan de l'Aiguille.

127.a   Eugster Couloir (TD+).
From the 'demi-lune' on the Mallory (3350m), you can ski a direct and very steep (especially at the top) descent when the north-west couloir is full of snow. Skiers who have done this route quite often have to set up rappels because the snow can be very hard between the deep gullies and the rocky steps. The slope gets up to 56°. The first descent was by Laurent Giacomini in June 1977. It can come into condition more quickly than the Mallory, but there can also be more snow slides.

At the start and roped up, but on telemarks...

127.b   Primi Vici (TD+). First descent of the Tournier Spur by Edouard Baud and Benoît Fanara in April 2003 (45-55°/1100m, 2 rappels in the lower section). Another line has been skied close to the Frendo Spur (55° minimum, ED+). The descent passes in the north-west face of the spur. Cross the section of mixed climbing using rappels and stay on the right. Via the snow slopes, below the seracs again, cross a final steep wall and the bergschrund. This descent was skied for the first time in June 1977 by Laurent Giacomini and Jean-Marc Boivin. It has been repeated at least once, although it is very rarely in condition.

128 AIGUILLE DU MIDI   3842m
Rond Glacier   D

3790m		February-May		45-50°/800m	
30m + 50m		235, 237		2	
1530m + 1300m		2-3hrs		SP	
North/west		4.2			

Some years, the north-west face of the Aiguille du Midi has dozens of visitors who come to play in the winter powder snow. Often the wind fills in the depressions and hardens the moguls formed by the skiers and snowboarders, and the slope becomes exposed again. You should also be aware of the orientation of the second west slope, which can contain hard snow in the morning, from the spring onwards. On the other hand, it is not unusual to ski this face with 50cm of fresh snow. The Glacier Rond gets it name from the lower glacier and not in fact the hanging glacier above. Other, new routes have recently been skied for the first time here (left bank of the hanging glacier and also a mixed face more to the west, after the middle crest).

Old setting off point on Rond Glacier (below Abri Simond)

From Chamonix take the Aiguille du Midi cable-car up and, via the east tunnel, descend the start of the ridge to the Vallée Blanche. Put your skis on as soon as possible and get warmed up on the first south-east facing slope (40°). Go round the south face of the Aiguille du Midi and climb up for 50m to the left of the Abri Simond. The traverse across the west face to reach the top of the north slope, is exposed. Ski on the left-hand headland (cable) at first to get used to the gradient of the slope. Further right, there is sometimes ice showing through the snow. Join a small col downhill and, via a very steep section, go to the top of the large west couloir. The left bank is steeper but often in better condition. From the final cone at the bottom of the couloir (bergschrund), head back right and stay near the rocky face. The cones at the bottom of the couloirs partly fill in the bergschrund and the crevasses. Cross the Glacier Rond and follow the track that goes to the Grands Mulets Hut (ref.32) and climb up for 30mins to the same height as the Glaciers cable-car. If the snow conditions allow, you can continue your descent to Chamonix (125.d to the Mont Blanc Tunnel). Otherwise, go back to the Plan de l'Aiguille.

128.a   West couloir (TD). From the bottom of the first north slope, cross the bergschrund and continue on the right bank of the hanging glacier. Climb and walk up (60m) right towards a notch. From here the west couloir looks narrow and very steep at the top (scoped this out during one of my reconnaissance trips in the 1970s, first complete descent by Pierre Tardivel in 1994 from the north face, TD). A short down-climb gets you to the couloir and you can now ski it straight down to the Glacier Rond. The icy steps exceed 55° for a few metres. The average gradient of the central section at the back ('heart') of the slope is 50°/200m.

128.b   Cunningham Couloir (TD). Also known as the Passerelle Couloir, you can rappel directly into it from the footbridge (passerelle) between the two stations on the Aiguille du Midi, or you can reach the notch at the top of it via the east ridge. This descent is a very good example of how to interpret data regarding the gradient of a slope. The centre and bottom ('heart') of the couloir is given a gradient of about 45°, whereas the actual slopes that you ski on the left bank exceed 55° and the snow on them is often hard! In short, this is not a very attractive route and that is why, having skied the first (probable) descent with a client in 1979, I have never been back to this couloir.

129 AIGUILLE DU MIDI   3842m
Cosmiques Couloir   D

⚑ 3790m	🏔 February-May	↳ 45°-50°/800m
↗ 20m + 50m	📷 235, 237, 244	⚠ 2
↘ 1500m + 1300m	🕐 2-3hrs	⊕ HP
✦ North/west	🎿 5.1

James Couttet

Chamonix hosted the 1960 World Ski Championships and from that moment on James Couttet (who had won in Engelberg in 1938) devoted his life to the creation and development of the Les Bossons ski area. The chairlift and drag-lift give skiers access to various pistes with almost 400m of height gain. To guarantee snow cover, water is taken from the Taconnaz Glacier to feed the snow canons. Moreover, the night skiing is an excellent bonus to the valley's attractions. Born and bred in the village of Les Bossons and as well as being a champion skier, James Couttet was also a talented mountaineer and climbed with, among others, Rébuffat and Lachenal. He was an all-round 'montagnard' and worked hard to preserve the authenticity of the mountains and their inhabitants. It was a great privilege to have known him. And it seems a litt-

Descent of the north ridge of the Dôme

le superfluous to add that his pure and honest approach to life was as precise and well-controlled as his ski turns!

———————

From Chamonix, via the Aiguille du Midi, follow route 128 to the col between the Cosmiques Hut and the Abri Simond. Set up a rappel (up to 50m some years) to cross the first few metres of mixed ground in the narrow couloir. Ski on the right bank, pass below the rocks and soon after use the west face. The couloir narrows towards the middle and where it widens out again you can join the Glacier Rond route (via route 128 to the Plan de l'Aiguille or routes 129.a or 129.b). From the tunnel you can ski right of the road via the summer tack down to the Aiguille du Midi car-park.

129.a   Descent via Taconnaz Glacier (AD). From the foot of the couloirs, and if there is good snow cover, you can ski the Taconnaz Glacier. At La Jonction area head left and make your way through the seracs and crevasses (you will need to roped together for this). From the Gîte à Balmat, descend the first north-facing slope that ends in a rocky section, then traverse left at the level of the small col (2221m) before the Bec du Corbeau. Traverse and ski the large west combe, head left (bands of rock downhill of you) and join the right bank of the Taconnaz Glacier (risk of avalanche in the afternoon). Via the line of moraine and the piste/track to the water supply points for the snow canons, join the pistes of Mont Blanc Glacier and Les Bossons ski area.

129.b   Direct descent via the Bossons Glacier (AD). At the bottom of the couloirs, follow the variant above. From the Gîte à Balmat, go to the small col (2221m). Stay on the north face and ski the length of the combe. At the bottom, head left 100m before the edge of the glacier to follow the narrow east-facing couloir, opposite the Plat du Glacier. There is a very slightly ascending traverse towards the right bank. Leave the glacier and, via a clearing in the woods, pick up the Cherro trail that leads to the right of the tunnel entrance area. There are other variants on the right side.

130 MONT BLANC DU TACUL   4248m
North face   AD

3790m	April-October	35°-40°/400m
1070m	216, 237	2
3470m	4-6hrs	SP
North	3.3	

It may seem something of a paradox, but you can ski on the Mont Blanc du Tacul at any time of the year except during the winter months. It can be very dangerous in winter, as the snow builds up here and does not stick to the slopes very well. Nevertheless, devoted ski-mountaineers bump into each other quite often here, and, among the big names of extreme skiing, Dominique Neuenschwander deserves a mention. This discrete and committed skier from Geneva advocates a pure form of extreme skiing and refuses to use 'mechanical means' on his routes (helicopters...). He has been scouring the world's mountain ranges for steep slopes to ski since the 1970s, and his first descents in the Mont Blanc Massif include the Gigord Couloir, the Aiguille Carrée (Grands Montets Ridge), the Domenech-Jaccoux Route (west face of Mont Blanc), and a route that links the east and west couloirs of the notch on the Dames Anglaises…

North face of Mont Blanc du Tacul

From Chamonix, via the Aiguille du Midi, descend the start of the east ridge. Ski down the first large slope on the right (there is sometimes a bergschrund to jump) or follow the normal route of the Vallée Blanche to the foot of the ridge. Go to the Col du Midi and then ski to the Cosmiques Hut (open some of the winter). The first slopes to climb towards the right can often be up to 40° before the crevasse. The next wide section is less steep. Now head right (crevasses) to go round the upper seracs, or alternatively climb straight up! At 4100m follow the ridge to the final section of rocky ramparts (30m of mixed climbing with crampons) before the summit. The descent follows the same route down and, depending on the season, you can ski back down to Chamonix via the Vallée Blanche. However, in general, when Mont Blanc du Tacul is stable and can be skied safely there isn't much snow left in the Vallée Blanche. Therefore, you usually have to take the Aiguille du Midi cable-car back down to Chamonix.

131 MONT MAUDIT   4465m
North face   D

⚐	3790m	🏔	April-October	⤵	45°/150m
↗	1430m	📷	238, 239	⚠	2
↘	1430m	🕓	5-7hrs	⊕	HP
✦	North	⚡	4.3		

The descent of the north face of Mont Maudit can be said to be serious, given that if there is not a track in, your decision to carry on will depend on both your knowledge of this kind of mountaineering and your experience of high-mountain terrain. You will need more than just solid technique and competent control of your skis, therefore, to ensure a adequate safety margin for this tour, and there will be other factors to take in to account (dig a snow pit, 'coin suisse' – another means of testing the snow's stability). In the top section (gradient of up to 45°) any fall could be extremely serious and there is always the risk of slab avalanches and serac fall (the cause of several accidents each year) in the lower two thirds of this route.

Take the Aiguille du Midi cable-car from Chamonix to the top station. Descend the ridge and put your skis on above the south-east combe. Follow route 130 to reach the shoulder on the Mont Blanc du Tacul (4100m), then descend to the Col Maudit. You usually go to the right of the seracs, then up the face to the bergschrund (4300m). You reach the shoulder uphill of the Col du Mont Maudit via the small face on the right (45°/80m). Traverse south to go round the rocks and climb up the steep slope to the summit staying close to the easy ridge. Your choice of descent route will depend on the conditions you will have

Mont Maudit, north face

131.a

131

observed on the way up. If in doubt, follow the your route of ascent via the shoulder. The north face is made skiable by the fact that the powder snow stays here temporarily. If the snow is hard, the 45° start below the summit is very serious.

131.a   North-east ridge (D). Depending on the snow conditions and the risk of serac fall, you can climb directly up the north-east ridge from the Col Maudit. The climb gets a bit more technical (AD, ice and mixed climbing, 3 to 4 pitches) and exposed as you reach the top of the Kuffner Ridge. You can also climb directly up the north face, under the summit, rather than going to the shoulder (risk of windslab avalanches, 40-45°/120m).

132 MONT BLANC   4810m
Traverse   AD

⚐ 3790m		🏔 May-July		�☐ sections of 40°
↗ D1 + D2: 1400m		📷 239		⚠ 2
↘ D1 + D2: 2800m		☺ D1 + D2: 11hrs		⊕ SP
✦ North		✗ 4.1		

Although it looks so close when you are down in the Chamonix valley, Mont Blanc remains a very high mountain that is covered in glaciers. Despite its kindly appearance and the gentle atmosphere of competition created by the sheer volume of visitors to the mountain, you should not underestimate this route. Even if the record for going from Chamonix church to the summit and back (part of the descent involved some judicious bum-sliding!) is just 5hrs and 10mins… On skis, if you are fit and well-acclimatised, this route can quite often be done in day (there and back from the Aiguille du Midi). To do that, however, you need to be very fast, there has to be a track already in, you need a good and reliable weather forecast and you need to choose a day in spring when the days are longer.

D1 From Chamonix go to the Aiguille du Midi and follow ref.27 to the Cosmiques Hut.

D2 From the hut go to the Col du Midi and then follow route 131 to the shoulder on Mont Maudit. You will sometimes need to wear crampons on the traverse to the Col de la Brenva as it can be exposed (ice and slab avalanches). After the col, the Mur de la Côte acts as a reminder of the laws of altitude! Depending on the snow conditions, go round the Petits Rochers Rouges on the right or join the middle section of the long final headland to the summit. If you are running late, are tired, or the weather doesn't look good, you can join the centre of the north face and the Grand Plateau below the Rochers Rouges (at around 4550m) and you will need a snow stake as you will probably have to set up a rappel.
From the summit if the west ridge looks in good condition, you can put your skis on straight away. Otherwise, in crampons and preferably roped together, downclimb for about 150m to find an area that looks easier to ski. Go down the right of the ridge and join the Grand Plateau via La Tournette, the Bosses and the Vallot Hut. Now follow 134 to the Grands Mulets and the Plan de l'Aiguille.

132.a Start on the north face (AD). Traverse beneath the west ridge (bergschrunds) and then join the ridge below the Tournette rocks. This is a variant to use if the ridge has a high cornice and is icy or if the face is not in condition until lower down, on the Grand Plateau (35° then 40°/100m).

132.b Return via the Corridor (AD). Descend via the Mur de la Côte (45°/100m). Then, leaving the Col de la Brenva on your right, ski the huge combe ('Le Corridor') watching out for the deep crevasses. From 4150m you have to go left to find a way through the steep section (seracs, possible rappel depending on the conditions). Watch out for serac fall down the north face of Mont Blanc when you get to the Grand Plateau. Follow route 134 to the Grands Mulets rock outcrop and on to the Plan de l'Aiguille.

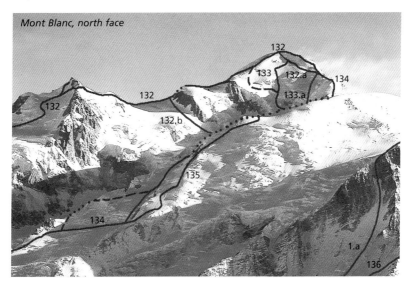

Mont Blanc, north face

Mont Blanc, bad weather threatens...

133 MONT BLANC   4810m
North face   D

⚑ 3790m	🏔 May-July	⛷ sect. of 45°, 30-35°/650m
↗ D1 + D2: 60m +1300m	📷 239	⚠ 2
↘ D1 + D2: 200m +2800m	🕐 D1 + D2: 9hrs	🏔 HP
✦ North	🎿 4.2	

Heli-drops from Italy into France were allowed up until 1981. As a result, some weeks in spring the north face of Mont Blanc would look like a piste with mogul fields. As I recall, the same President of France who was one of the first people to use a helicopter to access and to ski this face with the guide André Contamine in the 1960s, was the man who subsequently banned them. The first official descent was by the guide Lionel Terray and the skier Bill Dunaway for the purposes of a film in 1953. Spring 2001 saw huge numbers of skiers on the north face owing to great conditions (no need to rappel). The sheer weight of traffic in the area made the route into a very regular slope and my son Christopher and I were able to ski to the Plan de l'Aiguille from the summit in an hour. I

Arnaud van Schevensteen, the first one-legged person to climb and ski Mont Blanc!

should point out that the evenness of the slope allowed us to ski the route as if it was a piste, skiing fast and putting in wide turns, and generally making the most of the great snow conditions!

D1   From Chamonix, via the Aiguille du Midi, go to the Cosmiques Hut (ref.27). From here you can study the north face.

D2   Follow route 132 to the summit of Mont Blanc. The descent starts imme-diately below the summit. Ski a little to the left so as to pick up a slight couloir to cross the upper bergschrund. This is a not an extreme slope, but it is relatively exposed as the snow here is often hard. The gradient of the slope slackens off and you go round the large crevasse to the left (check it out beforehand). Come back to the centre of the face into a huge funnel-shaped area that often has an ice wall in it. (Be prepared to set up a rappel.) The route now follows the depression on the left with a large band of seracs above it. There are now about another 100m at 40°, then you cross the Grand Plateau. Follow route 134 or climb up towards the Dôme to descend the north ridge (aesthetic route for which you have to add an hour to the basic timing for the route, see route 135).

133.a   Traverse towards Les Bosses (D). After the first 200m of the face, tra-verse left towards the 'bosses' ('humps') on the normal route on Mont Blanc. Once you know that the route is ok all the way down, this descent of the north face is fantastic (between 40° and 50°/400m). Up until 2002, this route was sheltered from the seracs uphill of it. However, following an enormous shift in the seracs it is possible that before long this route will become extremely exposed as it is now in the line of potential serac falls.

On the north face of Mont Blanc

134 MONT BLANC   4810m
Normal route   AD

⌐ 2310m	🏔 April-June	⤵ sections of 35°
⬈ D1 + D2: 740m + 1760m	📷 235, 239	⚠ 2
⬊ D1 + D2: 2600m	⏱ D1 + D2: 3h$^{1/2}$ + 8$^{1/2}$hrs	SP
⬗ North	🎿 4.3	

Because of its altitude and exposed glaciated terrain (crevasses, serac fall), skiing Mont Blanc is a long and committing route. Nevertheless, bearing in mind these difficulties, the attraction for the ski-mountaineer remains the fact that this is the highest, one of the best and one of the most committing routes in the Alps.

If you have to descend to the Mont Blanc Tunnel (or, for the purists, if you start at the Mont Blanc Tunnel), you must ski beneath the power cables that are supported by the pylons for the old Glaciers cable-car, as the risk of avalanche is minimised here and controlled Gasex explosions carried out all around this area. This is especially true if you find yourself caught in bad weather.

The hardest thing about skiing this route, is sticking to the timings. You should follow the timetable given below.

– start from the Plan de l'Aiguille before 10 o'clock in the morning,
– be on the section below the Aiguille du Midi before midday (same goes for the return journey),
– reach the summit around 9 o'clock the following morning and return around 11 o'clock.

Finally, it is much better not to stop at the Vallot Hut, unless it is absolutely necessary. The hut is too high!

D1   From Chamonix follow ref.29 to the Grands Mulets Hut.

D2   From the hut, head towards the Dôme du Goûter to cross a first crevassed area at around 3200m. The main danger here comes from the risk of seracs falling from the Dôme du Goûter. Climb a little way up the left bank of the glacier, then, after making your way through the crevasses, move back to the centre of the glacier via an obvious headland and then move to the right bank. Try to stay on the left-hand side (crevasses) as you cross the Petit Plateau, so as to stay away from the seracs. A steep climb gives access to the Grand Plateau (deep crevasse on the side). Now head right and follow a regular slope up to the Col du Dôme (4237m). From here there is a steep and icy section that leads to the Vallot Hut. Ski-tourers rarely go to the summit with their skis on. The quality of the skiing on the descent is limited by the hard, windblown snow and the tricky and exposed ground you have to cover, especially on the ridge in the final section. It is now 2hrs to the summit (between 1/2hr and 1hr on the way down).

The descent follows the same route you took up back to the Grands Mulets, then to the Plan de l'Aiguille.

Note: There is a very real and obvious danger of serac fall at the point where you cross the Petit Plateau. If possible, it is preferable to follow the harder route up via the north ridge of the Dôme du Goûter (route 135).

135 DÔME DU GOÛTER   4304m
North ridge   D

⚑ 2310m	🗺 April-June	⌐ 40°-45°/400m
⬈ D1 + D2: 740m + 1250m	📷 239, 244	sections of 50°
⬊ D1 + D2: 2000m	⏲ D1 + D2: 3$^{1/2}$ + 7hrs	⚠ 2
⊕ North	⚔ 4.1	⊕ HP

This highly aesthetic route on the north ridge was very popular before heli-
drops were banned in the area. In fact, it ought to be both climbed in the summer and skied in the winter more often. Following this route also means you can
avoid the objective dangers of the normal route on the Petit Plateau. The descent
is 'airy' without being totally extreme and remains one of the most impressive
routes on Mont Blanc. As long as you have had a chance to check out the conditions beforehand, you can descend lower down the north face. There is a large
crevasse that cuts the slope in half. You can also cross the ridge at its eastern end.
The magnificent summit of the Dôme du Goûter and its 4304m sits a little in the
shade of its illustrious neighbour, but nevertheless makes a great objective in its
own right, especially this direct route to the summit via the north ridge.

D1   From the Plan de l'Aiguille follow ref.29 to the Grands Mulets Hut.

D2   From the hut climb via the Mont Blanc route (134) towards the foot of the
north ridge, which you go round from about 3150m. The wide headland narrows
(bergschrund) and you will have to walk up in crampons for over 300m (vertical
height gain) to reach the Pointe Bravais (4057m), at the top of the ridge. The summit of the Dôme du Goûter is about an hour up from here. If you have seen the
route on the way up, the descent should not pose any problems. However, if you
decide to ski this route after having climbed up to Mont Blanc, you should stay
near the ridge and slightly to the left. There are often windslab formations and
ice in the steepest section.

On the north ridge of the Dôme du Goûter

136   GLACIER DU BOURGEAT   3060m
Trappier Couloir   AD

⌶	1800m	🏔	February-March	⤵	40°-45°/400m
↗	1250m	📷	244	⚠	1
↘	2000m	⦿	5hrs	⊕	SP
⊕	North/west	🎿	4.1		

This superb route, often used by Monsieur Trappier, a passionate local ski-tourer, offers a 2000m descent on an even slope of powder snow. Accessing this route, however, can be dangerous after large falls of snow followed by strong winds.

From Les Houches take the Bellevue cable-car up and follow the line of the Tramway du Mont Blanc (see route 1). After the Col du Mont Lachat, join the second steep combe at around 2200m. Traverse directly left, then climb up a sustained slope to start with and then on a steep headland that overlooks the Arandellys gully (summer path to the Dérochoir). Head into the next small and steep valley on your left. At its eastern end, a slope followed by a double couloir towards the right allow you to cross the rock band (2800m). Depending on the snow cover, descend slightly and, via the thalweg of an ancient glacier, head back up and east. You can see, below and to the right, the Baraque Forestière des Rognes (2768m). Cross the Glacier de la Griaz. Sometimes no more than blocks of blue ice, you can go round the top of this, but it makes the crossing quite dangerous. Join the obvious ridge of the Trappier Couloir at around the point marked 3029m on the map. Behind this point there are several relatively steep couloirs that give access to the main couloir (almost 45°). Follow the main couloir for about 500m. If the central gullies are too deep, you can join on the left, via a notch, a small steep couloir that runs parallel to this. The snow conditions are better here. Come back right on a huge cone at the bottom of the

Mont Blanc from the Aiguillette des Houches

couloir at around 1600m. Keep well to the left on the wooded slopes, and via a series of steep densely wooded steps, you will reach the bottom of the main slopes. Stay on the left bank of the Torrent du Bourgeat and go to Les Granges and Saint-Antoine on the Les Houches road. In this case, it is easier to stay on the right bank of the mountain stream and go back to Taconnaz via Le Tremblay.

136.a   La Griaz ravines (AD). At the bottom of the Bourgeat valley (at around 1800m), keep traversing left (trees and steep couloirs). This brings you out at the north-west crest below the Bec à l'Oiseau. Descend into a series of wild ravines, at the foot of enormous avalanches that have come down from the La Griaz and Les Arandellys areas. Via the left bank of the Torrent de la Griaz (track near the road), you can rejoin Les Houches. This is quite an athletic variant! The less agile skiers may end up spending quite a while here…

137 MONT LACHAT   2115m
North-east ridge   PD

1800m	Winter	sections of 35°
316m	3hrs	1
1100m	2.3	DP
North		

This short route is great for the start of the season and can be done after the first falls of snow. In this case, the climb up in skins following the track is a great training route and a good route to do if the weather is not looking good. Despite the sounds of the nearby valley, as you enter this area you quickly feel like you are in the wilderness and only the chamois feel at home here…
The north-east face, between the Col du Mont Lachat (buildings) and the Roche Fendue headland, is an averagely steep slope covered in dry grass where the snow builds up. Despite the fact that there is a track that crosses this slope, it regularly becomes avalanche-prone. You can also do this tour with snow-shoes from the bottom up to at least the Baraque Forestière des Arandellys, at around 1800m.

From Les Houches, via the Bellevue cable-car, follow the Tramway du Mont Blanc (traverse of a steep couloir on the Bioannassay face) or follow more or less the line of the west crest of Mont Lachat. From the summit, start your descent on the north-east face. You will quite soon come up against a lot of shrubs and bushes (cables and pylons). You end up at the Baraque Forestière des Arandellys via a series of steep slopes. A little downhill of here, traverse left via the track that you follow to the Bellevarde pastures. On your descent of this track there are two avalanche couloirs, which you should cross with care.

137.a   Roche Fendue (F). At the start of winter, before the lifts are open, you can set off from Les Houches (Route des Gens, between the church and the Mairie or Town Hall). At the end of the road, follow the track (Baraque Forestière des Arandellys). The climb, which you can do using skins, is quite athletic. The recommended descent route is via the Roche Fendue and route 136.

138 LE PRARION-VAUDAGNE   1967m
Traverse   PD

⌐ 1850m	⬚ December-March	⌐ 35°/50m
⬈ 110m	◔ 2hrs	⚠ 1
⬊ 1950m	⤨ 2.1	⊕ DP
⬨ North-east		

Over the last few decades 'moyenne montagne' skiing in the Northern Alps has become a bit tricky. There are several reasons why skiing at lower altitudes has become more difficult. For example: the locals no longer use the forest under-growth as firewood, and the price of spruces has dropped while forestry work has become devalued and underpaid. As a result, there are all kinds of bits of brushwood growing all over the place, which is not good for skiers, least of all over the last few years when the winter's snowfall has hardly been heavy enough to regularly and properly crush the dead wood. Our ancestors worked incredibly hard to clear and to tame the mountains. They pulled up stumps, flattened banks and moraines, redirected mountain streams and dug tracks. When skiing first began, we made use of these 'organised' mountainsides, but over the last few years our high mountain pastures have disappeared along with the tracks that used to lead up to them. The solution is to maintain the ski areas. This is what the ski instructors in the Morzine-Avoriaz ski area decided to do. Volunteer, they give up one or two days each summer to clear the forest areas that have been overrun by unwanted vegetation.

From Les Houches, via the Prarion gondola, go to the start of the crest that leads to the Prarion. Between the trees and via a final step that steepens up, you arrive in 35mins at the summit. Descend via the north ridge that narrows. There is a steep and narrow section before the slope widens out again. In the same direction, between the trees you end up at the Col de la Forclaz. Follow the track, on the right, that goes back to Les Chavants. In the best snow conditions you can ski the right side of Le Prarion, near the gondola. After only a few minutes of climbing you can join this great off-piste run on the north/north-east slope.

138.a   Col de la Forclaz (F). Just as with the Mont Lachat route, this tour can be done in snow-shoes or with skins without using the gondola. Follow the tracks that lead up from Les Chavants (or from the small villages of Vaudagne and Le Châtelard) to the Col de la Forclaz. All of these tracks are signposted and are in the forest. From the Prarion 'belvedere', or panoramic viewpoint, you get great views of the whole of the north and west faces of the Mont Blanc Massif, as well as part of the Contamines area. From Le Châtelard, starting at Les Brions (1051m) it should take 3 1/2 hrs. Watch out as certain sections of the route can be dangerous if there are heavy snowfalls or there is a thaw (this is a useful consideration, as this route is often put aside as a poor weather-day alternative).

AIGUILLES ROUGES

PRACTICAL INFORMATION

Chamonix Tourist Office: 04 50 53 00 24 / www.chamonix.com
Compagnie des Guides: 04 50 53 00 88 / www.cieguides-chamonix.com
Ass. Int. Guides du Mont Blanc: 04 50 53 27 05 / www.guides-du-mont-blanc.com
Summits: 04 50 53 50 14 / www.summits.fr
Office de Haute Montagne: 04 50 23 22 08 / www.ohm-chamonix.com
PGHM: 04 50 53 16 89
Weather forecast: 08 92 68 02 74 / www.meteo.fr
Snow report: 08 92 68 10 20

SKI LIFTS

Brévent: 04 50 53 13 18
Flégère: 04 50 53 18 58

ROAD ACCESS

From Annecy, Geneva or Sallanches follow the A40 (or N205)
to Chamonix.

Previous page: A memorable winter's day high above the Chamonix Valley.

The Aiguilles Rouges chain could have suffered from being so close to its illustrious neighbour, the Mont Blanc Massif, but in fact the huge variety of routes on offer here means that the two ranges complement each other. From easy tours to narrow couloirs, from routes with easy access from ski lifts to numerous possible traverses, the Aiguilles Rouges is an integral part of the Mont Blanc region. Thanks to this ease of access and the great circuits that can be done in this area, this is also the starting point for trips heading north: to Sixt, Flaine and Les Portes du Soleil; or to the east and Switzerland: to the high limestone Alps via the Col de la Tour Salière and the Barberine cols; not forgetting, of course, the great routes on the Bel Oiseau, the Dent de Fenestral or Fontanabran between Finhaut and Les Marécottes. Moreover, this chain of crystalline rock (gneiss) also offers superb views of the whole of the Mont Blanc Massif, which are both breathtakingly beautiful and, more importantly, are a great opportunity for getting a look at routes for the future. The other advantage the Aiguilles Rouges has is that you can easily choose the best side of the chain to ski on, as the ski lifts and the pistes are all on the south side and the best descents are to be had on the 'wild' north side where the snow stays in excellent condition for a long time. The secondary ranges of the Perrons and Luisin-Emaney don't have ski lifts and usually get skied at the beginning of the season, for road access to the Emosson Dam, as the snow cover is general better here (the area is near the very wet valleys of Haut Faucigny).

139 AIGUILLETTE DES HOUCHES   2285m
From Le Brévent   PD

⚑	2525m (ski lift)	🏔	January-March	⌐	sect. of 30-35°
↗	160m	📷	249	⚠	1
↘	400m + 890m	🕐	3-4hrs	⊕	DP
✦	South-west	🎿	2.3		

Aiguillette des Houches

139.a   139

The Aiguillette des Houches is a lovely descent with a short climb, and can be done from the start of the season up to March. If you are considering skiing it, you should take into account the fact that it faces west and its quite sustained slope is exposed to the setting sun.

Don't be fooled by these gentle-looking slopes. They can be extremely dangerous as was evidenced by the huge Charousse avalanche that swept the whole of the face below the Aiguillette, ripping through the railway line and coming to halt at the level of the Autoroute Blanche in the valley...

From Chamonix, take the cable-cars up to Le Brévent. Join the west face and then cross a steep step on the left (leads to the entrance of the ENSA Couloir). Now climb up slightly and join the ridge that marks the boundary of the Chamonix face of the mountain (start of the EMHM, Bellachat etc couloirs). Another steep step (hut on the left) leads to the Col Bellachat. Ski along the side of the mountain to pass under the Aiguillette du Brévent and continue towards the Aiguillette des Houches. The start of the descent is just before the end of the crest. Join a steep combe that faces Mont Blanc and descend, continuing rightwards to get the best snow conditions. After a steeper traverse, continue left on to a large headland or right to the large couloir. Lower down, in the trees, pick up and follow the track that leads to La Flatière and Le Bettey, where I recommend you leave a car (in doing this you can check out the route from the road when you drop off the car).

139.a   Access via Le Coupeau (F). Rather than using the lifts to get to the start of the route, you can access the Aiguillette via its west face. From Le Coupeau, follow the track that leads to the Chailloux chalets, and then access the Aiguillette via the west crest. This is a more varied and aesthetic route despite the steep section at the level of the highest fir trees. For an alternative set of views and orientation you can follow the track from La Flatière up to the Chalets du Plan de la Cry and then go through the forest to the west crest ($2^{1/2}$-3hrs).

140 LE BRÉVENT   2525m
Tour of the north face   PD

⌐ 2525m (ski lift)	🪓 Winter	⌐ sections of 35°
↗ 350m	📷 251, 252	⚠ 1
↘ 1050m + 900m	🕐 3hrs	⊕ DP
⊕ All	⤨ 2.3	

The Brévent lifts were constructed in 1928 to carry tourists up to the top of the Brévent in the summer rather than for skiers. At that time, skiing down from the Brévent was considered quite an achievement!

You can quickly access several routes from the Brévent, unless of course the lift is closed for security reasons. It is quite a unique off-piste arena up here, but over the last few years there have been pretty mediocre falls of snow at the beginning of the season. As a result of this quirk of nature and the lack of properly cold weather, descents of the 1500m couloirs and sustained slopes here are becoming increasingly rare. On the other hand, the numbers of freeriders on

ENSA Couloir

the upper slopes of the Autel, Charlanon and the Aiguille Pourrie have been steadily increasing. Moguls seem to form really quickly on these descents, especially near the lifts and it feels like a non-stop show sometimes. On the south side the steep couloirs such as the Bellin (under the lift cables), the ENSA (further left, 40-50°/150m), the EMHM (exposed middle section) and the others further west, less commonly in condition, can be skied from the beginning of the winter if the snow cover is good. It is better to ski these when they have powder snow in them, as they are more dangerous and steep when the snow is hard (quite exposed if you fall). Beware, these are avalanche couloirs!

From Chamonix take the lifts up to the Brévent and follow the start of the pistes down to the Brèche du Brévent (2398m, rock climbing area on the left). Traverse via various short descents and climbs to the Col du Brévent (2368m). Via the combe before the Pointe de Vioz, descend the steep north face either to the left or to the right of a small central spur (risk of slab avalanches). Come back near a band of rock and, at around 2050m, start to climb up and right. After a long diagonal traverse, cross the hillocks below the Lac Cornu. Now go round to the right of the lake (if the ice is well formed on the lake you can also traverse across it). Climb up to the Col de la Glière (2461m) and from there either follow the Combe de la Glière back to La Flégère or cross the Col du Lac Cornu (via the south-west

On the north side of Le Brévent

or steeper south-east couloir) and join the Charlanon pistes at Le Brévent. If the conditions allow, you can even ski back down to Chamonix via the pistes or through the wood.

Traverse to the Col de la Glière

140.a

140.a   Aiguille de Charlanon (PD). You can also climb, before the Lac Cornu, to the Aiguille de Charlanon, and follow the same route down to ski the north face. You can then pick up route 140 and cross the lake or traverse the Aiguille to the north-east. Two couloirs on the south face are skiable. One is exposed and narrow and is downhill and west of the Aiguille (50°/80m). The other is wider and less steep and starts to the east, after the traverse of the summit of the Aiguille (40°/150m, rarely in condition!).

140.b   Pont d'Arlevé – Moëde Chalets (PD). Follow route 140 to the Col du Brévent and continue into the north valley, staying right, below the rocks. After a flat section, follow the path north across this steep and avalanche-prone slope (flattened bushes) to the Pont d'Arlevé. After the bridge (1597m), traverse and climb up to the Moëde Chalets. Now follow the summer path that leads to the Plateau d'Assy (long way to go to leave a car...).

140.c   Col de Bérard (PD). From the Pont d'Arlevé (via route 140.b), stay on the left bank of the Torrent de la Diosaz and climb up the length of the valley to the Col du Bérard (2460m) via the Balme Chalets. Descend into the east valley to get to the village of Le Buet (SNCF rail station), 5hrs.

141 AIGUILLE POURRIE — 2561m
South-west couloirs — PD

⌶ 2525m (ski lift)		🏔 Winter		↳ 50°/50m	
↗ 200m		📷 254		⚠ 1	
↘ 1300m + 1000m		🕐 3hts		⊕ DP	
✤ South-west		🎿 4.3			

Quite apart from its renown as a skiing area, the Aiguille Rouges is also a natural reserve. The reserve is hourglass shaped and, roughly speaking, it covers the north facing areas from the Col de Bellachat to the Aiguille du Belvédère (bounded by the Torrent de la Diosaz and the Col de Salenton), and from the Col des Dards to the bottom of the Bérard valley (including north and south faces down to the main road). Officially founded in June 1972, the reserve manages a rich and fragile landscape, flora, fauna and woodland. Even though the snow in winter hides some, or all, of this natural heritage from us, ski-mountaineers must respect the area as this delicate environment and its inhabitants should not be disturbed. Remember that the wildlife is particularly vulnerable at this time, and although it may be camouflaged the least disturbance can cause enormous expenditure of energy by an animal. As it flees its perceived attacker it could waste valuable energy, which can lead to exhaustion and even death... So, be careful and respect the area and its inhabitants!

From Chamonix, take the Brévent lifts up and follow the pistes to the Brèche du Brévent then the Col (see route 140). Descend via the east face (Autel slopes) above Planpraz (40°/100m), then follow the pistes to the Col Cornu chairlift. At the top of the chairlift, walk up a small steep couloir (10mins). After a kind of headland, you arrive at the Col du Lac Cornu (2414m). Follow the west ridge and choose one of the narrow south-west facing couloirs (40-45°/80m) opposite the top of the chairlift. If the snow is not good enough for this, go to the top of the north face (a few metres of walking or skiing below the summit). There is almost always powder snow here. You can ski down to Flégère via the Combe de la Glière and take the cable-car back to Brévent.

141.a Traverse to the Col de la Glière (2461m, F). From the Col du Lac Cornu,

there is a slight ascending traverse on the north-west face of the Aiguille Pourrie via the top of a steep valley (ever-present risk of unstable slabs balancing above the rock band) to the Col de la Glière. If this traverse looks a bit hazardous owing to large amounts of snow having been deposited here by the wind, then descend into the hollow to climb up the valley to the west of the col (need skins). Descend on to the east side of the col (steep for 50m) then ski down to Flégère via the Combe Lachenal.

141.b Col des Lacs Noirs (2610m, F). From the Col de la Glière you can continue the traverse to the Col des Lacs Noirs (easy climb up). From the col a regular slope of about 35° joins the bottom of the Combe de la Glière.

Col de la Glière

142 AIGUILLE DE LA GLIÈRE   2852m
East face   PD

2385m (ski lift)		Winter		35°-40°
500m		254		1
1000m + 800m		4hrs		SP
South-west		3.1		

There are some good short routes on the Aiguille de la Glière, which often come into condition quite quickly. It is also worth remembering that there was summer skiing up here in the 1970s thanks to the large amounts snow built up by avalanches, which stayed on the mountain until quite late into the summer, and two little drag-lifts.

From Les Praz de Chamonix, via the Flégère cable-car and the Index chairlift. Go up and right to use the transversal moraine that comes back into the centre of the slope below the Verlin Gendarme (pass on your left). A short steep climb left takes you to the upper combe that you climb to the left of the summit (don't climb to the summit itself, 45m of IV, rappel). The descent follows the same route back down, or you can follow a direct couloir (narrow) below the upper combe (40°/50m).

142.a   Descent west to the Col des Lacs Noirs (AD). This route is a bit steep at the top. Either climb up to the first col (40°/50m) or go to the real Col des Lacs Noirs (35° for a few metres and then 30° to the Combe de la Glière).

From the Aiguille Pourrie to the Aiguille de Praz Torrent

142.b ● **Traverse onto the west side of the massif via the Combe du Pouce (AD).** The slope is steep at the top (40°/100m). Go round the Aiguille du Pouce and the Tête du Béchat (2593m). Now traverse rightwards at this height (around 2250m) via a series of steep ledges (exposed). After the Combe de la Balme go to the Combe d'Envers de Bérard (about 1900m). Climb up to the Col de Bérard (1 1/2 hrs to the col at 2460m and return via Le Buet). Climb the combe de La Balme to the Col des Aiguilles Crochues (2704m, 2hrs) to get back to Flégère.

142.c ● **Traverse via the Floria Glacier (AD).** At the height of the Verlin Gendarme, continue in the couloir to the east ridge and go down to almost the height of the Col de la Floria (2752m). Via the quite narrow north couloir (40°/150m), descend to the Floria Glacier. Stay on the left (crevasses on the right) and go round he main section of the glacier to come back right into the skiable slopes. Stay right to pick up route 142.b.

143	AIGUILLE DE LA FLORIA	2888m
	East ridge	AD

⌐	2385m	🏳	Winter	⌐	40°-45°/100m
↗	500m	📷	257	⚠	1
↘	1200m + 800m	⏱	4-5hrs	🖐	SP
✦	South-west	🎿	4.1		

As with many of the peaks in the Aiguilles Rouges, there are only really difficult routes from the summit of the Aiguille de la Floria. Depending on the snow cover, the descents here often require some down-climbing for a few metres or the use of a rope.

From Les Praz de Chamonix, via the Flégère cable-car and the Index chairlift, follow the Crochues-Bérard route (number 144). At the south col (2701m), start walking up the north-east slope early on keeping as close as possible to the east ridge. You will have to traverse towards the right from time to time and then you reach a small notch before the final steep snowy ridge. Follow the same route on the descent (sections of 45°), then pass your tracks up and continue into the Combe des Aiguilles Crochues or towards Bérard.

Telemarking, the purest form of skiing!

143.a   West side (D). From the summit descend right to the south-west ridge and ski the west couloir that steepens up. Pick up a deep couloir on the left (rope useful) and follow it to the Floria Glacier, then join route 142.c. The slopes on the south-east face of the east and west notches on the Petite Aiguille Floria can be skied but it's not great skiing. Moreover, the cornices on the ridge look pretty threatening (50°/100m, snow cover varies).

143.b   East couloir (AD). From the summit, descend the east couloir. It has a narrow section and is barely skiable at the beginning of the winter because of the small rock band at the start. Continue into the Comb e des Crochues (pistes).

144 CROCHUES-BÉRARD   2701m
Traverse   PD

⌐ 2385m	⛰ December-May	ᗱ sections of 35°
↗ 480m	📷 254, 257	⚠ 1
↘ 1570m	◔ 4-5hrs	⊕ SP
✦ All	⚔ 2.3	

The Bérard Valley has also been declared a nature reserve and joined the Aiguilles Rouges Reserve in 1992. Carpeted with flowers in summer, the valley is a high level destination for snow-shoers in the winter. There are some glorious days in the winter and spring when the paths of the snow-shoers, or 'trappeurs', sweating their way up the valley, cross, more or less amicably, those of the skiers as they hurtle down in a narrow and direct line on the descent... We are all friends of the mountain, so a bit of tolerance and patience is required towards others. Besides, we don't own the mountain and we should do our best to preserve the peace and tranquillity of the place!

From Les Praz de Chamonix, take the Flégère and the Index (2385m) lifts up. Climb 100m up and away from the top of the lift station, then go round to the right of the foot of the south spur of the Aiguille de la Floria. A new draglift was opened in the winter of 2002 that takes you to exactly this spot. Traverse onto the large cone beneath the south col (2701m). Access to the left-hand notch is on foot. Descend to

Crochues ridge

the other side of the col, head right and go to the start of the long traverse beneath the Aiguille du Belvédère. The slopes here are not great and there is often a lot of avalanche debris (falls and slips here could have serious consequences).

Aiguille du Belvédère and the Pointe Favre

After a kind of ledge you get to the Col de Bérard via its south-west side (35mins of climbing). There is an easy descent in the large combe down from the col, and after a series of huge snow-fields you get to the Bérard Valley. Follow the track to the village of Le Buet (SNCF railway station). The north notch of the Crochues (2704m) is not used, but its south face can be skied (cornice, 45°/80m).

144.a   Col des Dards (2790m, AD). Descend onto the north side of the Col des Crochues and head right and as high as possible below the rock face of the Aiguilles Crochues. Climb up with skins towards the Aiguille du Belvédère and you will quickly see the steep access to the diagonal ledge that leads to the south notch of the Col des Dards. Be careful not to climb up into the first couloir, as you will then have to traverse the summit of the Crochues from right to left. This is possible, but is a longer route. Also, don't let yourself get drawn into trying to go to the main col, which is near the Belvédère as it has a section of difficult climbing in it (15m of II and IV). There is a great descent via the Lac Blanc side and on the return you end up back in Flégère (145.a).

Grande Floria and the Combe des Crochues

144.b   Aiguille de Bérard-Brèche Bévoty (2600m, PD). Rather than climbing up to the Col de Bérard from the shoulder at 2300m, continue to the heart of the combe that comes down from the col and then climb up the opposite slope. The climb up is quite steep for 50m and it is easier if you go up the slight combe. As you near the end of the climb, look out for the rocky notch on your right that you reach on foot. The direct descent now joins up with the relatively sustained slopes that lead to the Bérard Valley (40 mins more than going via the Col de Bérard).

144.c   Pointe Alphonse Favre, north/north-west couloir (AD). From the top of the Pointe Alphonse Favre, continue eastwards along the ridge. At the level of the large rocks on a small plateau, traverse for about 60m to the north and join the couloir on the left that narrows (40°/100m). Rejoin route 144.

145   POINTE ALPHONSE FAVRE   2788m
Mort Glacier   AD

⌶	2385m	🏔	January-May	⌐	35°/350m
↗	500m + 350m	📷	257, 260, 261	⚠	1
↘	250m + 1550m	🕐	5-6hrs	🚹	SP
✦	North	🎿	3.3		

In the heart of the Aiguilles Rouges and invisible from Chamonix, the Pointe Alphonse Favre has one of the best descents in the valley. There are certain connoisseurs who zealously keep this route a secret and would like to have it for themselves. Given the increasing numbers of people visiting it over the past few years, I would say they haven't been doing a very good job! The technical grading of the route means that it can be skied by a large number of people and it has the bonus of always having excellent snow conditions as it doesn't see ray of sun for the whole winter. Moreover, if you are prepared for the interesting alpine climbing to reach it, you can ski this route from the summit. First climbed by Alphonse Favre, a Genevan geologist, on 13 August 1887.

From Les Praz de Chamonix, follow route 144 (Crochues-Bérard traverse). Start the descent from the Col des Aiguilles Crochues and look out for the couloir that you need to climb, which you will see after the cliffs on the south face of the Aiguille du Belvédère. The start of the couloir is on a large cone after the last spur and you climb up using skins or on foot (if there is already a track!). The couloir narrows before the final crest. From here, on the left before the subsidiary summit, you can ski a steep couloir that faces north/north-west (145.b) and has good snow (narrow at the start, rocks more or less covered, 45°/50m then 35-40°/250m, arrive downhill of the Col de Bérard on the Envers de Bérard side). Continue left, close to the west crest. There is another descent on the north side, but it is less easy to find if you haven't checked it out before (see route 145.b). Stay on the west side and cross a step (often mixed, II) that is last obstacle before the summit. On the descent, go to a small col, then traverse to the top of the Mort Glacier and follow it to the bottom of the Bérard valley. The top of the slope barely exceeds 35°.

145.a   Le Belvédère (AD). From the small col below the summit, continue along the west headland of the Aiguille du Belvédère, then at around 2850m the route for skiers is blocked by the 'grosse marche' or the 'big step' (several exposed steps, rock climbing, III, to go to the summit of the Belvédère, 2hrs round-trip). The complete descent of the Mort Glacier starts via the right-hand headland, then joins the steep combe (slabs possible). There is also a difficult section on the north face, on the Bérard Glacier (ropes, sling and ice-axe useful in case you choose the wrong route!). I don't advise you do this route if you don't know where you are going.

145.b ■ North/north-east couloir of the Pointe Alphonse Favre (AD). 45°/50m and 35-40°/250m.

146 COL DU BELVÉDÈRE   2780m
South-east face   F

⚑ 2385m	🗻 January-May	⤵ 30°/50m
↗ 420m	📷 254, 260, 261	⚠ 1
↘ 900m + 800m	⏱ 4-5hrs	⊕ SP
✦ South	🎿 2.3	

In addition to being the highest summit in the Aiguilles Rouges, the Aiguille du Belvédère is also something of a geological curiosity. Situated in the heart of this crystalline massif (gneiss), the summit plateau of the Belvédère is actually limestone and is the remains of the Morcles sheet. This sedimentary layer, the original base of the Chamonix Valley, was thrust upwards during the period of alpine upheaval that reached as far as the neighbouring Haut Faucigny chain. You can traverse the summit on skis although there is a difficult section across the north ridge. This is actually more like mountaineering as there is an exposed section of down-climbing before you ski the steep Mort Glacier (145 or 145.a). There are two other routes that you can ski from the summit of the Belvédère, but it is essential that you check them out before skiing them as they can be very variable depending on the condition of the snow in them. One is in the middle of the north face and you have to pick out the line of descent beforehand, and the other faces more to the east and its slopes are often exposed.

On the Col du Belvédère

From Les Praz de Chamonix, take the Flégère and Index lifts. At the top station of the Index lift, head north-east (can use drag-lift here too) and, via a long traverse broken by short sections of climbing up, go to the Combe des Aiguilles Crochues. Now traverse, at the same height, round the south base of the Crochues and continue diagonally to the Lac Blanc (2352m). Pass the lakes and zigzag up the back of the valley. After a kind of ledge and a final step you reach the col with relative ease. The descent of this face presents no difficulties, although the snow here transforms very quickly and is not always in good condition.

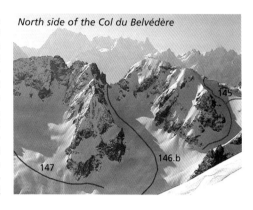

North side of the Col du Belvédère

146.a   Col des Dards-Aiguilles Crochues (F). Follow route 146 and well above the lake head left of the Belvédère towards the Col des Dards, further left for the summit of the Crochues (2837m). On the descent, there is often powder snow on this north-east face and it is certainly better quality than the snow on the Col du Belvédère. From the col you can check out the top of route 144.a on the north side.

146.b   North-west face (AD). One of the best descents in the massif, this traverse of the col onto the north-west face has become a classic route. If you find you have to put the track in or the snow is crusty or hard, it is customary to use a rope and secure it to the rock on the right (piton). After about 100m that are between 40 and 45°, the gully gets considerably bigger and the slopes on the right and the left, down to the kind of ledge in the glacier, are more stable. Stay on the left to avoid the crevasses and continue into the huge Bérard valley. This brings you out in the village of Le Buet (see route 144).

147 COL DE BEUGEANT 2807m
North face AD

2385m (ski lift)		January-May		35°/50m
900m		260, 261, 264, 265		1
1600m		5-6hrs		SP
North		3.1		

The Col de Beugeant is a classic route and is well known to the local tourers. In fact, just for the record, an 'athletic' tourer from Argentière amused himself by skiing it more than 500 times, managing to do it three times in one day! Joël Devouassoux, one of the valley's pure 'montagnards', is quite at home up here and overtakes other tourers as they strain to get to their objective weighed down by superfluous equipment. He is also very happy to make new tracks around the mountain and to surprise the chamois who, possibly recognising him, are used to these stealthy and silent passages across the snow. Are these images from a film by Samivel? Or rather a scene from a Frison-Roche story where nature's rigours and truths become simple values, which are most apparent to those who willingly receive her gift of beauty when she offers it…

From Les Praz de Chamonix, take the Flégère and Index lifts. Follow route 146 to the Lac Blanc. From just above the hut, go to the bottom of the Combe de Beugeant (at around 2500m) via a series of headlands and heading slightly left. Watch out, some sections can be exposed if a lot of snow has built up on the east face. You can also cross the Lacs Blancs without having to go to the new hut, by heading right after 2500m, which takes you to the left side (as you climb up) of the Combe de Beugeant. Via the centre of the combe, you reach a kind of a slight ledge on the left and you can see a line of ledges that you can follow up to the Col de Beugeant (100m of easy but exposed rock-climbing, use a rope to be safe and use the rock spikes to put in runners). If you continue climbing up the combe,

you reach a notch above a narrow gully that is not very skiable (take a rope). From the relatively narrow col, the descent on the north side is quite steep to start with. Now head left to cross a small col (Le Chardonnet, 2530m). Keeping a little to the left, you quickly join the large powder-filled slopes that stretch down to the Bérard valley.

Climbing up to the Col de Beugeant

147.a   Col de l'Encrenaz (PD). From the Col de Beugeant, there is a traverse down and beneath the Aiguille des Chamois and the Aiguille Martin to the Col de l'Encrenaz. The start of the descent on the east side is a bit rocky. Now ski down the whole valley, either via the Torrent de l'Eau Noire and the Col des Montets (149.a, not be done at the beginning of the season as the risk of avalanche is too high), or by traversing left to ski the distinct headland of the Tête de Praz Torrent. The slopes below and left are often exposed (build-up of windblown snow that rests on a steep slope of bushes and rhododendrons). If you head left through the larches you can get to Le Buet and the SNCF railway station, otherwise you can pick up the road.

Beugeant, north face

147.b   Encrenaz-Bérard (PD). Stay on the north side and on the left, below the Col de l'Encrenaz. Via the sustained slopes and heading slightly right, you can ski down directly to the Bérard valley if there is lots of snow. If not, head right in the large valley that comes down from the Aiguille de Mesure (route exposed to big powder and spring avalanches).

148 AIGUILLE DE L'ENCRENAZ   2887m
North face   AD

⌐ 2385m	⊠ February-May	⌐ 40°-45°/150m
↗ 600m	⌾ 264, 265	△ 1
↘ 1500m	☉ 5-6hrs	⑨ SP
✦ All	⚟ 4.1	

Aiguilles Rouges 'balcony'

1I was at the Posettes (Le Tour ski area) when I spotted a route that crosses the notch between the Aiguilles de l'Encrenaz and Martin and goes down the north-east face of Encrenaz, with its large couloir that is always in the shade. At the start of one winter (January) when it was cold and there was lots of snow, I climbed up this slope and found a way through on the right of the chimney below the summit. I had to climb up a kind of gully (section of 65°). 80m higher up, I was on the summit. I had to leave a sling in so that I could rappel back down past the icy section (rope for a 25m rappel, possible with crampons and ice-axe). I have been back to this route several times with aspirant guides and with clients and it is easier to climb up on the south side. The rest of the descent is a magnificent 400m couloir and the slope varies from 40° to 30° at the bottom. Seen from the Montenvers, these three couloirs look very enticing, but the snow conditions in them are often disappointing. Once you have skied the couloir on the Encrenaz there's not much point in skiing the others, as they are very similar, unless of course it's the panoramic view that you are after.

From the Les Praz de Chamonix take the Flégère cable-car and then the Index chairlift. Descend eastwards and follow route 146 to the Lac Blanc. Above the new Lac Blanc Hut, there is an easy climb to the foot of the large south combe beneath the Aiguille de la Persévérance (2450m). Go right of the most rocky-looking ridge south of the Aiguille as you climb up the combe. Join the central couloir that comes down from the notch between the Aiguille Martin and the Aiguille de l'Encrenaz. Go down to the foot of the couloir and follow a long traverse left towards route 147a.

148.a ▪ **North-east couloir (D).** At its start, from the notch between the Martin and the Encrenaz, the couloir is 40°/50m but there is a cliff in the way. Side-slip to the left of the spur and set up a rappel (minimum 30m high) to cross this rocky or icy convexity. You now join the large couloir and route 149.

149 COL DE L'ENCRENAZ
East face

2579m
PD

1430m		February-April		sections of 35°
950m		265		1
950m		4-5hrs		SP
East		3.1		

The route described here is not dependent on the cable-cars and their opening hours while the tough climb up to the col is varied and you get the added bonus of the odd sideways glance from a bemused chamois or bouquetin. Having said that, you can access this route from the Flégère lift system: climb up to the Lac Blanc and continue to the foot of the south spur of the Aiguille des Chamois. A long traverse around the foot of the various Aiguilles now takes you to the deep Encrenaz combe.

From Chamonix follow the N506 up to the Col des Montets and continue in the direction of Vallorcine. About 800m after the col stop after the first bridge (point marked 1431m on the map). Climb up the east face, through the larches, heading left in the middle and then following the right bank. Now go up the steep valley and join the bottom of the crest that separates the Aiguille de Mesure from the Aiguille Morris. Follow the crest to about 1900m. Head left below the rocks at the base of the Aiguille de Mesure and join the Combe de l'Encrenaz, which you climb to the col (might have to cross a few rocky sections on foot). There are various different routes that

Bérard valley

you can take on the descent, and your choice will depend on the usual criteria – quality and quantity of the snow, effects of the sun and heat, personal choice, time of year etc. The classic descent follows the route that you took on the way up.

149.a   Nant de l'Eau Noire (AD). Direct descent of the valley of the Torrent de l'Eau Noire to the Col des Montets (short sections of 40°, narrow).

149.b Aiguille Martin, Chardonnet Couloir (PD). From the Col de l'Encrenaz, climb up the north face of the Aiguille Martin to about 2620m below the Col de Beugeant and join route 147 in 20mins and ski the Bérard valley via Le Chardonnet.

149.c   Aiguille Morris, north face (D). You can ski the north/north-west face of the Col de l'Aiguille Morris. Take equipment for a short rappel in the middle to cross a band of rocks (section of 50°). On the other hand, the climb up the south side is steep and difficult.

Aiguille de l'Encrenaz, north couloir

149.a

147.a

148.a

150 AIGUILLE DE MESURE   2812m
East face   D+

1330m		March-May		sections of 55°
980m		265		2
980m		5-6hrs		SP
East		5.1		

You can get a really good view of this face from the Le Tour ski station. I climbed up and probably did the first descent of the east face of the Aiguille de Mesure one 4th April, and I had very good snow cover. A morning start from Le Buet means you can be on the east face quite early on. You can start from La Flégère and traverse under the Aiguilles Rouges if you want to traverse the east brèche or notch sometimes known as the Brèche de Praz Torrent. As it is a descent on the north side the timing will be ok.

From Le Buet (first small village behind the Col des Montets) or via route 147 in reverse, climb up the steep slope to below the Aiguille de Praz Torrent (at around 2100m). Go up and into the combe that finishes below the east face of the Aiguille de Mesure. Climb up the Aiguille on the left at first then via a ledge and now climb in a kind of Z shape to join the central promontory. Follow the promontory and head left again onto the slopes/couloirs that lead to the summit. On the descent of the route you have seen on the way up, you may have to use a rope before the small face that is crossed by a band of rocks at its base. You can't be sure that the slab will hold under your weight. You can continue your descent directly back to Le Buet or you can traverse the east brèche, or notch, of the Aiguille de Mesure (see route 150.a).

150.a   Traverse to the north side via the east brèche (2480m, D+). At the bottom of the large combe (2150m) head left of the large gendarme on the right of the summit of the Aiguille de Mesure. The couloir that leads to the notch is not too steep on this side. On the north side, however, it is narrow and very steep and there is not often a lot of snow in it. You will have set up one, two or even three 25m rappels here, the last one being entirely unavoidable (50m rope, pitons, snow stake). The skiable slope varies from 50° to 40°/200m. There is a long couloir on this big and wild north face that joins the Bérard valley and Le Buet. If you rappel past the top section of the couloir that is quite unpleasant as it is narrow and difficult, then this descent is a D. It is better to set off from Le Buet if you want to ski this descent, while starting from the Flégère lift system is better for doing the traverse of the east brèche as well as the descent of its north side.

Aiguille de l'Encrenaz and the Aiguille de Mesure

151	**LE BUET**	**3096m**
	South-east side	**PD**

⛏	1330m	🏔	December-May	↳	sections of 35°
↗	1770m	📷	267	⚠	1
↘	1770m	⏱	6hrs	⚕	SP
⊕	East	🎿	3.1		

By 1981 there were only four sites in the Massif where heli-drops were allowed: the Dôme de Goûter, the bergschrund on Mont Mallet, Pointe Isabelle and Le Buet. The status of the last of these sites was temporarily uncertain following the

President Valéry Giscard d'Estaing's helicopter trip to Le Buet with his family in April 1980. I accompanied the group, which was led by the guide James Couttet, and had the privilege of skiing of great descent through firm snow left over from Easter of that year. Although we had the 'tact' to be dropped off a little

Valéry Giscard d'Estaing on Le Buet

below the summit so as not to get in the way of the ski-tourers who were already there, the latter were nevertheless outraged. The ensuing political and ecological polemic saw the end of heli-drops on Le Buet, and the following winter drops in the three other sites were also banned. This remains a questionable decision given the number of helicopter trips that are authorised to take supplies of beer and food to the huts for the ski-tourers, and the complimentary helicopter rides for the media, plus the essential life-saving rescue flights that are a part of daily life in the valley. The authorities in neighbouring countries seem to be able to sensibly manage the numbers of flights and heli-drops in their protected sites in such a way that the mountains remain accessible to everyone, even to less fit or less well-trained ski-tourers. It should, however, be remembered that back in the 1970s there was total chaos concerning the myriad heli-drop and collection points that had been authorised across Savoie and something had to be done. After all, there are limits... Owing to its proximity, its 1700m climb and long not very technical descent though a series of small valleys, Le Buet remains a coveted summit, which attracts a number of committed ski-tourers every year.

From Le Buet (first small village behind the Col des Montets) climb up the whole of the Bérard valley. At first follow the track on the right bank of the mountain stream, then traverse below the Rocher de la Source (at around 1530m). Continue up via the left bank to the Pierre à Bérard Hut (1924m, covered in snow). Now head towards the Aiguille de Salenton. Pass below the col and go to the right of the Aiguille. Soon after this join the last shoulder that leads to the summit on Le Buet. Follow the same route down on your descent. If the conditions allow (good spring snow), you can ski the small valleys that come down from the summit ('Creux aux vaches', a few steep sections) or pick your way through the bands of rock towards Mont Oreb. Watch out, there are the couloirs that are steep at the bottom and avalanche-prone slopes...

151.a   Col de Salenton (2526m, PD). This is a route that crosses from the Diosaz side to the Bérard side. If you are looking for an 'athletic' route, you can go up Le Buet from La Flégère or Le Brévent (traverse the Aiguilles Rouges via the Col des Crochues and then follow the Balme valley). Either of these options are equally 'doable', especially in winter when the snow stays cold and you can ski the descent in the afternoon. The Col de Salenton itself makes a nice objective for the day and is a good training or introductory route (take off 1 1/2 hrs from the Le Buet route).

151.b   Col des Cochons (2485m, PD). This route is shorter than the previous one. The col is between the Aiguille de Bérard and the Col de Salenton, almost directly above the hut. It has a regular slope (30-35°/ 250m) and it is better to ski this route with good snow.

151.c   North-east face (D). If it wasn't for the high ever-present cornices on the summit of the Le Buet, you could ski some fantastic routes on this sunny

Mont Oreb seen from Les Posettes

face. Do this in the spring and climb up from the Tré les Eaux valley and follow the depression of one of the couloirs on the face. Now, to be less exposed, join the summit crest (40-45°/350m) on the right via a nearby crest.

152 MONT OREB
South-east face

2634m
TD

⬆ 1330m		🗻 March-April		🦥 50-55°/300m	
↗ 1300m		📷 267		⚠ 3	
↘ 1300m		◷ 5hrs		⊕ HP	
✦ South-east		🎿 5.3			

Mont Oreb seen from Les Posettes

151.c

152

In the 1980s I 'entertained' myself by skiing the south side of Mont Oreb. It was quite late in the spring and I accessed the top via the west ridge. The descent was broken by three rock steps, and I had to set up two small rappels. The final traverse half way though the descent took me to the large couloir that comes down from the west shoulder (flat titanium piton marked AB for the rappel). 700m slope with exposed sections of between 45 and 50°.

From Le Buet (first small village after the Col des Montets) and via the hamlet of La Poya, climb up the start of the Bérard valley to just after the south face of Mont Oreb. Climb up the valley that goes round to the left of Mont Oreb to join a distinct ridge that, via a series steep sections and grassy slopes, takes you to the wide Cristaux Ridge. You should ski the descent quite early in the day, before the sun makes it too dangerous. Further left (to the west), there is a straight couloir that can be quite fun despite being narrow and another one to the north-east.

153 POINTE DE LA TERRASSE   2734m
South-east face   PD

1350m		January-April		40°/100m	
1400m		268		1	
1400m		6hrs		SP	
South-east		3.2			

The Loriaz chalets sit on a superb balcony (2020m, hut open in the summer), which deserves a visit and you can even spend the night there. You can pitch a tent or bivouac (igloo) near the chalets and take in the splendid sunset, and see the magnificent sunrise over the Massif while getting an early start the next day. The day before you could even treat yourself by skiing the very pleasant north-east combe. Climb to the promontory (marked at 2360m on the map) of the Aiguille du Charmoz.

From the hamlet of Le Couteray (between the Col des Montets and Vallorcine, on the left after Le Buet and 15mins walk from the SNCF railway station), follow the track to Loriaz, which you reach after several zigzags. Continue to the flat section in the middle of the valley and then head left. You either go straight into the north-east couloir that is difficult to climb in powder snow, or preferably the Col de la Terrasse that you reach on the right after a final steep section (often on foot). From the col, go round and to the left of the crest and go to the Pointe de la Terrasse via the Col de Sassy (cornices). The direct descent of the north-east couloir is sustained but the snow is usually excellent. Otherwise follow the ascent route.

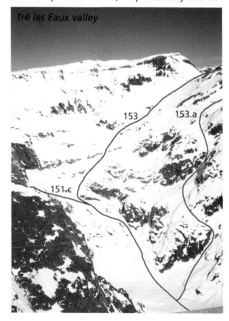
Tré les Eaux valley

153.a Tré les Eaux (AD). From the Pointe de la Terrasse, descend into the west face that gets progressively steeper. The descent follows a gully to the far right that takes you above the bands of rock. Watch out as the snow sits on slopes of dry grass and the area is prone to avalanche in the afternoon. Stay close to the large valley, below the Col des Corbeaux and the Rochers du Châtelet lower down. Head left again, between the last bands of rock and go to the large flat areas of the Tré les Eaux valley. Descend this valley on the left bank of the mountain stream. At the bottom, there are two possible routes: either climb up a bit and follow the summer path (section with chains and ladders), or continue down the middle of the mountain stream to 1700m and join the woods on the left bank (Tête des Combasses, chalets). Before set-

Loriaz chalets

ting off down the depression that marks the mountain stream (can have poor snow cover at the beginning of the winter), you can climb up 100m (steep) on the right and join the Bérard valley lower down and on the south side.

154 COL DE LA TERRASSE   2648m
Swiss side   PD

⚑ 1350m	▨ December-May	⌐ 35°
↗ 1300m	◷ 5hrs	⚠ 1
↘ 1300m	⤉ 3.1	⊕ DP
✦ North-east		

Veudale gorges

The Col de la Terrasse can be skied easily and is in good condition from the first falls of snow. Later on in the winter you can traverse it via Tré les Eaux. Nevertheless, this descent is committing and the exit into the mountain stream can be tricky when there is poor snow cover and can be exposed if there is a risk of avalanche. You should only ski this route if you have seen it first and know what the conditions are like in it. On the other hand, if you return via the same route it makes a pleasant descent. Other option: 153.

Go to Finhaut in Switzerland and, if possible, follow the road up to Léchère (otherwise there's a further 100m of height gain). Go up to the Emosson Dam. Cross the dam and start to move up left in the second small valley. After a first ledge, head up towards the Veudale Gorges, which you climb (steep at the start) to get to a long second ledge/flat area. Continue right and go to the limestone promontory (can see dinosaur tracks here, but not with the snow!). Via the slight valleys and on the south you get to the Col de la Terrasse. The descent follows the same route back down or you can go further right via system of steeper slopes/couloirs that also lead to Veudale Gorges. Cross the dam and after

On the Finive Glacier, near the Emosson Dam

the climb up to the Col de la Gueulaz, take the right-hand combe (Golettes Gorges) that leads directly to the hairpin bend (1707m, tunnel) and follow the road down to Finhaut. Follow the track to Barberine. If the slopes are avalanche-prone, it is safer to take the road from the dam to Finhaut (train to Le Buet).

154.a ▪ Brèche des Perrons (2495m, PD). Pass the first flat area at the Veudale Gorges (at around 2200m), head diagonally left (small wall/dam) and join a narrow valley that leads to the Brèche des Perrons. This is a shorter descent but is on the same side of the mountain, which often has excellent snow conditions (PD, 4-5hrs). The direct descent to Barberine should be done when the snow is stable (start of a winter when there's not much snow or on a spring morning). The slope below the dam (south-east) is steep and prone to avalanche.

155 BEL OISEAU   2643m
East face   AD

⚑ 1350m		🏔 November-April		⤷ 35°
↗ 1400m		📷 271		⚠ 1
↘ 1500m		☺ 6hrs		⊕ DP
✦ All		🎿 3.1		

At the far end of the Aiguilles Rouges and the Aiguilles des Perrons, there is a small crystalline range. Situated entirely in Switzerland, the three modest summits of Bel Oiseau, Fontanabran and Le Fenestral are perched above the pretty village of Finhaut. The last of the three, Le Fenestral, which faces the sun, was for several decades a haven of peace and quiet for the final victims recovering from tuberculosis. That is why there are several large stone buildings in this area, set away from the tourist centres. At the beginning of the winter, the skier can find three main routes here and just under a dozen averagely difficult variants which are quick to access that make their between the woods, alpages and wide combes. The steep slopes through the woods and the avalanche couloirs have thankfully not attracted many adventurers and it looks like the excessive development of our natural sites might not extend to this small corner. The first summit after the Emosson Dam has the nice-sounding name of Bel Oiseau ('Handsome Bird'). This remarkable viewpoint is in such a spot that you get great views of the routes on the Envers des Perrons, the Finive Glacier, the Pic de Tenneverge and the Col de la Tour Salière, as well as of several descents on the north side of the Trient Glacier and the Col de Balme.

Normally, the road is cleared of snow up to the hamlet of La Léchère (1440m). From here, go to the right of the chalets and head horizontally to the right bank of the first steep-sided valley (avalanche couloir). At the first bushes, cross the couloir and join the track that follows the Torrent du Besson. Go to the plateau on which the Fenestral alpage sits (1797m, pleasant rocky viewpoint where you can stop for your first break on the way up or on the way down). Continue up the steepest valley and head left at around 2100m and take the east combe that leads to a subsidiary summit (2614m). If you want to go to the main summit of Bel Oiseau (2643m), traverse left to about 2400m to join the Col de Bel Oiseau (2460m), then head up the north side through some rocks to the summit. The descent via the same route follows requires you to follow this long traverse. To access the other routes, on the other hand, continue to the west summit (2628m).

South faces of Bel Oiseau and the Dent de Fenestral

155.a East/North-east couloir (D-). Access to this couloir is just to the north of the summit. As it is quite steep at the top and narrow in its lower section, this couloir needs to have good snow cover for you to be able to ski it. The snow here is generally good at the start of winter. You have to get a look at the route as you climb up to be sure you can cross the narrow section (40-45°/250m).

155.b South couloir (AD). Direct from the summit, join a couloir that narrows 100m below to form a gully. It then widens out again down to the Emosson Dam road (45°/100m). Watch out, this is an avalanche couloir!

155.c South-west face (AD). Take the slope opposite the dam that goes from 30 to 40°. To negotiate a few rocks you have to head a little to your right. You soon have to traverse back left (above 2200m) to stay uphill of the bands of rock. You end up at the end of the road to the dam (to the east of the entrance to the tunnel).

155.d North-west combes (PD). From either the Col du Bel Oiseau or the summit, take the pleasant regular combes to the north and stay on the right. The slope steepens up above Barberine (old dam). To get back to the end of the Emosson Dam, follow the road (roughly 600m) and use the tunnel (very steep ladders at either end) to get to the road that takes you to La Léchère or Finhaut.

156 FONTANABRAN-FENESTRAL Traverse 2678m PD

⚐ 1350m	🗺 January-April	⊿ sect. of 35-40°
↗ 1360m	📷 271	⚠ 1
↘ 1360m	⏱ 5-6hrs	⛑ SP
⌖ All	⛷ 3.1	

You can access Fontanabran via La Léchère as per the previous route, as you can now climb up the south combe that comes out between the two summits. For Fontanabran, continue via a kind of headland and 200m higher up you reach a subsidiary summit of the highest point in the chain. To get to the Dent de Fenestral you have to descend a little to the right then take a short climb up to the north notch from where you see the deep Comba Rossa. The traverse to the north side and into the Val d'Émaney and the return via Les Marécottes is not often done as there is a risk of frequent avalanches here. There are other very pleasant tours that you can do here via the Barberine, Émaney and Tour Salière Cols, but I haven't included them in this guide.

From La Léchère, follow route 155 and continue up the large combe to the col on the left of the Fenestral rocks. You can rock-climb to the summit via a steep and not very snowy step. The descent can be down via the same route, but you have to be aware of how, where and when the snow warms up and make sure you don't find yourself in the wrong place at the wrong time.

156.a   Comba Rossa (PD). From Finhaut, follow the Emosson Dam road and take the first forest track on the right. Follow this through the forest and, when you get to above the larches, go up towards the combe that nestles between two rocky ridges. At the top climb to the left-hand notch, which is steep and narrow at the top. This variant access route is quite convenient and less monotonous than the other approach route from La Léchère. The tour that descends via the Comba Rossa is a great route to do early on in the season (climb up via Fontanabran, pass the Col de Fenestral and descend via the steep Comba Rossa).

Daybreak

We now leave the crystalline massifs of the Mont Blanc and the Aiguilles Rouges to enter the high limestone massifs that stretch to the Bernese Oberland.
Among many others possibilities, a few ideas:
– traverse of the Dents du Midi by the Golette starting in Les Marécottes;
– traverse through the Col de la Tour Salière from Emosson;
– the Tenneverge;
– the Finive glacier via the 'Œil de Bœuf', etc.

Edouard Baud

Following in the footsteps of his two grandfathers, both guides and one a ski champion, Edouard dedicated his life to the noble passion of top level skiing and mountaineering. By granting him access to this shared passion, I also exposed him to its risk and its dangers. Combining his spirit, strength and technique and my experience, we shared the delights of skiing the most beautiful Alpine classics, and reached the serenity of the lofty Himalayan summits. At the height of his dreams and of our plans, aged 24, Edouard was brutally snatched away by a collapsing serac. Through cruel and fatal timing, nature asserted her sovereignty over man's precaution, technical expertise or good faith. Too short a life has met with unyielding fate at the top of the Gervasutti couloir on this Spring 2004 morning. The smile, the glow of youth, of a son, a brother, a firm friend, stays engraved in our hearts.

'Better to be lost to one's passion, than to lose one's passion'.

INDEX OF ROUTES AND VARIANTS ACCORDING TO LEVEL OF DIFFICULTY

(with route or variant route numbers)

277

Tita Neire (Col de), 48a
Tondu (Mont) Nant Blanc face, 17a
Tondu (Mont) Tour, 18
Tondu (Mont), Col des Chasseurs, 17b
Tondu (Mont), Pain de Sucre, north-east, 17
Toule (Aiguille de), north-west face, 109
Tour (Aiguille du), normal route, 66
Tré la Tête (Aiguilles de), south face circuit 26
Tré la Têté (Col de), 25a
Tré la Tête (Têtes de), north couloir, 9b
Tré les Eaux 153a
Tricot (Aiguille de), via Tricot Glacier, 3b
Trient Glacier, right bank, 53b
Triolet (Col du), west face, 97
Triolet (Petite Aiguille du), west/south-west face, 97a
Tufs (Col des), 20a
Van (Pointe du), east couloir, 64a
Van (Pointe du), north couloir, 64b

AD+
Dolent (Mont), Gallet Ridge, 45
Noire Glacier, traverse, 107
Orny (Pointe d'), Arpette Couloirs, 57
Scie (Col de la), 24a
Tré la Tête (Aiguille Nord de), north-west face, 12
Trident (Col du), north-east face, 114

D-
Bel Oiseau, east/north-east couloir, 155a
Dolent (Mont), notch north of Maye Hut, 45b
Grande Lui (west face), 50
Infranchissable (Col de), traverse to Col de Miage, 11b
Plateau (Brèche Nord du), 75a
Rochefort Ridges, traverse, 108b

D
Amône (Col de 1'), south-west couloir, 78
Argentière (Aiguille d'), Barbey Couloir, 51, 74a
Argentière (Aiguille d'), Milieu Glacier, 74
Argentière (Col d'), south-east face, 46b
Bionnassay (Aiguille de), north face, 3
Bionnassay (Col de), Italian face, 30a
Blaitière (Brèche de), Contamine Couloir, 124b
Blaitière (Brèche de), Spencer Couloir, 124
Blanc (Mont), Aiguilles Grises, 30
Blanc (Mont), north face, 133
Blanc (Mont), traverse towards Les Bosses, 133a
Brenva Glacier via Tour Ronde, 37a
Buet (Le), south-east face, 151c
Cardinal (Brèche du), west couloir, 89a
Chardonnet (Aiguille du), Forbes Arête, 69
Courtes (Col des), north-east couloir, 79
Courtes (Les), north/north-east couloir, 81
Cristaux (Col des), north-east couloir, 80
Croulante (Aiguille), south couloir, 96b
Éboulement (Aiguille de 1'), south couloir 100

Encrenaz (Aiguille de 1'), north-east couloir, 148a
Floria (Aiguille de la), west side, 143a
Fourches (Col des), east couloir, 53a
Glaciers (Aiguille des), east face, 24c
Goûter (Dôme du), north ridge, 135
Gruetta (Mont), south face, 42
Hirondelles (Col des), 42a
Jorasses (Col des Grandes), 101b
Lex Blanche (Aiguille de la), north-west face, 13
Lex Blanche (Col de la), north face, 25b
Maudit (Mont), north face 131
Maudit (Mont), north-east ridge, 131a
Midi (Aiguille du), Cosmiques Couloir, 129
Midi (Aiguille du), Rond Glacier, 128
Moine-Nonne (Brèche), 90a
Morris (Aiguille) north face, 149c
Neige (Dôme de), north face, 14
Orny (Petite Pointe d'), north-east couloir, 57a
Passon (Aiguille du), north-east couloir, 70e
Passon (Aiguille du), south-west couloir, 70c
Portalet (Le), north face, 55
Reilly (Col Adams), south-west couloir, 70d
Ronde (Tour), east col, 113a
Ronde (Tour), normal route, 111
Ronde (Tour), west col, 114a
Tacul (Aiguille du), north-west shoulder, 103
Talèfre (Col de), west couloir, 98
Tour (Aiguille du), Table Couloir, 67
Tour Noir (Col du), north -east face, 76a
Tour Noir (Col Supérieur du), 47b, 76c
Tournier (Pointe), east couloir, 79a
Tricot (Pointe Inférieure de), east couloir, 4d
Trident (Col du), Brenva Glacier, 37
Verte (Col de l'Aiguille), south-west couloir, 92a
Verte (Petite Aiguille), Chevalier Couloir, 86
Verte (Petite Aiguille), north face, 86a

D+
Allobrogia (Pointe), north face, 45a
Argentière (Aiguille d'), X Couloir, 73
Bérangère (Aiguille de la), west couloir, 9c
Courtes (Les), south/south-west couloir, 96a
Dorées (Aiguilles), Copt Couloir, 54
Droites (Les), east summit, 93a
Durier (point marked 3358 m), south couloir, 40
Géant (Dent du), 40b
Goûter (Aiguille du), Payot Ridge, 1b
Infranchissable (Col), east face, 29a
Jorasses (Grandes), south face, 41
Lanchettes (Aiguille des), north couloir, 16a
Mallet (Mont), shoulder, west slope, 106
Mesure (Aiguille de), east face, 150
Mesure (Aiguille de), traverse to north face, 150a
Miage (Col de), west/north-west face, 5b
Miage (Dômes de), Métrier Ridge, 6
Nonne-Evêque (Brèche), south-west couloir, 90
Pierre à Joseph (Pointe Supérieure de), descent via Pierre à Joseph Glacier 99b

INDEX OF ROUTES AND VARIANTS

HUT INDEX